MICHIGAN
ITS LAND AND
ITS PEOPLE

JAMES KILLORAN

STUART ZIMMER

MARK JARRETT

JARRETT PUBLISHING COMPANY

EAST COAST
19 Cross Street
Ronkonkoma, NY 11779
516-981-4248

WEST COAST
10 Folin Lane
Lafayette, CA 94549
510-906-9742

1-800-859-7679 ❖ Fax: 516-588-4722
www.rwmg.com/jarrettpub

ISBN 1-882422-31-7

Printed in the United States of America
by Malloy Lithographing, Inc., Ann Arbor, Michigan.
First Edition

10 9 8 7 6 5 4 3 2   00 99 98

ABOUT THE AUTHORS

James Killoran is a retired New York City Assistant Principal. He has written *Government and You* and *Economics and You.* Mr. Killoran has extensive experience in test writing for the New York State Board of Regents in Social Studies and has served on the Committee for Testing of the National Council of Social Studies. His article on Social Studies testing has been published in *Social Education,* the country's leading Social Studies journal. In addition, Mr. Killoran has won a number of awards for outstanding teaching and curriculum development, including "Outstanding Social Studies Teacher" and "Outstanding Social Studies Supervisor" in New York City. In 1993, he was awarded an Advanced Certificate for Teachers of Social Studies by the N.C.S.S.

Stuart Zimmer is a retired New York City Social Studies teacher. He has written *Government and You* and *Economics and You.* He served as a test writer for the New York State Board of Regents in Social Studies, and has written for the National Merit Scholarship Examination. In addition, he has published numerous articles on teaching and testing in Social Studies journals. He has presented many demonstrations and educational workshops at state and national teachers' conferences. In 1989, Mr. Zimmer's achievements were recognized by the New York State Legislature with a Special Legislative Resolution in his honor.

Mark Jarrett is a former Social Studies teacher and a practicing attorney at the San Francisco office of Baker and McKenzie, the world's largest law firm. Mr. Jarrett has served as a test writer for the New York State Board of Regents, and has taught at Hofstra University. He was educated at Columbia University, the London School of Economics, the Law School of the University of California at Berkeley, and Stanford University, where he is a doctoral candidate in history. Mr. Jarrett has received several academic awards, including Order of the Coif at Berkeley and the David and Christina Phelps Harris Fellowship at Stanford.

ALSO BY KILLORAN, ZIMMER AND JARRETT

The Key To Understanding Global Studies
The Key To Understanding U.S. History and Government
Mastering Global Studies
Mastering U.S. History and Government
Comprende Tu Mundo: Su historia, sus culturas
Historia y gobierno de los Estados Unidos
Mastering Ohio's 9th Grade Citizenship Test
Mastering Ohio's 12th Grade Citizenship Test
Los Estados Unidos: Su historia, su gobierno
Nuestro Mundo: Su historia, sus culturas
Ohio: Its Land and Its People
Ohio: Its Neighbors, Near and Far
Principios de economía
Texas: Its Land and Its People
New York: Its Land and Its People
North Carolina: The Tar Heel State

ACKNOWLEDGMENTS

The authors would like to thank **Dr. Janet Alleman** of Michigan State University, East Lansing, who reviewed the manuscript and wrote the foreword to this book. Dr. Alleman is a leading national authority on elementary education.

The authors would further like to thank **Dr. Roger Rosentreter** of the Department of History at Michigan State University, East Lansing, and Editor of *Michigan History Magazine,* who reviewed the history sections of this book.

The authors would also like to acknowledge the help of the following Michigan teachers who reviewed the material and reading level of this book. Their comments, suggestions and recommendations proved invaluable.

Candice Chatfield, Teacher
Winans Elementary School
Waverly Community Schools

Sally Hudgins, Teacher
Moores Park Elementary School
Lansing Schools

Sonya James, Teacher
Gundry Community School
West Ottawa Schools

Colin Ripmaster, Teacher
Lakewood Elementary School
Flint Schools

Sally J. Redinger, Teacher
Mattawan Later Elementary School
Mattawan Consolidated Schools

We would further like to thank **Dr. Joel Fischer** for his work on the history section and his useful comments on the entire manuscript. In addition, we would like to thank **John Curry,** Michigan State Photo Archivist and **Caroline Scholfield,** librarian. Both helped in obtaining many of the photographs used in this book. Finally, the authors would like to thank **Hanna Kisiel** and **Julie Fleck** for their many suggestions and insightful comments in editing the manuscript.

Cover design by Burmar Technical Corporation, Albertson, N.Y.
Artistic illustrations by Ron S. Zimmer.
Maps and graphics by C.F. Enterprises.
Layout, maps/graphics and typesetting: Burmar Technical Corporation, Albertson, N.Y.

This book is dedicated to ...

my wife Donna, and my children Christian, Carrie, and Jesse. ..... *James Killoran*
my wife Joan, and my children Todd and Ronald. .... *Stuart Zimmer*
my wife Goska, and my children Alexander and Julia. .... *Mark Jarrett*

FOREWORD

This should be an exciting year for you in Social Studies. You will learn about our State of Michigan. You will be introduced to its people, its places, form of government and vast resources. You will learn how generations of Michiganders have met their needs and solved their problems. Their struggles and achievements have made Michigan the outstanding place it is today.

I encourage you to talk to other members of your family about what you read in this book. Use local resources such as your public library or community museum to help Michigan's story come to life. It can be fun to learn what happened in early times and how things have changed. Maybe you will even have an opportunity to visit some of the many places described in this book.

As a citizen of Michigan, you already have a voice in how our state is governed. For example, you can speak to relatives and friends, write to government officials and send your views to newspapers and magazines. As an adult you will be able to vote and run for public office. You will have to earn a living. This book will help prepare you for these and other important duties that lie ahead. It will also engage you in exciting activities that help you learn to cooperate with others and to communicate your ideas.

Besides providing a rich background about our state, *Michigan: Its Land and Its People* will help prepare you for the MEAP Test in Social Studies that you will be asked to take next year. The content and activities of this book have been carefully designed to help you do your best when you take this important test.

I hope that, after reading this book, you will join me by becoming an avid Michigander. You are about to join a long list of people who have known and loved the Wolverine State. Welcome!

Janet Alleman
Professor of Education
Michigan State University
East Lansing, Michigan

PHOTO CREDITS

(LC) Library of Congress; (NA) National Archives; (MSA) Michigan State Archives; (MTB) Michigan Travel Bureau; (MATB) Mackinaw Area Travel Bureau; (FMC) Ford Motor Company; (TDT) Texas Department of Transportation; (JA) Jarrett Archives. (t) top; (m) middle; (b) bottom; (r) right; (l) left; (c) center.

COVER: Pictured Rocks, Lake Superior, Michigan (Superstock Photos)

OPENING ACTIVITY: **Pg. 1:** MSA

UNIT 2: **Pg. 14:** JA; **15:** © Michigan Bell Telephone Company, 1964. All Rights Reserved; **24:** Jackson Convention and Tourist Bureau; **35:** © Stewart Milstein; **36:** © Stewart Milstein; **37:** (t) © Stewart Milstein, (b) Greater Lansing Convention and Visitors Bureau; **39:** (t & b) © Tom Buchkoe; **44:** MTB; **45:** (t) © Michael M. Smith, (b) MATB; **47:** (t) MATB, (b) © Tom Buchkoe; **48:** Holland Area Convention and Visitors Bureau; **51:** Bay Area C.V.B.; **52:** © Tom Buchkoe; **54:** (t) Traverse City V.C.B., (b) © Stan Chaldex; **55:** © Tom Buchkoe; **56:** (t) Traverse City V.C.B., (b) Mackinaw Area Tourist Bureau; **57:** (t) © Randall McCune, (m) MSA, (b) JA; **58:** (t) JA, (b) © Vito Palmisano; **59:** (t & b) JA; **60:** (t) Kalamazoo Air Museum, (m) MSA, (b) MTB; **61:** (t) Holland Area Visitors and Convention Bureau, (b) JA; **63:** United Nations Photo 157447 / P. Sudhakaran; **64:** JA.

UNIT 3: **Pg. 73:** (t, l) JA, (t, r) MSA, (b) MSA; **75:** LC; **78:** MSA; **79:** MSA; **80:** (t) MSA, (b) New York State Archives; **81:** MSA; **82:** MSA; **83:** MSA; **84:** MSA; **85:** (t & b) MSA; **88:** Mackinaw Area Tourist Bureau; **89:** JA; **91:** LC; **92:** MSA; **93:** (t) © Michigan Bell Telephone Company, 1964. All Rights Reserved, (b) MSA; **95:** (t) © Michigan Bell Telephone Company, 1964. All Rights Reserved, (m) MSA; **97:** LC; **98:** LC; **100:** (t) LC, (b) Capitol Historical Society; **101:** LC; **106:** Capitol Historical Society; **107:** LC; **108:** (t) MSA, (m) MSA, (b) Capitol Historical Society; **109:** MSA; **110:** MSA; **111:** MSA; **114:** MSA; **116:** MSA; **117:** MSA; **118:** (t & b) LC; **119:** LC; **120:** MSA; **121:** (t & b) MSA; **122:** MSA; **124:** MSA; **126:** (t & b) MSA; **127:** Mackinaw Area Tourist Bureau; **128:** Post and Grape Nuts are registered trademarks of Kraft Foods, Inc. Photos used with permission; **129:** Post and Grape Nuts are registered trademarks of Kraft Foods, Inc. Photos used with permission; **133:** (t) MSA, (b) FMC; **134:** (t) MSA, (b) FMC; **135:** (t & b) FMC; **136:** FMC; **137:** FMC; **139:** MSA; **140:** LC; **141:** (t) MSA, (b) LC; **142:** (t & b) MSA; **143:** © Vito Palmisano; **147:** LC; **153:** MSA; **154:** © Vito Palmisano; **156:** (t) LC, (b) MSA; **157:** (t) LC, (b) MSA; **158:** MSA; **159:** MTB; **162:** LC; **168:** JA; **169:** © Stewart Milstein; **171:** JA.

UNIT 4: **Pg. 175:** (t) Grand Traverse Pioneer and Historical Society, (b,l) MSA, (br) Greater Lansing C.V.B.; **182:** MSA; **183:** JA; **185:** © Vito Palmisano; **187:** (t) MSA, (b) JA; **188:** JA; **190:** (t & b) MSA; **192:** MSA; **195:** JA; **196:** Holland Area C.V.B.; **198:** (t,m,b) LC; **199:** MSA; **200:** (t) JA, (b) MSA; **201:** LC; **204:** (t & b) LC; **206:** MSA; **207:** MSA; **208:** (t) New York State Governor's Office, (b) LC; **209:** (t) MSA, (b) Motown Museum; **214:** (t) JA, (b) Mackinaw Area Tourist Bureau.

UNIT 5: **Pg. 225:** (t) MSA, (m) Traverse City V.C.B., (b) FMC; **226:** LC; **231:** JA; **233:** © Stewart Milstein; **288:** (t) TDT, (b) JA; **289:** (t) MSA, (b) High Point C.V.B.; **235:** JA; **237:** MDT; **240:** © Randall McCune; **241:** (t) Perdue Farms, Incorporated, (b) © Tom Buckhoe; **242:** FMC; **243:** © Vito Palmisano; **244:** MSA; **245:** (l) © Tom Buckhoe, (r) Mackinaw Area Tourist Bureau; **246:** JA; **248:** MSA; **248:** (t) MSA, (b) JA; **252:** (t) MSA, (b) © Tom Buckhoe; **253:** © Vito Palmisano, (b) © Randall McCune; **254:** JA; **259:** MSA.

UNIT 6: **Pg. 261:** (t, l) The White House, (t, r) Bay Area C.V.B., (b) JA; **362:** NA; **266:** (t & b) JA; **269:** LC; **270:** LC, **271:** (t) LC, (b) NA; **272:** LC; **275:** LC; **276:** LC; **278:** U.S. Capitol Historical Society; **279:** (t) The White House, (b) Bureau of Engraving and Printing; **280:** Collection of the Supreme Ct. of the U.S.; **281:** JA; **282:** JA; **283:** (l) MSA, (r) JA; **282:** JA; **285:** JA; **286:** JA; **287:** (t) Michigan Governor's Office, (b) JA; **288:** MSA; **289:** JA; **290:** (t) JA, (b) MSA; **291:** (t) Jackson V.C.B., (b) Kalamazoo County V. & C.B.; **295:** LC; **296:** (t) LC, (b) : Collection of the Supreme Ct. of the U.S.; **299:** Collection of the Supreme Ct. of the U.S.

UNIT 7: **Pg. 303:** (t, l) JA, (t, r) LC, (b) JA; **372:** © Goska Jarrett; **316:** LC; **317:** TDT; **318:** © Stewart Milstein.

CLOSING ACTIVITY: **Pg. 411:** JA.

PICTURE GAZETTEER: **Pg. 345:** (t & b) JA; **346:** (t, r) JA, (m, l) JA, (m, r) JA, (b) JA; **347:** JA; **348:** (t, r) JA, (b) JA.

TABLE OF CONTENTS

UNIT 3: AMERICAN HERITAGE

UNIT 4: PEOPLE IN SOCIETY

UNIT 5: ECONOMICS

UNIT 6: GOVERNMENT

UNIT 7: CITIZENSHIP

CLOSING ACTIVITY

SKILL BUILDERS

LANGUAGE ARTS SKILL BUILDERS

FAMOUS MICHIGANDERS

FAMOUS PLACES IN MICHIGAN

REFERENCE TOOLS

MAPS

THE IMAGE I HAVE
OF MICHIGAN IS ... ?

OPENING ACTIVITY This school year you will learn about Michigan—its land and its people. You will also learn about your community and nation. This book will involve you in many new and interesting activities. The authors hope you enjoy your journey through its pages.

AN IMPORTANT NOTE: This is an interactive textbook. You will be asked to participate in many exciting activities as you learn and apply new information. Even though there are empty spaces on some pages, **you should not write in this book.** Instead, do all of your writing on a separate piece of paper or in a notebook.

Introduction

WHAT DOES "MICHIGAN" MEAN TO YOU?

Before we start our journey together, let's find out what images or thoughts **you** have about Michigan. Millions of people have an image of Michigan as the place where the automobile industry began. When other people hear the name "Michigan," they may think of the state where the Mackinac Bridge is located. What does Michigan mean to **YOU**?

The Mackinac Bridge.

THINK ABOUT IT

List or draw the images and thoughts that "Michigan" brings to your mind.

When I think of Michigan, I think of ...

Next, compare your thoughts about Michigan with those of your classmates.

Now you are ready to begin your journey. The first unit of this book will give you some handy tools for studying and learning—making your trip a more pleasant and rewarding one. Later units will introduce you to the geography, history, culture, economy and government of Michigan and its communities.

UNIT 1

KEYS TO LEARNING WITH SUCCESS

In this book you will learn about Michigan and the United States. You will also learn skills necessary to pass local and state examinations. This new information will be especially helpful next year, when you take a state test in the fifth grade. The test will ask you to remember information you learned this year in school. The unit you are about to read provides you with some of the keys that will help you to become a more successful student.

1: VISUALIZING ("PICTURING") IMPORTANT INFORMATION

In Social Studies examinations, you are often asked to understand and apply important terms and ideas. To help you learn and remember new terms and ideas, you will be asked to complete two Vocabulary Cards at the end of each activity in this book.

Vocabulary Cards are index cards with questions on them. As you go through the activities in this book, you will develop your own set of cards to use for studying. Each Vocabulary Card has two parts:

❖ **Front of the card.** The front is for writing about the term or idea.

❖ **Back of the card.** The back is used to create a "picture" of the term or idea.

THE FRONT OF THE CARD: WRITTEN INFORMATION

On the front of each card, you will be asked to describe a term or define an idea. When you learn a specific term, like the Declaration of Independence, you should describe it on the card and explain why it is important. Here is an example:

Example #1

> Declaration of Independence
>
> What is it? (Description)
>
> It is a document written mainly by Thomas Jefferson in 1776. It announced to the world that America wanted to be independent from Great Britain.
>
> Why Is It Important? (Explanation)
>
> The document stated the basic idea that governments are created to protect people's rights. It serves as a basis for our government.

When you learn about a new idea, like **democracy,** you will usually be asked to define the idea and to give an example of it.

Example #2

> Democracy
>
> Define the term.
>
> Democracy is a form of government in which citizens have a "voice" in public decisions. Citizens vote for people to represent them in their government.
>
> An Example: The government of Michigan is a democracy. Its members are elected by the voters of the state.

THE BACK OF THE CARD: VISUAL INFORMATION

Pictures are often easier to remember than words. On the back of each card, you will be asked to draw a picture about the information on the front. Making your ideas into pictures will help you remember and understand these terms. Let's see what the information on these same two Vocabulary Cards might look like when put into picture form.

Although you will find **two** Vocabulary Cards to complete in each activity, you should create an additional card any time you find a word or phrase you think is important.

2: USING MNEMONIC DEVICES

Another way to remember factual information is to use a mnemonic (nē' monik) device. **Mnemonic devices** are word tricks that help you to remember. They are especially useful when you have to remember a list of items—such as planets, continents, cities, rivers or important historical events.

THE KEY WORD METHOD

A helpful mnemonic is to form a single word by using the **first** letter of each word on a list or in a group. For example, you might think of a word to help you remember the names of the five Great Lakes: **H**uron, **O**ntario, **M**ichigan, **E**rie and **S**uperior. One such word might be: H-O-M-E-S .

H	—	O	—	M	—	E	—	S
u		n		i		r		u
r		t		c		i		p
o		a		h		e		e
n		r		i				r
		i		g				i
		o		a				o
				n				r

THE KEY SENTENCE METHOD

Another method to recall something is to create a key sentence. For example, the flags of four nations flew over Michigan at different times: France, Spain, England and the United States.

1. **Think of a word that rhymes with or reminds you of the name of each nation:**

   ❖ **United States** – United (both words start with "**un**")

   ❖ **France** – Frank (both words start with "**Fran**")

   ❖ **Spain** – speaks (both words start with "**sp**")

   ❖ **England** – English (both words start with "**engl**")

2. **Now put these words together to form a sentence that will help you to remember them. For instance:**

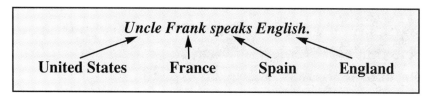

3: WRITING ESSAYS

Sometimes you may be asked to write an **essay**. An essay is made up of several paragraphs on a common theme. To write a good essay you need to know how to organize your thoughts. It takes practice and skill to write well.

STEPS IN THE WRITING PROCESS

The writing process is not one big step, but several small steps. Let's take a look at each major step in the writing process:

❖ **Step 1: Prewriting**

Begin by asking yourself, "Why am I writing this?" Your answer will determine what and how you write. For example, the purpose of your writing may be to provide information, to persuade or to tell about an event. Next, jot down your ideas on what you plan to write about. Cross out any ideas that do not fit. Look at each item carefully. Then put the ideas you want to use in the order you wish to present them. This list of ideas is sometimes called an **outline.** Organizing your ideas on paper is similar to making a "blueprint" for building a house. Your outline is the blueprint for your essay.

❖ **Step 2: Drafting**

A "draft" is simply your first or preliminary writing. In the drafting stage, you begin to carry out your blueprint. Try to imagine that your first draft resembles a "cheeseburger." Your cheeseburger will have a top bun, a slice of cheese, patties of meat and a bottom bun.

The top bun states your main topic. It introduces the reader to what you are going to write about.

The cheese slice is your lead-in. The lead-in connects your statement of the main topic with the body of your essay.

The patties of meat are the main ideas and supporting details. Imagine that each "patty" of meat shows one of the ideas listed on your outline. Here is where you explain each idea.

The bottom bun is the end of your essay. It summarizes what you have said.

❖ **Step 3: Revising**

Revising is one of the most important parts of the writing process. You need to read over your first draft to see if you have included all your main ideas. In the revising step, you take out things you have written that do not seem to fit. You also add new sections where something seems to be missing. Move sections around if they do not seem to be in the right place. The ideas in your essay should all relate to your main topic. The points you make in your essay should flow easily from one to another.

❖ **Step 4: Editing**

Editing is sometimes called proof-reading. In this step you check your essay for errors or make last-minute changes. Editing allows you to "fine-tune" your essay for grammar, punctuation, spelling and style. Look up words or grammar rules that you are not sure about. Correct any mistakes you find. Some writers like to read their work aloud to hear how it sounds.

Sometimes you may have an opportunity to share your essay with other members of your class. Sharing written work with your classmates allows you to get reactions to what and how you wrote. The process of having classmates review your essay is called **peer editing**. Peer editing provides important feedback to help you further improve your essay.

❖ **Step 5: Publishing**

Publishing means to "make public." In this final step, you make your finished work available to others to read. Some people publish their finished work in newspapers, books and magazines. Others "publish" their work by showing what they have written to friends or by handing it in to the teacher.

APPLYING THE STEPS IN THE WRITING PROCESS

Let's apply what you have just learned to the following writing assignment.

> Write a short essay explaining why it is important
> for you to get a good education.

STEP 1: PREWRITING

Remember to begin by thinking about the purpose for your writing. Here, you want to explain why it is important for you to get a good education. Your essay should give reasons why a good education is important. Now, think about all the reasons that you can for having a good education and jot them down.

Outline

Purpose: To explain why it is important for me to have a good education.

Points:
   A. A good education will make me more aware of the world around me.
   B. A good education will help me to get a good job when I get older.
   C. A good education will help me to be a good citizen.
   ~~*D. A good education is not easy to get.*~~

Conclusion: My future depends on getting a good quality education.

As the illustration above shows, you were able to come up with four ideas. After thinking further, you decide to make a change. You decide that the last idea on your list—"a good education is not easy to get"—does not fit with the main idea. You simply eliminate it by crossing it out.

Next, you organize your remaining ideas into what you believe is the best order for writing your essay. Here, you start with what is most immediate. A good education makes you more aware of the world today. Then you turn to the future. A good education will help you to get a job and to become a good citizen. Once you decide that this is the best order for presenting your ideas, you are ready to move on to the next step in writing your essay.

STEP 2: DRAFTING

Now let's expand the ideas in your outline to create a first draft. Put them into essay form by using the "cheeseburger" method:

> *In society it is important for me to go to school.*
>
> *There are some reasons why this is so.*
> *One of the most important reason for a good education is that it makes me more aware of the world around me. In Social Studies I learn how people live in the past. In sceince, I learn how my body works.*
>
> *A good education prepares me for getting a job. In school I learn to read for later work. Another reason to have a good education is that I will learn about citizenship. A good education prepares me to face important jobs such as voting, holding office and paying taxes.*
>
> *Therefore, it is important to have a good education. Having a good future depends on my getting a good education today.*

Top Bun (*Topic Sentence*). The first sentence of your essay is your introduction. It states the main topic of the essay. Notice how the topic sentence lets your reader know what you are writing about.

Cheese Slice (*Connecting Sentence*). The "cheese" sentence helps the reader to follow your thoughts by connecting your introduction to the main body of the writing. Another lead-in you might have used is: *"The following information will show how this is true."*

Patties of Meat (*Main Sentences*). The "patties of meat" section is the main part of your essay. Here you give specific examples and facts to support each of the three main ideas in your outline.

Bottom Bun (*Ending Sentence*). Your last sentence should be similar to your opening topic sentence, except that it is now stated as a conclusion. The conclusion reviews what you have explained in the essay. Notice how the last sentence in the draft above ends the essay by reminding the reader of the importance of a good education. There are several other concluding sentences that you might have chosen: *"Therefore, we can see that ..."* or *"Thus, it is obvious that ...."*

STEP 3: REVISING

After you finish your draft, you should re-read and revise it.

> *In society it is important for me to go to school*
> (today) (very)
> *get a good education.*
>
> *There are ~~some~~ several reasons why this is so.*
>
> *One of the most important ~~of the reassons~~ reassons*
> *for a good education is that it makes me more* (my having)
> *aware of the world around me. In Social Studies*
> *I learn how people ~~live~~ lived in the past. In ~~sceince~~, science*
> *I learn how my body ~~works~~ work.* (nature and) (work)
>
> *A good education ~~gets me ready~~ prepares me for getting a*
> *job. In school I learn to read for ~~later~~ work.* (when I grow older) (will improve my reading and math skills) (future)
>
> *~~Another~~ A third reason to have a good education is that*
> *I will learn ~~about citizenship~~ how to become a good citizen. A good education ~~gets~~*
> *~~me ready~~ prepares me to face important jobs such as voting, holding*
> *office and ~~paying taxes~~ serving on a jury.*
>
> *Therefore, it is important ~~to~~ that I have a good education.*
> *Having a good future depends on ~~my~~ getting a ~~good~~ quality*
> *education today.*

Notice in this revising stage how certain words and phrases in your essay have been changed. For example, "serving on a jury" seems like a better example than "paying taxes." Getting a "quality" education, on the last line, sounds better than repeating the expression "good education." Also, notice how by re-reading your essay, you caught a misspelled word, "sceince," and were able to spell it correctly: "science."

STEP 4: EDITING

After revising your essay, you re-read it one last time. The purpose of this final editing is to correct any last errors you missed before. On your last reading, you discover that you wrote "reassons." You should have written "reasons"—the correct spelling of the word. At this stage, you would correct this error.

STEP 5: PUBLISHING

The last step involves publishing or making your finished work available to others. Here is what your final essay looks like:

> In society today it is very important for me to get a good education. There are several reasons why this is so.
>
> One of the most important reasons for my having a good education is that it makes me more aware of the world around me. In Social Studies I learn how people lived in the past. In science, I learn how nature and my body work.
>
> A good education prepares me for getting a job when I grow older. In school I will improve my reading and math skills for future work.
>
> A third reason to have a good education is that I will learn how to become a good citizen. A good education prepares me to face important jobs such as voting, holding office and serving on a jury.
>
> Therefore, it is important that I have a good education. Having a good future depends on getting a quality education today.

4: PRE-READING HINTS

You have now learned some practical methods for understanding and remembering information. In the following units, you will learn a great deal about Michigan and the United States.

To help you through these units, each section will be introduced by an icon. An **icon** is a symbol—something that stands for something else. Think of each icon as your personal guide, telling you what to expect in each section of the activity. The following list identifies each icon.

Each activity usually begins with an introduction. Here you will learn what is required of you in order to carry out the activity.

These sections provide information for doing the activity. For example, you will be given information about Michigan's geography in order to create a map of what Michigan "looks" like.

These sections will introduce you to a new word or idea. For example, you will learn the definitions of the words "concept" and "generalization."

In these sections you will be asked to complete a task. For example, you might be asked to fill in a chart, write a paragraph or locate places on a map.

In these sections you will learn a new skill. For example, you will learn how to read a map, interpret a bar graph or pie chart, write a business letter or create an outline of a reading.

In these sections you will be asked to do research outside of the classroom. For example, you might be asked to read a book from the library, interview an adult or conduct a survey.

In these sections the activity comes to a close. You will be asked to think about what you have done in the activity, and how this helps answer the focus question that began the activity.

Throughout the text you will find pronunciation guides. These follow important new words. A key that explains the use of symbols in the pronunciation guide is found in the Glossary at the end of the book.

MICHIGANDER OR MICHIGANIAN?

In 1996, the *Detroit Free Press* conducted a survey of people living in Michigan. They asked people what they preferred to be called: Michiganders or Michiganians. The results of the survey showed that people preferred Michigander by almost three to one over Michiganian. This book will use what people in Michigan most prefer—Michigander.

GEOGRAPHY

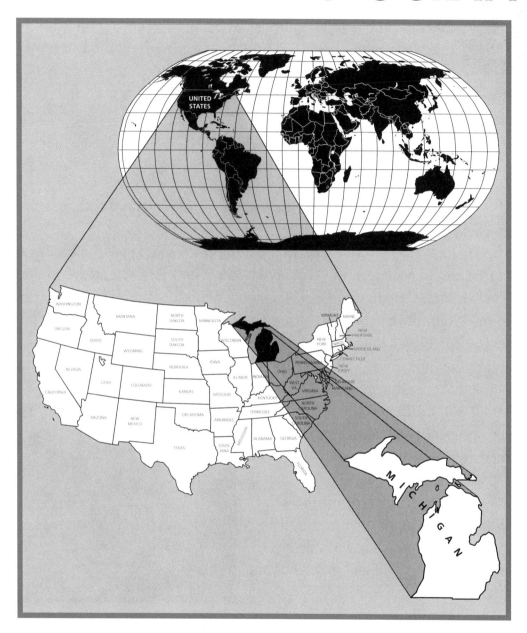

*W**here* we live often determines *how* we live. The study of geography came from the need to know "where." Geography tells us where different places are and what they are like. This knowledge is important because we come into contact with people and products from many different places.

13

A FUTURE STATE IS FORMED

What was it like when the Earth first began? No one knows for sure. Scientists believe that almost five billion years ago the Earth was a mass of molten rock and hot gas. Gradually, the molten rock and hot gases began to cool. As the surface cooled, the crust of the Earth became solid. There were earthquakes and volcanoes. Minerals such as copper and iron ore formed. No plants or animals lived at this time.

Gases in the atmosphere surrounding the Earth eventually turned to rain. Parts of the Earth became covered with water. What is present-day Michigan became covered by shallow seas. Sand, clay and lime settled in layers.

About three billion years ago, the first simple plants and bacteria appeared in the water. These sea creatures later decayed. The decayed creatures formed the petroleum and natural gas present today. Many millions of years ago, the Earth's fragile crust in the area of Michigan was shattered by the eruption of volcanoes. Molten lava came to the surface. Boiling water carried copper into gaps and holes in the rocks.

Some 350 million years ago, great coral reefs developed in the warm, salty seas above Michigan. Later, these seas dried up. The corals died, and their skeletons turned to limestone. Salt deposits were left wherever the sea evaporated. In some places, the salt deposits measured hundreds of feet thick.

About 300 million years ago, Michigan was probably covered with thick jungles and fresh-water swamps. Ferns and other plant life developed. Giant insects, lizards and amphibians ruled the land. Later, the swamps dried up. Loose soil and mud covered the plants, which decayed. Under the weight of soil and rock, the former plants turned into coal.

Many of the dinosaurs that once roamed the Earth were among the largest known land animals.

About 200 million years ago, scientists believe dinosaurs and other giant reptiles dominated Michigan's landscape. Early birds and small reptiles also appeared. Then, 65 million years ago, the Earth was hit by a large asteroid—a huge rock or mass falling from outer space. After the asteroid crashed, a thick cloud of dust spread throughout the Earth's atmosphere. Many scientists believe this dust cloud blocked the sun's rays from reaching the land surface. Without sunlight, dinosaurs and other animals began to die out.

As recently as a million years ago, the climate became very cold. Rain turned to snow. The snow that fell froze into ice. Other snow piled on top, creating layers and layers of thick ice. The weight of the ice made the bottom layers very dense. These rivers of ice were known as glaciers. A great ice cap spread south from the Arctic across all of what is now Canada and Michigan.

The glaciers advanced slowly, scraping the Earth's surface like giant bulldozers. They swept away everything in their path. Trees, rocks and soil were carried along by them.

Thousands of years passed. The Earth grew warmer again, and the glaciers began to melt. Plant and animal life returned to Michigan. But then the weather grew cold and warm several times. Each time there was a new "Ice Age," the glaciers returned to Michigan. The last Ice Age ended only 10,000 years ago.

In Michigan, the glaciers dug out huge basins as they slowly retreated north. When the glaciers melted, they left behind large piles of rocks, sand, gravel and clay. The basins became giant lakes, even larger than the Great Lakes of today. Slowly, the lakes drained through rivers into the ocean.

Fields of grass grew in the rich soils. In time, large elephant-like mammals, known as mammoths, developed. The mammoths grazed on open grasslands and swamps in the area of Michigan. They had long curved tusks. Mastodons, similar to mammoths, ate leaves and shrubs. There were also large beavers, musk ox, caribou, wolves and moose. Although no exact date is known, many scientists feel that around 8,000 years ago the first people started to arrive in the area of present-day Michigan.

A herd of mammoths graze in a swamp.

How did these different natural forces affect Michigan's landscape and geography? What physical features would Michigan inherit from these changes in the Earth's surface? What natural resources are now found in abundance in Michigan? In this unit you will learn the answers to these and other questions about Michigan's geography.

CAN YOU PLEASE GIVE ME SOME DIRECTIONS?

2A You just read about the distant past. Now think about the future. In this activity, you will learn how geographers locate places on the Earth. Look for the following important words and phrases:

▶ North and South Poles   ▶ Prime Meridian   ▶ Physical Regions

▶ Equator   ▶ Continent   ▶ Regions

A ▶ symbol appears in the margin where the **word** or **phrase** is first explained.

It is the year 2100. Friendly life-forms have been discovered on a far-off planet. They are eager to learn about the Earth. They understand our languages. These life-forms even allow their children to become pen pals with children from Earth. Imagine that you have been communicating with your pen pal, Zular, for almost a year.

Zular would like to visit you this summer. However, Zular needs to know exactly where you live in order to come to your house. You decide to use a computer to help you write directions for Zular. You hit the keys of your computer to bring up the instructions for the "Geography-Information" program. Here is the first thing you see on your computer screen:

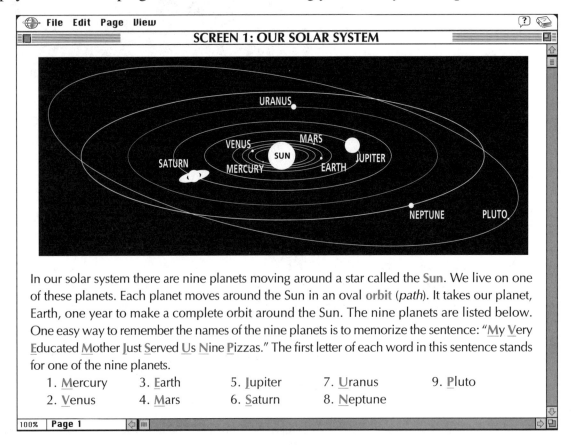

In our solar system there are nine planets moving around a star called the **Sun**. We live on one of these planets. Each planet moves around the Sun in an oval **orbit** (*path*). It takes our planet, Earth, one year to make a complete orbit around the Sun. The nine planets are listed below. One easy way to remember the names of the nine planets is to memorize the sentence: "My Very Educated Mother Just Served Us Nine Pizzas." The first letter of each word in this sentence stands for one of the nine planets.

1. Mercury   3. Earth   5. Jupiter   7. Uranus   9. Pluto
2. Venus   4. Mars   6. Saturn   8. Neptune

You decide to take notes after viewing each screen. You can use these notes later to help you write directions to your pen pal, Zular.

NOTES FOR MY LETTER:
The name of the planet that I live on is ___?___ .

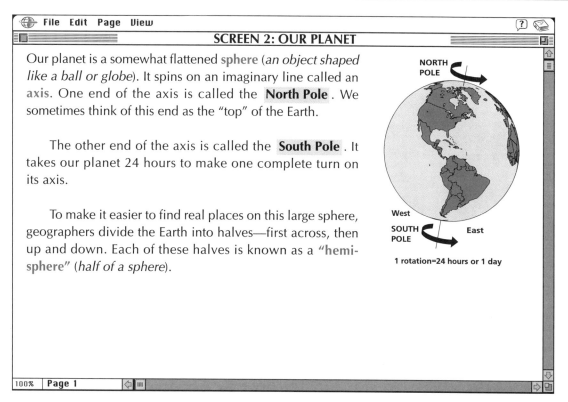

File   Edit   Page   View

SCREEN 2: OUR PLANET

Our planet is a somewhat flattened **sphere** (*an object shaped like a ball or globe*). It spins on an imaginary line called an **axis**. One end of the axis is called the **North Pole** . We sometimes think of this end as the "top" of the Earth.

The other end of the axis is called the **South Pole** . It takes our planet 24 hours to make one complete turn on its axis.

To make it easier to find real places on this large sphere, geographers divide the Earth into halves—first across, then up and down. Each of these halves is known as a "**hemisphere**" (*half of a sphere*).

NORTH POLE

West

SOUTH POLE   East

1 rotation=24 hours or 1 day

100%   Page 1

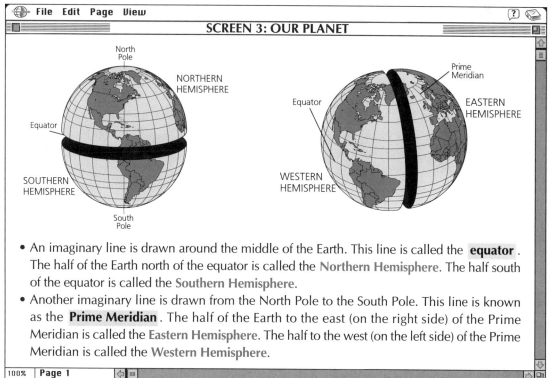

File   Edit   Page   View

SCREEN 3: OUR PLANET

North Pole

NORTHERN HEMISPHERE

Equator

SOUTHERN HEMISPHERE

South Pole

Prime Meridian

Equator

EASTERN HEMISPHERE

WESTERN HEMISPHERE

- An imaginary line is drawn around the middle of the Earth. This line is called the **equator** . The half of the Earth north of the equator is called the **Northern Hemisphere**. The half south of the equator is called the **Southern Hemisphere**.
- Another imaginary line is drawn from the North Pole to the South Pole. This line is known as the **Prime Meridian** . The half of the Earth to the east (on the right side) of the Prime Meridian is called the **Eastern Hemisphere**. The half to the west (on the left side) of the Prime Meridian is called the **Western Hemisphere**.

100%   Page 1

NOTES FOR MY LETTER:
I live in both the ___?___ Hemisphere and the ___?___ Hemisphere.

File Edit Page View   ? 📖
SCREEN 4: CONTINENTS AND OCEANS

Continents are the major land masses of the world. Geographers have divided these land masses into seven continents. In order of size, they are: **Asia, Africa, North America, South America, Antarctica, Europe** and **Australia.**

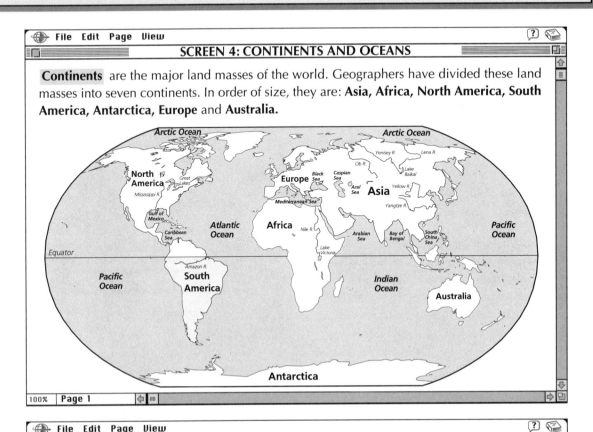

100% Page 1

File Edit Page View   ? 📖
SCREEN 5: CONTINENTS AND OCEANS

The continents of North America, South America and part of Antarctica are in the Western Hemisphere. Europe, Africa, Asia, Australia and part of Antarctica are the continents of the Eastern Hemisphere. Often mapmakers will draw the division between the Eastern and Western Hemispheres slightly west of the Prime Meridian. This is done to show all of Europe and Africa in the same hemisphere.

The Earth is the only planet in our solar system with a lot of water. The Earth has fresh water in lakes and rivers, and salt water in oceans. Human life depends on water—for drinking, farming, fishing, manufacturing and transportation.

Most of the Earth's surface is covered by oceans. An **ocean** is an extremely large body of salt water. Minerals in the water give it a salty taste. There are four main oceans:

- the **Atlantic Ocean**
- the **Pacific Ocean**
- the **Arctic Ocean**
- the **Indian Ocean**

100% Page 2

NOTES FOR MY LETTER:
I live on the continent of ___?___ , located between the ___?___ Ocean and the ___?___ Ocean.

✔ CHECKING YOUR UNDERSTANDING ✔

Use the map and information in screens 4 and 5 to answer the following questions:

1. Which continents are located completely in the Southern Hemisphere?

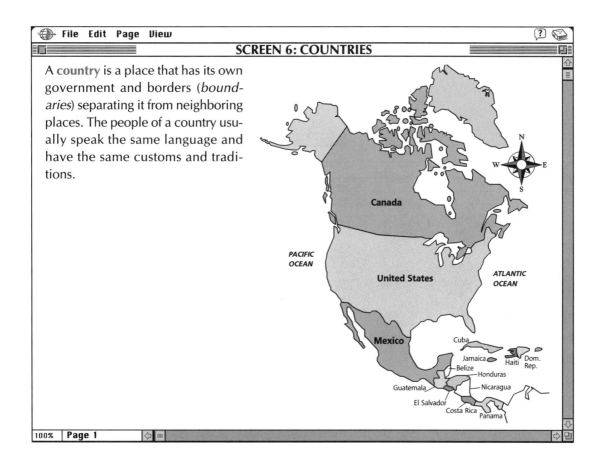

File   Edit   Page   View

SCREEN 6: COUNTRIES

A **country** is a place that has its own government and borders (*boundaries*) separating it from neighboring places. The people of a country usually speak the same language and have the same customs and traditions.

Canada

PACIFIC OCEAN

United States

ATLANTIC OCEAN

Mexico

Cuba

Jamaica   Haiti   Dom. Rep.

Belize

Honduras

Guatemala   Nicaragua

El Salvador

Costa Rica   Panama

100%   Page 1

NOTES FOR MY LETTER:
The country in which I live is called ___?___ . It is located directly north of a country called ___?___ . It is located south of a country called ___?___ .

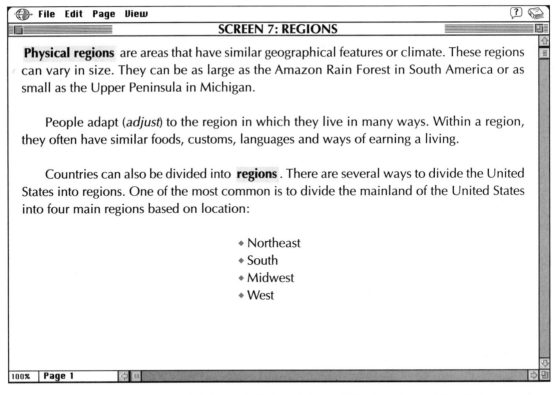

File   Edit   Page   View

SCREEN 7: REGIONS

Physical regions are areas that have similar geographical features or climate. These regions can vary in size. They can be as large as the Amazon Rain Forest in South America or as small as the Upper Peninsula in Michigan.

People adapt (*adjust*) to the region in which they live in many ways. Within a region, they often have similar foods, customs, languages and ways of earning a living.

Countries can also be divided into **regions**. There are several ways to divide the United States into regions. One of the most common is to divide the mainland of the United States into four main regions based on location:

- Northeast
- South
- Midwest
- West

100%   Page 1

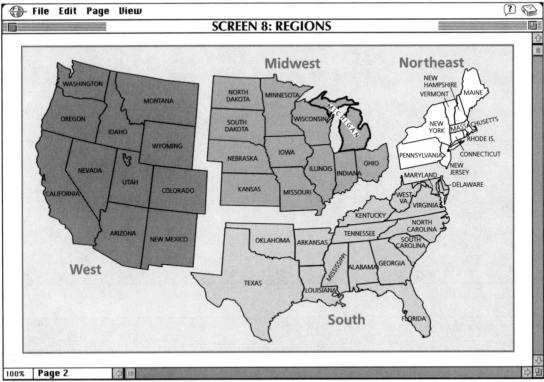

File   Edit   Page   View

SCREEN 8: REGIONS

100%   Page 2

NOTES FOR MY LETTER:

The region I live in is known as the ___?___. The number of states in this region is ___?___. The names of these states are ___?___.

SCREEN 9: STATES AND COUNTIES

Most countries are divided into smaller political units known as states or provinces. The United States is divided into 50 **states**. Can you locate the state in which you live?

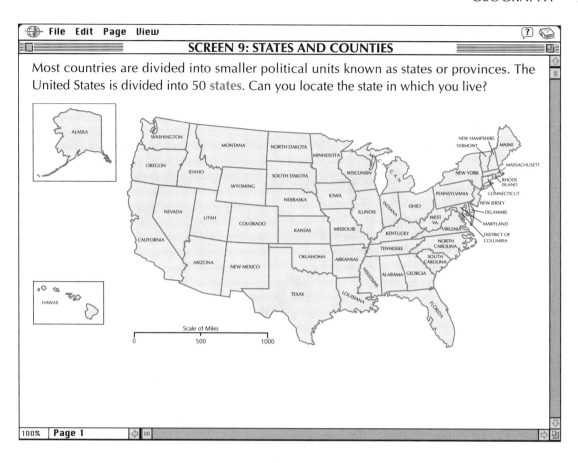

SCREEN 10: STATES AND COUNTIES

Each of the 50 states is itself divided into smaller units called **counties**. Michigan is divided into 83 counties. Can you locate the county in which you live?

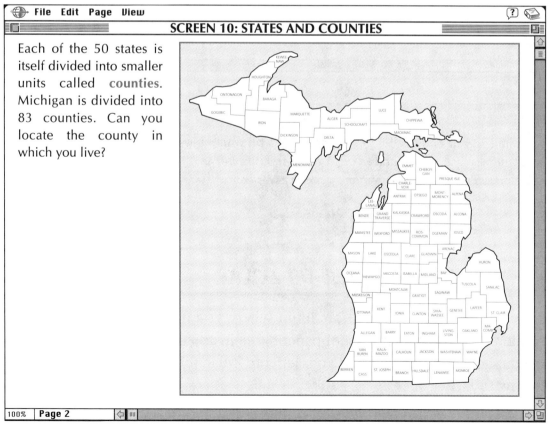

NOTES FOR MY LETTER:

I live in the state of ___?___ and the county of ___?___ .

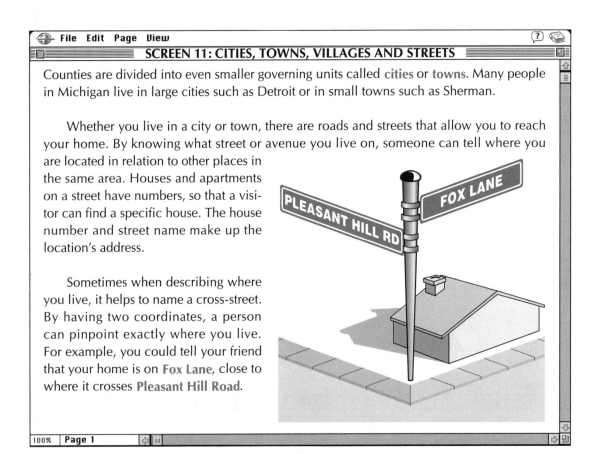

File   Edit   Page   View

SCREEN 11: CITIES, TOWNS, VILLAGES AND STREETS

Counties are divided into even smaller governing units called **cities** or **towns**. Many people in Michigan live in large cities such as Detroit or in small towns such as Sherman.

Whether you live in a city or town, there are roads and streets that allow you to reach your home. By knowing what street or avenue you live on, someone can tell where you are located in relation to other places in the same area. Houses and apartments on a street have numbers, so that a visitor can find a specific house. The house number and street name make up the location's address.

Sometimes when describing where you live, it helps to name a cross-street. By having two coordinates, a person can pinpoint exactly where you live. For example, you could tell your friend that your home is on **Fox Lane**, close to where it crosses **Pleasant Hill Road**.

100%   Page 1

NOTES

I live in the (city or town) of ___?___ . The street on which I live is called ___?___ . The nearest cross street is ___?___ . My house or apartment number is ___?___ .

Closing

WRITING A LETTER TO ZULAR

You now have enough information about where you live to direct someone else to your location. On a separate sheet of paper, write instructions for Zular explaining how to find your home. Before you start your letter to Zular, read the following hints for writing a **"how to"** letter.

Skill Builder

THE "HOW TO" FORM OF WRITING

A "how to" writing gives step-by-step directions to the reader about how to do something. "How to" writings can be about almost anything. For example, they can explain how to make a cake, assemble a toy or ride a bicycle. Here are some helpful hints on creating a "how to" writing.

HELPFUL HINTS

1. **Start with a theme statement.** This statement should explain what the reader will be doing. For example:

   Here are the directions for finding my house at 75 Fox Lane.

2. **Use a "bridge" sentence.** Sometimes you will need a connecting sentence to introduce the reader to the details of what you are writing about. For example:

   If you follow my directions carefully, it should take an hour to reach my house.

3. **Write a step-by-step list of what to do.** Starting with the first step, explain to the reader how each step should follow another in order until the task is completed. Use words that show the reader you are moving from one step to another: "first," "next," "then," "later" and "finally." For example:

   First, take Interstate 75 going east. Then, get off Interstate 75 at the Pleasant Hill Road exit. Next, drive up the hill past two traffic lights. Finally, make a right turn at Fox Lane. Our home is the second house on the right.

4. **Point out what may go wrong.** Tell the reader about any problems that might occur and how to avoid them. For example:

   Some people have trouble seeing the street sign for Fox Lane, since it is partly hidden by a tree. You can recognize Fox Lane by the bank on the corner.

5. **Write a Conclusion.** Provide a closing sentence that ties together your directions. For example:

   If you follow these directions carefully, you should have no trouble finding my house. I look forward to seeing you soon.

Now that you better understand the "how to" form of writing, let's put your new skill to use. Review the notes that you took at the end of each computer screen. Use the information in your notes to write a letter to Zular, your pen pal from outer space.

INTER-GALACTIC COMMUNICATION

Dear Zular: [Greeting]

[Theme Statement]: _____

_____

[Bridge Sentence]: _____

_____

[Step-By-Step Instructions]: _____

_____

_____

[Conclusion]: _____

_____

Your pen pal, [Closing]

(sign your name)
[Signature]

FAMOUS PLACES: MICHIGAN SPACE AND SCIENCE CENTER

Michigan is home to more astronauts than any other state in our nation. Astronauts **Roger Chaffee, Jim McDivitt, Jack Lousma, Al Worden** and **Brewster Shaw** were all born in Michigan. Because of this close association with the space program, a Space and Science Center was built on the campus of Jackson Community College. At the Space Center, visitors can see a Mercury Redstone rocket, the Apollo 9 Command Module and other spacecraft.

Can you identify any of these spacecraft?

EXPANDING YOUR UNDERSTANDING

Creating Vocabulary Cards

Equator
What is the "equator"?
Which hemispheres does it separate?

Prime Meridian
What is the "Prime Meridian"?
Which hemispheres does it separate?

Locating Places on Maps

Make a copy of the map below. Then number the map boxes to identify (1) Northern Hemisphere; (2) Southern Hemisphere; (3) Eastern Hemisphere; (4) Western Hemisphere; (5) North Pole; (6) South Pole; (7) equator; and (8) Prime Meridian.

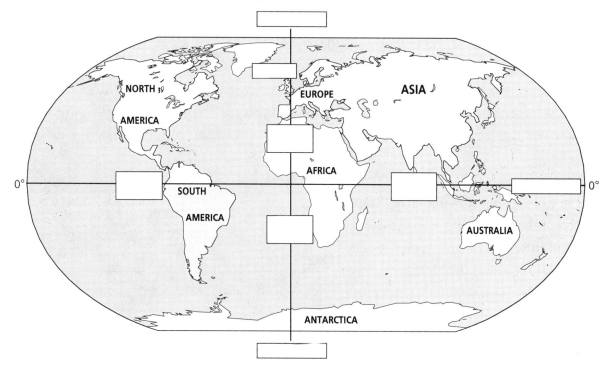

Describing Where You Live

Make a large copy of the diagram to the right. Starting with the outer circle, write the name of your nation, region, state, county and community. The outer circle has already been done for you. Complete the other four circles.

HOW GOOD A CARTOGRAPHER ARE YOU?

2B In this activity, you will learn how maps help us to locate places. Look for the following important words:

▶ Map ▶ Grid ▶ Legend (Key) ▶ Latitude
▶ Cartographer ▶ Symbol ▶ Scale ▶ Longitude

Your friend in California has sent a map of an imaginary community that he made as a school project. You look at his map and say to yourself: "This seems like an interesting project to do. I'm also going to make a map."

WHAT ARE MAPS?

▶ You ask your teacher for advice on how to begin. Your teacher explains that a **map** is really a small picture, diagram or model of a place. It shows where things are located. Your teacher says the easiest way to understand a map is by mapping things in a small area. She suggests you start by making a map of your desktop.

You draw a box to represent your desktop. Your teacher then puts three objects in different locations on the top of your desk. She says, "Now pretend you are a bird, flying over the desk. Can you describe *exactly* where the objects on your desk are located?"

You find this hard to do. Your teacher agrees that it is not easy. Your teacher tells you that the earliest
▶ **cartographers** (*people who make maps*) had the same problem.

To help locate places on a map, cartographers today usually make a grid similar to the one for the "desk map" to the right. A **grid** uses straight lines that cross each other. The crossing lines form rectangles. The rows along the top and side are given letters or numbers.

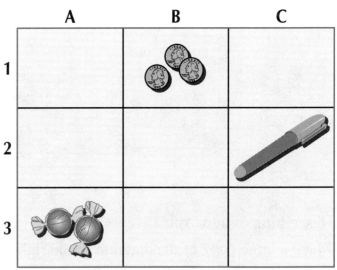

A GRID OF YOUR DESK

LEARNING TO USE A MAP

Maps are drawings, models or diagrams of a part of the Earth. They come in different sizes and shapes. A **political map** shows where countries, states and cities are located. Other maps show geographic features such as mountains, oceans and rivers. Still others show airports, parks and schools. A **globe** is a special kind of map. It is a three-dimensional sphere that shows the entire Earth.

THE TITLE

To understand a map, first look at its title. The **title** tells you what area or part of the Earth is shown on the map.

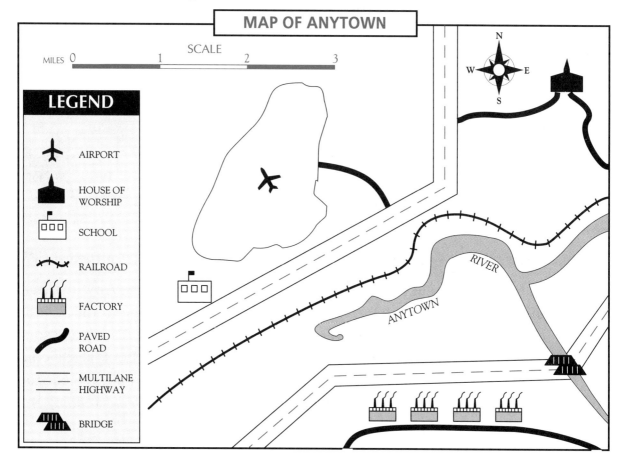

THE LEGEND

The secret to using any map is to understand its symbols. Instead of writing the word "highway," "railroad," "airport" or "school" each time one of these appears on the ▶ map, mapmakers use symbols to represent these things. A map **symbol** is a drawing that stands for an actual place or thing.

Symbols may appear as shapes, lines, dots, dashes or drawings. Each map will have ▶ its own unique set of symbols. Mapmakers provide a **legend** to explain in words what each symbol means. The legend "unlocks" the meaning of the symbols used on the map. For this reason, the legend is sometimes called the "**key**." For example, the symbol for an airport on one map may be entirely different on another map. Each symbol is explained in the legend, so you can tell what it means.

✔ CHECKING YOUR UNDERSTANDING ✔

1. What is the title of the map on page 27?

2. There are 8 symbols on the map of Anytown. On a separate sheet of paper, draw the symbol used for:

   ◆ a factory   ◆ a school   ◆ a bridge   ◆ an airport

DIRECTION INDICATOR

To make it easier to find directions on a map, mapmakers provide a **direction indicator**. It is often called a **compass rose**. The compass rose shows the four **cardinal** (*basic*) directions:

   ◆ **north** (N)   ◆ **south** (S)   ◆ **east** (E)   ◆ **west** (W)

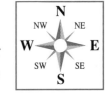

Sometimes we need to find places that fall in between the four basic directions. A compass rose may also show four **intermediate** (*in-between*) directions:

   ◆ **northeast** (NE)   ◆ **northwest** (NW)   ◆ **southeast** (SE)   ◆ **southwest** (SW)

Let's see how well you understand what you have just read. On the Anytown map, in which direction would you have to travel to go from the bridge to the school? Here are the steps to figure out the answer. Most maps show north at the top and south at the bottom, but you should check the compass rose to be sure. Look at the compass rose in the upper right hand corner of the Anytown map. If you traveled from the bridge (*in the eastern part of Anytown*) to the school (*in the western part*), you would be traveling west.

SCALE

Just as a model airplane is a small version of a large, real airplane, a map is a small diagram of a large, real place. If a map were the same size as the area it shows, it would be too large to use. Imagine a map of your school the same size as your school!

The larger the area represented, the less detail a map will usually have. For example, a map of the United States may show only outlines of the states and some cities. A map of your school can show much more detail, such as each classroom.

Mapmakers use a device called a **scale** to show what distances the measurements on a ◀ map stand for in real life. The scale can be used to figure out the distance between any two places on a map. Scales tell us the real distance, usually in miles or kilometers. Map scales are usually shown as a line marked: "Scale of Miles." Mapmakers may use one inch to represent (*stand for*) one real mile. On a map of a large area, one inch may represent 100 miles or more.

Let's see how we can go about finding the approximate distance from Detroit to Battle Creek. First, look at the map below. Put a ruler under the scale on the map. You will see that one inch on the scale of miles represents a real distance of 100 miles.

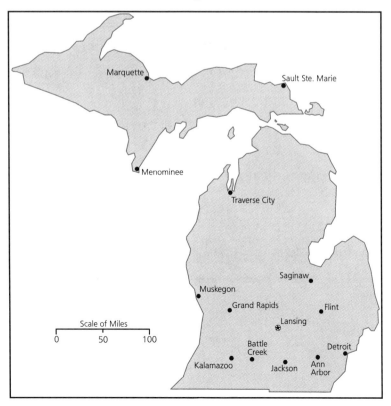

Put a piece of paper on the map. Line up the top edge of the paper until it touches both Detroit and Battle Creek. Mark both spots with a pencil or pen. Now use a ruler to measure this distance. It measures about an inch. One inch represents 100 miles. Therefore, the distance from Detroit to Battle Creek is about 100 miles.

✔ CHECKING YOUR UNDERSTANDING ✔

Let's practice the new skill you just learned. Using the map on the previous page, what would be the distance from:

- Marquette to Sault Ste. Marie?
- Flint to Traverse City?
- Kalamazoo to Saginaw?
- Grand Rapids to Ann Arbor?
- Jackson to Kalamazoo?
- Traverse City to Menominee?

Closing

DRAWING A MAP OF AN IMAGINARY TOWN

It's time for you to complete the task described at the start of this activity. You now have enough information to draw a map at least as good as the one your friend from California has sent. You decide you will map an imaginary town named after yourself. For example, if your name is Brian, you'll call the town **Brian**ville. If your name is Maria, the town will be called **Maria**ville. Use the following steps to create your map:

1. Decide how many different features you want to show on your map.
2. Think of where on the map you will place each feature.
3. Place each feature on your map.
4. Create symbols for a legend or "key" to explain the features on your map.
5. Add a direction indicator (*compass rose*) showing north, south, east and west.
6. Include a scale of miles.
7. Finally, put a title at the top of your map: MY MAP OF __?__ VILLE

EXPANDING YOUR UNDERSTANDING

Creating Vocabulary Cards

Map
What is a "map"?
Name four elements of a map.

Legend
What is a "legend"?
What is a legend used for?

Interpreting a Mileage Chart of Cities in Michigan

In this activity, you learned how to measure distances on a map. In addition to providing a scale, road maps often contain a **mileage chart.** The following mileage chart shows the approximate distances from one city to another on commonly used roadways.

MILEAGE CHART

	Ann Arbor	Battle Creek	Detroit	Mackinaw City	Manistee	Muskegon	Saginaw
Ann Arbor	•	76	38	272	232	166	86
Battle Creek	76	•	114	266	179	98	273
Detroit	38	114	•	281	242	188	96
Mackinaw City	272	266	179	•	164	231	188
Manistee	232	179	141	312	•	85	146
Muskegon	166	98	143	378	231	•	131
Saginaw	86	273	13	336	188	146	•

To find the distance from **Detroit** to **Mackinaw City** you will need to use the information on the chart.

❖ Find *Detroit* on the left-hand column. Using your left hand, hold a finger on the name *Detroit*. Then using your right hand, put a finger on *Mackinaw City*, along the top row.

❖ Now move your right finger straight down and slide your left finger straight across. Your fingers will meet at "281." Thus, it is 281 miles from Detroit to Mackinaw City.

Let's practice the skill of reading a mileage chart. What is the distance:

1. from Battle Creek to Saginaw?   **2.** from Muskegon to Ann Arbor?

◆ LEARNING ABOUT LATITUDE AND LONGITUDE ◆

In order to help find the exact location of any place on Earth, geographers have created two sets of imaginary lines—called "latitude" and "longitude" lines.

LINES OF LATITUDE

▶ **Latitude** (lat' i tood) is the name given to any of the imaginary horizontal lines that run *across* the Earth. A good way to help recall which way latitude lines run is to think of them as *steps* of a **lad**der, because lines of latitude run horizontally. They are sometimes called **parallels** because latitude lines run parallel to each other. Because they are parallel lines, they never meet.

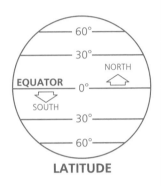

LATITUDE

Since a map or globe would be too confusing if *every* line of latitude were shown, mapmakers usually draw in only some latitude lines. The **equator** is the most important latitude line. It stretches all around the middle of the Earth. It is the same distance from the North Pole as it is from the South Pole.

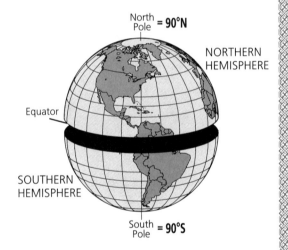

All other latitude lines are identified by how far north or south of the equator they are. Lines of north latitude are shown on areas north of the equator. Lines of south latitude are shown on areas south of the equator.

Each latitude line is assigned a number in degrees to show its distance from the equator. The symbol for **degrees** is °. Going in either direction from the equator, we mark latitude lines from 1° to 90°. An "N" or "S" is added after the number of degrees to show if the line is north or south of the equator. For example, a latitude line 87 degrees north of the equator would be written as 87°N. Lines south of the equator have an "S" after the number of degrees.

At the equator (0° degrees latitude) the climate is generally hot. The sphere of the Earth curves away from the Sun as you go towards the North and South Poles. As a result, the higher the latitude number, the cooler the climate will generally be. The angle of the Earth's tilt as it revolves around the Sun makes the seasons change.

❖ CONTINUED

LINES OF LONGITUDE

Longitudes (lon' ji tōōdz) are imaginary lines that run up and down the Earth. They are drawn as lines connecting the North Pole to the South Pole, and are sometimes called **meridians**. Unlike latitude lines, they are not parallel. All the longitude lines meet at both the North and South Poles.

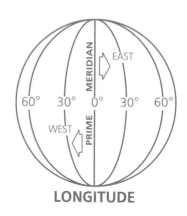

LONGITUDE

The **Prime Meridian** is the most important longitude line. Geographers use it to divide the Earth into two hemispheres (*east and west*). The half of the Earth west of the Prime Meridian is known as the Western Hemisphere, while the half to the east is known as the Eastern Hemisphere.

Like the equator, the Prime Meridian is identified as zero degrees (0°). Going in either direction from the Prime Meridian, we mark the longitude from 1° to 180°, adding **"E"** or **"W"** to indicate if it is east or west of the Prime Meridian.

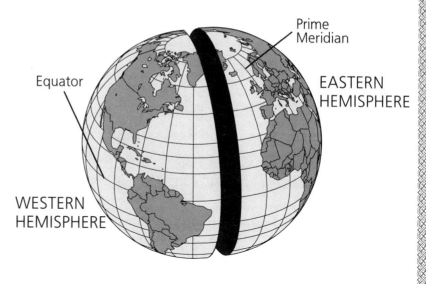

Because longitude lines are not parallel, they are not always the same distance from one another. At the equator, each degree of longitude measures a distance of about 69 miles. As the longitude lines come nearer to the North or South Pole, they get closer and closer together. Finally, all longitude lines meet at both the North and South Poles.

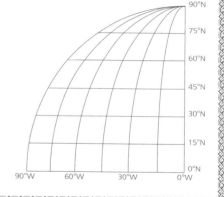

Using Latitude and Longitude to Locate Places in Michigan

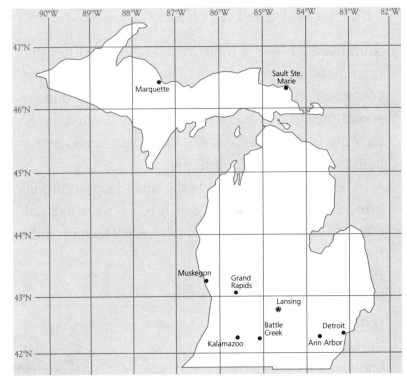

When latitude and longitude lines both appear on a map or globe, they form a grid pattern. By knowing the points at which latitude and longitude lines meet, you can locate any place on the surface of the Earth.

Look at the map on the right. What is the approximate latitude and longitude of Grand Rapids? To find out, put your finger on the dot representing Grand Rapids. Move your finger down slightly until it touches 43°N latitude—this line is 43° **north** of the equator. Next, move your finger from Grand Rapids slightly to the left, until it touches 86°W longitude. This line is 86° **west** of the Prime Meridian. Grand Rapids' location is close to where these two lines cross—at 43°N latitude and 86°W longitude. Because latitude is always "N" or "S" and longitude is always "E" or "W," we can simply write 43°N, 86°W.

Use the map above to identify the approximate location of:

1. Kalamazoo   3. Ann Arbor   5. Battle Creek   7. Marquette
2. Lansing   4. Detroit   6. Muskegon   8. Sault Ste. Marie

HOW DOES GEOGRAPHY AFFECT PEOPLE'S LIVES?

2C In this activity, you will learn about the five themes of geography. Look for the following important words and phrases:

▶ Geography   ▶ Absolute Location

▶ Five Themes of Geography   ▶ Relative Location

THE SUBJECT OF GEOGRAPHY

Geography includes not only the study of different places, but also the study of ◀ people, where they live and how they are linked to the world around them. Geographers have identified five themes to help us understand how the world and its peoples are linked. Each theme highlights one part of the study of geography. The **five themes of geography** are *location, place, region, human-environment interaction* ◀ and *movement*. Let's see how these apply to your school.

THE FIVE THEMES OF GEOGRAPHY

LOCATION

Location is where something can be found in relation to other things. Each continent, country, state and county has its own special "location." Even buildings have a location.

❖ **Absolute Location** is the exact position of a particular place on the Earth's sur- ◀ face. For example, the absolute location of your school is its unique address.

❖ **Relative Location** is the position of a particular place on the Earth's surface in rela- ◀ tion to other locations. Relative location uses such terms as *near, by* or *at the corner of* to identify the location.

QUESTIONS A GEOGRAPHER MIGHT ASK ABOUT YOUR SCHOOL

- What is the absolute location of your school?
- What is the location of your school relative to the nearest fire station?

Is your school located near a firehouse?

PLACE

Place refers to the qualities of a location that make it different from other locations. What is the place like where you live? Is it hot or cold? Dry or humid? Mountainous or flat? You will learn more about the geographic features that make a place unique later in this unit.

QUESTIONS A GEOGRAPHER MIGHT ASK ABOUT YOUR SCHOOL

- Is your school made of brick or wood?
- How many floors does it have?
- How many classrooms are there?

What are the special features of your school?

REGION

Regions are areas that have similar characteristics or features. Regions can be large or small. People within a region usually have more contact with one another than they do with people outside the region. One region can sometimes be considered to belong to an even larger region. For example,

❖ your **community** is a small region that is part of a larger region called a **county**.
❖ your **county**, in turn, is part of a larger region called a **state**.
❖ your **state** is part of an even larger region of states known as the **Midwest**.

QUESTIONS A GEOGRAPHER MIGHT ASK ABOUT YOUR SCHOOL

- In which community is your school located?
- In which county is your school located?
- In which state is your school located?
- In which region of the United States is your state located?

HUMAN-ENVIRONMENT INTERACTION

Human-environment interaction is the way in which the physical features of a place affect its people. It is also how the people affect the physical features. For example, people can change their environment by cutting down forests and building cities. On the other hand, the environment also shapes what people do, such as skiing on mountains.

QUESTIONS A GEOGRAPHER MIGHT ASK ABOUT YOUR SCHOOL

- How do students in your school dress during the winter months?
- How do students in your school dress during the summer months?

What time of the year was this photograph taken? How do you know?

MOVEMENT

People often interact with each other. They trade, travel and communicate to get what they need. Understanding this **movement** of goods, ideas and people from place to place allows us to learn about many different lands and cultures.

QUESTIONS A GEOGRAPHER MIGHT ASK ABOUT YOUR SCHOOL

- Name a product used in your school that was made in another country.
- Do you know any people who were not born in Michigan? If so, where did they originally come from?

Students expand their knowledge at the Impression 5 Science Center in Lansing. What do you think they are learning about?

In learning about any new area, you should keep five basic questions in mind:

❖ How does **location** affect the area?

❖ What kind of **place** is it?

❖ What **region** does the area belong to?

❖ What **human-environment interactions** have taken place?

❖ What **movements** of people, goods and ideas affect the area?

CONNECTING GEOGRAPHY TO WHERE PEOPLE LIVE AND WORK

You have just learned how the five themes of geography apply to your school. These themes apply to every place in Michigan. Often there is a strong connection between the geographic features of an area—such as its rivers, mountains and natural resources—and where people live and do business. Let's look at this connection by examining the city of Marquette.

MARQUETTE: A CASE STUDY

▶ **Marquette** is located on the Upper Peninsula, along the southern shoreline of Lake Superior. It is halfway between Sault Ste. Marie, on the eastern tip of the Upper Peninsula, and Duluth, Minnesota. With about 22,000 people, Marquette is the largest city on the Upper Peninsula.

Most of the Upper Peninsula is forest. Marquette is near thousands of lakes, streams and waterfalls. The land is more hilly than the Lower Peninsula. Twenty-five miles east of the city, visitors can see the spectacular Pictured Rocks National Seashore. These green and orange sandstone cliffs jut out into the waters of Lake Superior.

Marquette's climate is influenced by the Great Lakes. Lake waters warm the peninsula in winter and cool it in summer. The average temperature of Marquette is about 18°F in January, and 68°F in July. Because of winds and moisture from the lake, the city receives plenty of snow—about ten feet each year. The growing season is shorter than in the southern part of Michigan, and the soil is less fertile. Nearby farmers specialize in growing fruits like apples, but farming is not as important as it is in southern Michigan.

Father Jacques Marquette, a French explorer, first passed through this region in 1670. Later, this territory became part of the United States. When Michigan gave up land on its eastern frontier to Ohio in 1837, it received the Upper Peninsula in exchange. Seven years later, iron ore was discovered in the southwest part of the peninsula. By the 1880s, railroad lines were completed to carry the ore to Marquette, to be loaded onto ships. The ore was then shipped through the Great Lakes to Pennsylvania. In the late 1800s, the forests of the Upper Peninsula also supported an active lumber industry. Later, the location of a prison and a college brought new jobs to Marquette.

Today, the lifestyles of people in Marquette continue to be influenced by the city's location, resources and climate.

Marquette is far from other urban centers, but has easy access to them by water, highway, railroad and air. It is 500 miles north of Detroit. More than 7,000 students attend Northern Michigan University. The Cleveland Cliffs Iron Company, in nearby Ishpeming, employs a large number of workers.

Aerial view of Marquette.

Because of the beautiful forests, lakes and winter snow, people in Marquette enjoy nature and outdoor sports. In winter, people participate in cross-country skiing, sledding, dog-sledding and ice fishing. In summer, they go camping, fishing, swimming and boating. Visitors to Marquette also enjoy going to the Marquette County Historical Museum.

FAMOUS PLACES:
MARQUETTE COUNTY HISTORICAL MUSEUM

Marquette has its own historical museum. It has exhibits on Marquette's development. The museum has displays that examine the role of key industries in the area—shipping, logging and mining. There are several life-sized **dioramas**—a three-dimensional scene created by placing objects, figures and pictures in front of a painted background. One diorama shows a furnished Chippewa wigwam. Another diorama displays surveyors at work using early compasses.

THINK ABOUT IT

1. How has Marquette's location influenced its development?
2. How have the people of Marquette adjusted to their environment?

THE INFLUENCE OF GEOGRAPHY

Marquette's geographic features obviously influence how its people live. Is this also true for other places? Let's look at two other cities—Lansing and Detroit—to further see if geography affects how their residents live. For this project, the class will be divided into groups. Each group will research one city to find information about how its people live and how they have adjusted to their environment. To locate information, you may want to:

❖ use the Internet

❖ check the name of the city in an **almanac** under "Cities of the U.S."

❖ consult an **atlas** to find some of the geographic features of the city

❖ write or call the **Chamber of Commerce** of that city

❖ use **travel guides** that feature that city

❖ call the city's toll free **Travel Information** number to obtain information

Geographic Features	Lansing	Detroit
Is the city located near a major body of water?		
Are there any geographic barriers that stand in the way of its development?		
What are some of the city's main natural resources?		
Describe the climate of the city.		
What are the main occupations of its residents?		
What do the residents do for enjoyment?		
What features have attracted people to this city?		
What cultural features does the city provide?		
Other Questions: _____		

REVIEWING THE IMPACT OF GEOGRAPHY ON PEOPLE'S LIVES

Closing

Now that you have looked at three cities in Michigan, what conclusions can you draw? Write an essay focusing on the ways geography influences how people live.

EXPANDING YOUR UNDERSTANDING

Creating Vocabulary Cards

The Five Themes of Geography
List the Five Themes of
Geography.

Absolute and Relative Location
What is "absolute" location?
What is "relative" location?

Applying the "Five Themes" to Your Community

A good way to understand new ideas, such as the five themes of geography, is to illustrate them with a picture or drawing. How easily can you find examples in your own community that illustrate each of the five themes? Copy the five boxes below on a separate sheet of paper. In each box, draw or find a picture of something in your community that illustrates the listed theme. For example, to illustrate location, you might draw or attach a picture of a house with a large address sign.

Location:	
Place:	
Region:	
Human-environment interaction:	
Movement:	

WHAT DOES MICHIGAN "LOOK" LIKE?

2D In this activity, you will learn about some of the important physical features of Michigan. Look for the following important words and phrases:

▶ Peninsula   ▶ Weather   ▶ Climate

▶ Topography   ▶ Precipitation   ▶ Tables

One day you get a letter from a friend. She writes that she will be visiting you this summer. Before arriving, she would like to learn about the physical features of Michigan. She asks you to send her a description of the state's geography. But Michigan is so large that you don't know what to write.

TWO WAYS TO DESCRIBE MICHIGAN

You ask your teacher where to start. Your teacher says, "Before I help you, please draw a picture of what an apple looks like. Then write a brief description of what an apple looks like." That seems simple enough, you think.

MY APPLE DRAWING	MY APPLE DESCRIPTION
?	?

After you have completed the task, your teacher asks:

❖ Which was easier—drawing an apple or describing it?

❖ Which provides more information, the drawing or the description?

❖ Did they both provide the same kind of information? Explain your answer.

Ah! Now you understand what your teacher meant. To give someone accurate information about a place, it is sometimes best to provide both a picture **and** a description. You decide to send your friend a written description **and** a "picture" of Michigan.

You start by getting a book about Michigan from the library. The book has written descriptions of Michigan but no maps. You ask your teacher for help. She says that the written descriptions will allow you to play the role of a junior or "amateur" cartographer.

She tells you that modern cartographers often begin with photos of the region they intend to map, taken from an airplane or satellite. Then they examine the area, review other maps and conduct research about the region to fill in the details. Your teacher goes to her desk and hands you an outline map of Michigan. She says this map should help you to "picture" Michigan. Using the written descriptions in your library book will help you fill in the details on your outline map.

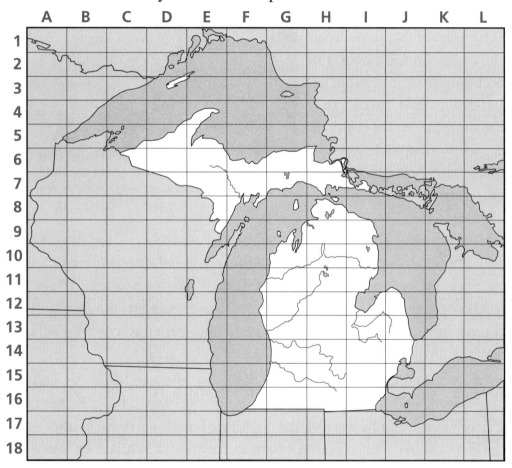

 THE GEOGRAPHY OF MICHIGAN

When you open your library book on Michigan, here is what you find:

SIZE
In size, Michigan ranks 23rd out of the 50 states in the United States. It is the third largest state east of the Mississippi River: only Florida and Georgia are larger. In fact, Michigan is larger than many countries. Michigan is also the tenth largest state in population.

▶   Michigan consists of two separate peninsulas. A **peninsula** is a piece of land almost completely surrounded by water but connected by one side to a larger piece of land. The northern part of Michigan is called the **Upper Peninsula**. It accounts for about 30% of the state's land area. The southern part of Michigan is called the **Lower Peninsula**. Its area is more than double the size of the Upper Peninsula. The total land area of both peninsulas is more than 58,000 square miles.

THE BOUNDARIES (BORDERS) OF MICHIGAN

Michigan is often referred to as the "Great Lakes State" because it is bordered by four of the five Great Lakes. Only Lake Ontario does not touch Michigan. Because most of Michigan borders the Great Lakes, the state's shoreline is longer than any other state's except Alaska's. If straightened, Michigan's shoreline would stretch from the Atlantic to the Pacific Ocean.

Lake Michigan and the Sleeping Bear Dunes.
Which state has a longer shoreline than Michigan's?

❖ **Water Boundaries.** To the north of the Upper Peninsula lies the largest of the Great Lakes, Lake Superior. (*To help you find places on the map on page 43, grid letters and numbers are shown. For example, Lake Superior stretches from B5 to H6*). Lakes Michigan (G8–16) and Huron (H8–L9), connected by the Straits of Mackinac, are to the southeast. To the southwest, the **Menominee River** forms the boundary between the Upper Peninsula and the state of Wisconsin.

The Lower Peninsula is bordered on the west by Lake Michigan and on the east by Lakes Huron and Erie and their connecting waterways. Lake Huron empties into Lake Erie (J16–L15) by way of the St. Clair River, Lake St. Clair (J15) and the Detroit River (J14). These bodies of water form the boundary between the Lower Peninsula and the Canadian province of Ontario (K14).

⌒   A NOTE ABOUT PROVINCES   ⌒

Just as the United States is divided into states, Canada is divided into political units called **provinces**.

❖ **Land Boundaries.** Michigan has a land border with three states. The states that border Michigan are **Indiana** (F17–H17) and **Ohio** (H17–K16) to the south of the Lower Peninsula, and **Wisconsin** (B6–E14) to the southwest of the Upper Peninsula.

FAMOUS PLACES: MICHIGAN'S LIGHTHOUSES

A lighthouse is a tall tower, built to provide a beam of light to guide ships in fog, haze or the dark of night. Michigan has more lighthouses than any other state. Most of its lighthouses were built between 1825 and 1900. Lighthouses were originally manned by the U.S. Lighthouse Service. Today, Michigan's lighthouses are all automated and equipped with modern technology. Improvements in radar have reduced the need for new lighthouses.

Point Betsie Lighthouse in winter.

THE AMATEUR CARTOGRAPHER

On your map, label the bodies of water that border Michigan. Also label Canada and the three states that border Michigan.

RIVERS, LAKES AND BAYS

Michigan is called a "water wonderland" because of its many rivers, lakes and bays. **Rivers** and **lakes** provide fresh water for drinking, farming, recreation, transportation and industry. Most Michigan rivers are found in the western part of the Lower Peninsula. Rivers in the Upper Peninsula are smaller and have rapids and waterfalls. Its largest river is the **Escanaba** (F7), which flows south into Green Bay, Wisconsin.

The Detroit River, the St. Mary's River and the St. Clair River (J14) are among the state's most important waterways. They connect the three upper Great Lakes with the St. Lawrence Seaway and the Atlantic Ocean. Other rivers include the **Muskegon, St. Joseph, Manistee, Tahquamenon**, and the **Kalamazoo.** The **Grand River** is the longest river in Michigan. Two major rivers in the east-

Tahquamenon Falls in the Upper Peninsula.
How many of Michigan's rivers can you name?

ern part of the Lower Peninsula are the **Saginaw** (*the state's shortest river*) and the **Au Sable River** (I10).

Lakes are bodies of fresh water surrounded by land. There are over 11,000 fresh-water lakes in Michigan. The largest one is **Houghton** (H11) in the Lower Peninsula. **Bays** are a part of a larger body of water that cuts into the land. The bays of Michigan include the Saginaw (I12), Grand Traverse (G9) and Whitefish Bays (H6).

THE AMATEUR CARTOGRAPHER

On your map, label some of the major rivers, lakes and bays of Michigan.

TOPOGRAPHY

▶ **Topography** (tə pog' rə fē) refers to the land forms of a place. Topography affects where people live and what they can do. Land forms are created in different ways. Michigan's land forms were created over millions of years. The state owes much of its present shape to the movement and pressure of glaciers. During the last Ice Age, the area was covered by glaciers. A **glacier** (glā' shər) is a very thick sheet of ice. As the glaciers slowly moved across Michigan, they dug holes in the ground. The holes filled with water when the glaciers later melted. The larger holes became the Great Lakes. The smaller holes became the thousands of small lakes that now cover Michigan.

Today, Michigan's topography has two distinct regions.

❖ **Great Lakes Plains.** The Great Lakes Plains include all of the Lower Peninsula and the eastern half of the Upper Peninsula. During the Ice Age, glaciers divided the Lower Peninsula into two different sections. The moving ice scraped the soil from the surface of the land and pushed it as far as the southern half of the Lower Peninsula. After that, the glaciers started to melt, leaving the rich soil behind. As a result, soils in the Upper Peninsula and northern parts of the Lower Peninsula are generally poor for farming. Richer soils are found in southern Michigan.

❖ **Superior Uplands.** The highest elevations in Michigan are found in the Superior Uplands. The land here is hilly or mountainous. Both the **Huron** and the **Porcupine** Mountains are located in this area. The highest point in the state is **Mount Arvon**.

More than 500 islands also belong to Michigan. Most of these islands are in the Great Lakes. Michigan's three largest islands are **Isle Royale** (D3), **Mackinac Island** (H7) and **Beaver Island** (G8).

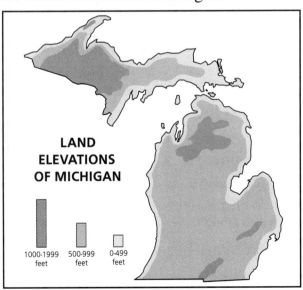

LAND ELEVATIONS OF MICHIGAN

1000-1999 feet   500-999 feet   0-499 feet

FAMOUS PLACES: MACKINAC BRIDGE

Five miles of water separate the Upper and Lower Peninsula at the Straits of Mackinac. Starting in 1923, ferries allowed people to move between the peninsulas. However, Michiganders dreamed of one day traveling from one peninsula to the other without a ferry. Serious problems first had to be overcome. Could a bridge five miles long be built? Would the bridge be strong enough

The Mackinac Bridge.
Which two pieces of land does the bridge connect?

to withstand the winds of 60 to 70 miles per hour? In 1950, studies showed that building such a bridge was possible. By 1957, the Mackinac Bridge had been completed.

THE AMATEUR CARTOGRAPHER

On your map, label the locations of Isle Royale, Mackinac Island, Beaver Island and the Mackinac Bridge.

WEATHER AND CLIMATE

We often hear people talk about the **weather**. Weather is a description of an area's current ◄ temperature, wind and sunshine. A key factor that plays a role in an area's weather is its temperature—how hot or cold it is. Weather also involves the amount of **precipitation** ◄ (pri sip i tā' shən)—the moisture that falls to Earth as rain, snow, hail and sleet.

Climate (kli' mit) is different from weather. Climate is the average of all the weather conditions over a long period of years. People are often attracted to an area with plentiful rainfall, mild temperatures, and sufficient sunshine. Climate also affects what farmers can grow. An area's climate is affected by its location, land forms and nearness to bodies of water. Michigan's climate is largely influenced by its location in the center of the North American continent and its nearness to the Great Lakes.

Young people ice-skating in Marquette.
What other wintertime sports do Michiganders enjoy?

Michigan's climate is generally warm or hot in the summer and cool or cold in the winter, depending on the location in the state. Since large bodies of water, like the Great Lakes, respond slowly to temperature changes, summer is cooler and winter is warmer than they otherwise would be. The average monthly temperature for January varies from 10°F (–12°C) in the northwest to 26°F (–3°C) in the south. Precipitation in the state is usually evenly spread throughout the year. It ranges from 26 inches in the north to 36 inches in the southern part of the state. In the winter, snowfall is often very heavy along the northern shores of the Upper Peninsula.

The **growing season** of an area is the period of time that crops are safe from frost that could kill them. In Michigan, the growing season varies from one part of the state to another. In the Upper Peninsula, the growing season can be as long as 150 days or as short as 70 days, depending on location. In the Lower Peninsula, the growing season is generally longer—from 80 to 170 days.

Tulip gardens in Holland, Michigan.
What other kinds of flowers grow in Michigan during the spring and summer?

Average Temperatures in Fahrenheit in two Michigan Cities				
Month	Detroit's Normal Daily High	Detroit's Normal Daily Low	Sault Ste. Marie's Normal Daily High	Sault Ste. Marie's Normal Daily Low
January	30.3°	15.6°	21.1°	4.6°
February	33.3°	17.6°	23.2°	4.8°
March	44.4°	27.0°	32.8°	15.3°
April	57.7°	36.8°	48.0°	28.4°
May	69.6°	47.1°	61.6°	38.4°
June	78.9°	56.3°	70.5°	45.5°
July	83.3°	61.3°	76.3°	51.3°
August	81.3°	59.6°	73.8°	54.3°
September	73.9°	52.5°	65.9°	44.3°
October	61.5°	40.9°	54.3°	36.2°
November	48.1°	32.2°	40.0°	25.9°
December	35.2°	21.4°	26.2°	11.8°

If you have trouble understanding this table, read the following Skill Builder.

Skill Builder
LEARNING TO INTERPRET A TABLE

A table is an arrangement of words or numbers in columns. A table is used to organize large amounts of data so that the information can easily be located and compared.

Tables usually contain different categories of information. Categories in the table on page 48 are found in the headings across the top and down the left-hand side. The first two categories listed along the top row of the table are: *Month* and *Detroit's Normal Daily High and Low.* The "normal daily high" is the average highest temperature in the course of a day for that month. Categories down the left-hand margin list the months of the year.

Suppose you wanted to compare the average Normal Daily High in July for Detroit and Sault Ste. Marie. How would you go about doing this?

◆ First, place a finger from your left hand at the top of the column *Detroit's Normal Daily High.* Slide your finger down this column until you reach the row for *July.*

◆ Using a finger from your right hand, find the column marked *Sault Ste. Marie's Normal Daily High.* Slide your finger down this column until you also reach the row marked *July.*

◆ The row for *July* allows you to compare the *Normal Daily High* in both cities. Thus, the *Normal Daily High* in Detroit is 83.3°F., while in Sault. Ste. Marie it is 76.3°F.

THE AMATEUR CARTOGRAPHER

On your map, locate the two cities in the table. Label each city's average temperatures (normal daily high and low) for January and July.

Closing
WHAT DOES MICHIGAN LOOK LIKE?

How well did you do as an amateur cartographer? Let's find out:

❖ First, compare the map you created with the one found on page 350.

❖ Then, describe any similarities or differences you find between the two maps.

❖ Finally, write a brief description of each item on your map on a separate sheet of paper. Include these descriptions when you send your map to the friend who asked you about Michigan's geography.

◆ THE GREAT LAKES ECOSYSTEM ◆

Within a physical region, such as a rain forest, desert or prairie, there is a balanced relationship between the land, water, atmosphere, plants and animals. This balanced relationship is known as an ecosystem. An **ecosystem** is a system in which plants, animals and the physical environment work together as a single unit.

 ## HOW AN ECOSYSTEM WORKS

The basis for any ecosystem is plant life. Plants trap the energy in sunlight. Plants also depend on nutrients from the soil and water from rain, snow or dew. Animals then eat plants to survive. After the animals die, bacteria, fungi, worms and insects break down the animal bodies and return their nutrients to the soil.

For example, the grasses, rabbits and coyotes on a prairie form a single ecosystem. Energy flows from the sun to the grasses. Rabbits feed on the grasses, and absorb their energy and nutrients. Coyotes eat some of the rabbits, and absorb their energy and nutrients. When the rabbits and coyotes die, bacteria and other decomposers make them decay. This decaying enriches the soil for the grasses. The activities of these plants and animals also affect both land forms and climate. Grass prevents the soil from eroding and produces oxygen, which goes into the air. Animals provide carbon dioxide, which helps trap heat.

THE FOOD CHAIN IN A PRAIRIE ECOSYSTEM

❖ CONTINUED

The **Great Lakes ecosystem** covers the Great Lakes and their surrounding areas. It includes eight states in the United States and two provinces in Canada. About 33 million people live in this ecosystem. The Great Lakes dominate the landscape of this ecosystem and influence its climate. One-fifth of all the world's fresh surface water is found here. The region's rainfall passes into streams and rivers, which drain into the lakes. Much of this water then evaporates from the lakes back into the air. Many birds, fish, insects, mammals and seeds travel from one part of this ecosystem to another.

In a sense, the Great Lakes ecosystem is made up of several smaller related ecosystems. Together, they support a vast variety of plant and animal life. Many of the species (*types*) of fish in the lakes are unique. Along the shores of the lakes are some the world's largest freshwater sand dunes. Plants and animals have adapted to this unique coastal environment by developing into new kinds of species. For example, the dune thistle and Lake Huron locust are found only in this area.

The Great Lakes ecosystem is located where the forests of the eastern United States, the pine forests of Canada and the grassy prairies of the Midwest all meet. The northern areas of the Great Lakes region are home to large pine forests. In the southwest of the region are the flat lands of the prairies.

Humans have had a tremendous impact on the Great Lakes ecosystem. They have cleared the land for growing crops, fished in the lakes and built large cities. Today, the Great Lakes ecosystem supports both industry and agriculture.

Sometimes these human activities have threatened the

Tobico Marsh is a 1,700-acre natural preserve in Bay City. *What role does plant life play in this marsh's ecosystem?*

ecosystem. For example, logging companies once cut down whole forests. Eventually, these companies planted new trees. Now, most of Michigan's northern forests are made up of "second-growth" trees. The greatest threat to the Great Lakes ecosystem today comes from pollution. Companies and cities have dumped chemicals into the lake waters. Many dumpsites in inland areas contain dangerous chemicals. For the Great Lakes ecosystem to survive, humans must learn to interact with their environment without injuring plant or animal life.

EXPANDING YOUR UNDERSTANDING

Creating Vocabulary Cards

Topography
Define "topography."
Give an example of a topographical feature.

Climate
Define "climate."
What is the climate of your area?

Describing the Weather in Your Area

In this activity, you learned the difference between weather and climate.

❖ Describe today's weather. Using a thermometer, give the temperature in Fahrenheit at two different times of the day.

❖ Record the temperatures in your area for five days. Take two readings each day, at about the same time of day. Then create a table showing those temperatures. Calculate the average temperature for all five days.

Features That Make a Place Unique

Each location on Earth has special features that make it different from other places. The special features of a place include the following:

❖ how hot or cold the place is, and how much rainfall it receives;

❖ whether the place is in the mountains, in a flat valley, on rolling hills or on a plain;

❖ the kinds of plants and animals that live there;

❖ whether the place has valuable natural resources; and

❖ whether the place is near or far from bodies of water.

Shorelines like this one along Lake Superior are part of Michigan's physical features.

Which features do you think have the greatest effects on how people live?

WHAT DO MICHIGAN'S REGIONS "LOOK" LIKE?

2E In this activity, you will learn to identify the regions of Michigan. Look for the following important words and phrases:

▶ Upper Peninsula   ▶ Lower Peninsula   ▶ Atlas

Your friend was happy with the map and written description you sent to describe Michigan. But she wants additional information about the regions and cities of your state.

MAIN GEOGRAPHIC REGIONS OF MICHIGAN

You already know that a **region** is an area with common geographic features. Most Michiganders think of Michigan as having two major regions: the Upper and the Lower Peninsula. In this activity, you will read about these two regions. You will also learn about each region's principal cities. To keep track of the two regions, make a larger copy of the chart below. Complete the chart as you read each section.

Geographic Region	Describe Its Location	Describe Its Main Physical Features	Identify Its Major Cities
Lower Peninsula	?	?	?
Upper Peninsula	?	?	?

Although Michigan is large in area, most people live in a few sections of the Lower Peninsula. In fact, more than 75% of the state's residents live on less than 5% of the state's land.

THE AMATEUR CARTOGRAPHER

In this activity you will find a blank outline map for each region. Photocopy or trace the outline to use for your own map. For each region, label its major cities, landforms and bodies of water. At the end of this activity, you will be asked to put these maps together to form a single map of Michigan.

MICHIGAN'S UPPER PENINSULA

▶ The **Upper Peninsula** is large in area, measuring 384 miles from east to west and 233 miles from north to south. In general, the Upper Peninsula has a short growing season and long, cold winters. Much of the area's snowfall does not melt until the start of summer.

Despite its cold winters, the Upper Peninsula is an outdoor paradise. There are twenty-four state parks, three state forests and several national parks. Campers, hunters, fishermen and hikers are all attracted to the beauty of its natural treasures—lakes and rivers, thick forests and a wide range of wildlife.

Because of its geography, the Upper Peninsula is not heavily populated. Only about 320,000 people make the area their permanent home. By comparison, the city of Detroit has three times as many people.

A major winter sport is ice-fishing.
What summer activities attract people to the Upper Peninsula?

THE TOPOGRAPHY OF THE UPPER PENINSULA

Although the Upper Peninsula forms one body of land, it consists of two topographical areas. In the western part of the Upper Peninsula, the land is higher than in the east. The highest elevations in Michigan are located here.

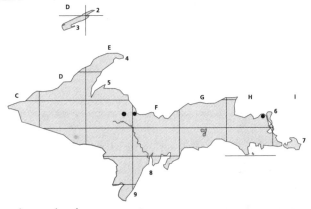

The eastern portion includes lowlands, swamps and hills. The colored cliffs of the **Pictured Rocks** along Lake Superior are found here. They were formed by retreating glaciers and waves washing against the shore.

The Upper Peninsula is often called Michigan's "Treasure Chest" because of its many important minerals and other natural resources. It also has a wide variety of wildlife. Deer, black bears, coyotes, porcupines, bobcats, beavers, owls, bald eagles and hawks all make the Upper Peninsula their home.

Kayaking by the Pictured Rocks.

PLACES OF INTEREST IN THE UPPER PENINSULA

The largest city in the Upper Peninsula is **Marquette** (F6), located on the shores of Lake Superior. In Marquette, tourists can visit the **Marquette Maritime Museum** and **Presque Isle Park**, one of the nation's largest urban parks. The park offers visitors a zoo, hiking trails, and beautiful sand and pebble beaches.

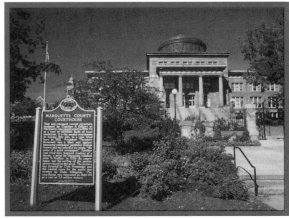

Marquette County Court House, built in 1902.
What other interesting sites are there in Marquette?

One of the most fascinating places to visit in the Upper Peninsula is **Sault Ste. Marie** (H6). Founded in 1668, it is Michigan's oldest city. Located on the Saint Mary's River, it is also the only gateway to Canada along a 300-mile stretch of border. Since the **Soo Locks** opened in 1959, foreign ships have been an important part of the city's life. Visitors take boat rides through the canal to watch the waters being raised twenty-one feet to the level of Lake Superior.

Skiing is one of the popular outdoor sports that brings people to the Upper Peninsula. When **Ishpeming** (E6) was first founded, it was a mining area. The miners brought with them a love of skiing. To amuse themselves, the miners would ski and jump down snow-covered mounds of rock piled high from the mines. In 1887, the sport of ski jumping was introduced to the United States at Ishpeming. Today, the **National Ski Hall of Fame and Museum** is located here. Big Powderhorn Mountain, Indianhead Mountain and Cooper Peak are other well-known ski resorts in the Upper Peninsula.

Isle Royale (D3) is the largest island in Lake Superior. Almost 45 miles long and seven miles wide, it is surrounded by hundreds of smaller islands. Located 22 miles from the mainland, it takes a six-hour ferry ride to reach the island. On the island, there are no roads, and wheeled vehicles are prohibited. The island remains the home of moose and wolves. **Isle Royale National Park** has kept its natural character and still appears much as it did hundreds of years ago.

THE AMATEUR CARTOGRAPHER

On your map, give a title to the region and label Marquette, Sault Ste. Marie, Ishpeming and Isle Royale.

MICHIGAN'S LOWER PENINSULA

▶ The **Lower Peninsula** is shaped like a large oven-mitten. The thumb is separated from the rest of the mitten by Saginaw Bay. The Lower Peninsula is bounded on the west by Lake Michigan, and on the east by Lakes Huron and Erie. Lake St. Clair, and the St. Clair and Detroit Rivers form the border between Michigan and Ontario, Canada.

Extending south from Saginaw Bay, a lowland depression divides the Lower Peninsula into two sections. South of the depression, the land rarely rises more than 200 feet above sea level. North of the depression, the land rises gradually to elevations ranging from 1,200 to 1,700 feet above sea level.

Retreating glaciers played a key role in shaping the Lower Peninsula. In the northern part, glaciers scraped the surface of the Earth. Today, this area has sandy soils lacking many nutrients. In the southern part of the peninsula, the glaciers left behind rich soils. As a result, the southern Lower Peninsula is known for its agriculture. As elsewhere, the area's geographic features help determine how its people earn a living and enjoy themselves.

Cherry trees in bloom in the Lower Peninsula. *Why are soils in the Lower Peninsula more fertile than soils in the Upper Peninsula?*

THE NORTHERN LOWER PENINSULA

The natural features of the Northern Lower Peninsula— its bays, rivers and islands—make it an attractive place to live or visit. One of its most famous features is the Mackinac Bridge, which connects the Upper Peninsula to the Lower Peninsula. In the shadow of the bridge is **Fort Michilimackinac**, a reconstructed French Fort and trading post from the 1700s. During the summer, programs are presented by guides dressed in period clothing.

Fort Michilimackinac with Mackinac Bridge in the background.

Several important islands are located just off the northern coast of the Lower Peninsula. One of the most interesting is **Mackinac Island** in Lake Huron. Among the famous sights on the island is the **Grand Hotel**. This four-story building, with its celebrated white pillars, opened in 1887.

The Grand Hotel on Mackinac Island.

Before Mackinac Island became a part of the United States, it belonged to Native Americans, the French and then the British. The island was called *Michilimakinac*, or "great turtle," by the Native Americans. In 1780, the British built **Fort Mackinac** on the island to secure the area against American colonists during the American Revolution. The fort has been restored and now is a popular museum.

A two-and-a-half-hour ferry ride from the Lower Peninsula brings visitors to **Beaver Island**. This island was once home to **James Jesse Strang**. Strang claimed to be the successor to Joseph Smith, the founder of the Mormon Church. Strang declared himself King of Beaver Island in the 1840s. Today, the island is home to about 400 residents.

Traverse City (G10) is located at the foot of the Grand Traverse Bay. The city is one of Michigan's most popular vacation sites. Traverse City is famous for its annual Cherry Festival.

The Sleeping Bear Dunes attract thousands of visitors each year.

Another popular site on the Lower Peninsula's western shore is **Sleeping Bear Dunes** at Glen Haven. This stretch of shoreline along Lake Michigan includes beautiful beaches, hiking trails, lakes, rivers and campgrounds.

Located at the base where the "thumb" meets the rest of the mitten is **Bay City** (I12). At one time, Bay City was a major lumber town. Today, the city still retains much of its lumber-town flavor. Visitors enjoy viewing fancy homes built by lumber mill owners when the city was a mill town. The Saginaw River links Bay City to its neighbor, **Saginaw** (I13). Like Bay City, Saginaw was also once a lumber town. Today, Saginaw is home to several General Motors plants.

Homes of lumber mill owners line Center Avenue in Bay City's Historic District.

Just south of Saginaw is **Frankenmuth** (I13), Michigan's most popular tourist destination. Each year Frankenmuth attracts more than three million visitors. The town was founded by Lutheran missionaries in 1845. Visitors come to see Frankenmuth's Old World-style architecture, Bavarian festival, German beer halls and shops. They also love to roam through the world's largest Christmas store. It is not surprising that Frankenmuth is often known as "Michigan's Little Bavaria."

One of the many restaurants in Frankenmuth.
What style of architecture do many of Frankenmuth's buildings have?

THE AMATEUR CARTOGRAPHER

On your map, give a title to the region and label Mackinaw City, Mackinac Island, Beaver Island, Traverse City, Bay City, Saginaw and Frankenmuth.

THE SOUTHERN LOWER PENINSULA

The Southern Lower Peninsula is noted for its industries. Manufacturing developed in this area because of its location midway between mineral resources and east coast markets.

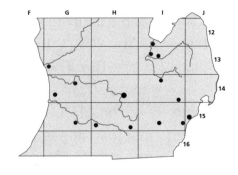

Detroit (J15), located on the Detroit River, is in the southeastern part of the Lower Peninsula. The city was founded in 1701 by **Antoine de la Mothe Cadillac.** Detroit is Michigan's largest city, and the sixth largest city in the United States. It is the urban center of Michigan. Almost fifty percent of the state's population lives in Detroit or in nearby suburbs.

Detroit is the heart of America's automobile industry and is often called the "Motor City." The city is famous for its **Renaissance Center** and the **Detroit Historical Museum.** The museum has a permanent display that helps visitors to understand the development of the automobile. Detroit has one of the finest art collections in the world at the **Detroit Institute of Fine Arts.** Overlooking the Detroit River is **Fort Wayne,** built in the 1840s and 1850s. The fort resembles a fortress from the Middle Ages.

A view of Detroit from Windsor, Canada.
What attractions draw visitors to the city of Detroit?

A three-mile island, known as **Belle Isle Park**, is situated in the middle of the Detroit River. This splendid park has a children's zoo, an aquarium and other attractions. The park also has a marvelous view of Detroit's skyline of tall buildings.

The cities of Flint, Pontiac and Dearborn are all located near Detroit. Like the Motor City, they are closely linked to the automobile industry. The area around **Flint** (I14) was once used by Native Americans for hunting and farming. Europeans later built a fur-trading post here. Flint is sometimes thought of as the birthplace of the modern labor union movement. Today, Flint has some of Michigan's finest cultural exhibits housed in the **Sloan Museum** and the **Flint Institute of Arts.**

The conservatory in Belle Isle Park.
What takes place at a conservatory?

Pontiac (I14) is named after a famous Native American chief. It is home to the Pontiac Division of General Motors, which makes Pontiac cars. **Dearborn** (I15) is the suburb of Detroit where Ford Motor Company's main factory is located. **Fair Lane**, in Dearborn, was once the home of Henry Ford.

FAMOUS PLACES: GREENFIELD VILLAGE

At age sixty, Henry Ford began to collect older buildings and their contents to show how ordinary Americans lived in the past. Ford spent millions of dollars to show how the growth of technology had changed the nation. Visitors can see where aviation began at the Wright Brothers Cycle shop. The village contains the farmhouse where Ford was born and the factory where he manufactured his first cars. Ford also brought Thomas Edison's laboratory to Greenfield village.

The shop where the Wright Brothers built their first plane.

Ann Arbor (I15), 38 miles west of Detroit, was founded in the 1820s. The city was named after two women, Ann D'Arbeur and Anne Rumsey. They were early pioneers in the area. Today, Ann Arbor serves as the main campus for the University of Michigan. The university also has three excellent museums: the **University Exhibit Museum** (*a natural history museum*), the **Kelsey Museum of Archaeology**, and the **University Art Museum.**

Farther west is the city of **Jackson** (H15). In 1854, Jackson was the meeting place for a group of politicians and citizens who wanted to prevent the spread of slavery. The meeting led to the birth of a new political party, the Republicans. Today, the Republican Party is one of the nation's two main political parties. The **Michigan Space Center** is also located in Jackson.

West of Jackson is the city of **Battle Creek** (H15)—"Cereal Center of the World." In the 1900s, W.K. Kellogg and Charles W. Post began companies that sold breakfast cereals. They located their factories in Battle Creek because grain-growing prairies were nearby. Visitors to the city can see the **Kimball House Historical Museum**, a restored house with exhibits about abolitionist Sojourner Truth. Battle Creek is also known for the **Kingman Museum of Natural History**.

Further west is the city of **Kalamazoo** (G15). The city is named after the Kalamazoo River. The name comes from the Native American word *Kikalemazo*, or "bubbling water." The city is home to the **Kalamazoo Aviation History Museum**. Pharmacia & Upjohn, a pharmaceutical company, General Motors, and several paper-making factories play a key part in the city's economy.

Not far from Kalamazoo is **Lansing** (H14), the state capital. Lansing is named after Charles Lansing, a hero of the American Revolution. In the 1840s, Michigan's leaders decided to move the capital from Detroit to Lansing. Detroit had been captured by the British in the War of 1812. Many Michiganders felt it would be easier to

The Space Museum at Jackson.

One of Kellogg's earliest plants in Battle Creek.
Why did Kellogg and Post open plants in Battle Creek?

The Kalamazoo Aviation History Museum.

defend the state capital if it were moved farther inland. Besides being the center of Michigan's government, Lansing is home to the **Michigan Women's Hall of Fame**. Ransom Olds built his first automobile in Lansing. **Michigan State University** is located nearby in East Lansing.

The town of **Grand Rapids** (G14) was first established in the 1820s by Louis Campau, a fur trader. As logging expanded throughout Michigan, Grand Rapids became a key furniture-making center. Logs floated down the Grand River to mills located in Grand Rapids. Because of its furniture-making, the city is known as the "Furniture Capital of America." Today, Grand Rapids is Michigan's second largest city. Its factories produce auto parts, paper supplies and electrical appliances. President **Gerald Ford** grew up in Grand Rapids.

If we continue our path west of Grand Rapids, we come to **Holland** (G14), near Lake Michigan. Holland was founded in the 1840s by Dutch settlers. Dutch people are from Holland, a country in northwestern Europe. Each May, more than half a million visitors come to Holland's **Tulip Festival**. People also enjoy visiting the **Windmill Island Theme Park**, which has an authentic Dutch windmill made in Europe.

Holland, Michigan.
What is Holland known for?

Muskegon (G13) is located directly north of Holland, on the shores of Lake Michigan. It has much to offer residents and tourists. The **Silversides**, a submarine from World War II, is anchored in Muskegon. The Silversides sank 23 enemy ships. **Hackley House** and **Hume House**—two gems of Victorian architecture—are also found in Muskegon. The **Fire Barn Museum**, with its 1923 fire pumper, hose carts and other antique firefighting equipment, is also part of the excitement of Muskegon.

Hume House was built during
Muskegon's lumbering period.

THE AMATEUR CARTOGRAPHER

On your map, give a title to the region and label its major rivers. Also label the cities of Detroit, Flint, Pontiac, Dearborn, Ann Arbor, Jackson, Battle Creek, Kalamazoo, Grand Rapids, Lansing, Holland and Muskegon.

YOUR FINAL TASK

After reading about each region of Michigan you completed a map for that region.

❖ Now cut out and combine all three sections onto another piece of paper.

❖ Do your sections fit together to form a map of Michigan?

❖ Compare your completed map to the map of Michigan in the back of this book.

  ◆ Are the two maps similar?
  ◆ If not, you should make corrections to your map.

❖ To complete your map, paste or tape the sections of your map onto a large sheet of paper. Now draw scenes of your favorite places in Michigan on the margins outside the map.

EXPANDING YOUR UNDERSTANDING

Creating Vocabulary Cards

Upper Peninsula	*Lower Peninsula*
Describe the "Upper Peninsula."	*Describe the "Lower Peninsula."*
Identify some of its most	*Identify some of its most*
interesting places.	*interesting places.*

Examining People's Impact on the Environment ————————

In this unit, you have studied how people are often affected by their environment. The reverse is also true. People can have an important impact on their environment. The following news stories provide some recent examples where people have had an important effect on their environment. See if you can determine how these changes in the environment may in turn affect the people of Michigan.

❖ **Brazil.** Rain forests provide much of the world's oxygen. In the 1980s, Brazil began cutting down and burning its rain forests more rapidly than before. Brazilians hoped to sell the wood and to grow food on the newly cleared land. However, heavy rains quickly washed nutrients out of the soil, making farming difficult.

- *Locate Brazil on a map of the world.*
- *What impact did these changes have on the local environment?*
- *What impact might these developments have on Michiganders?*

Part of former rain-forest destroyed in Western Brazil.

❖ **Kuwait**. In 1990, Kuwait, a country with rich oil fields, was invaded by Iraq. Countries around the world condemned the invasion. The United Nations sent troops to force Iraq to withdraw. As the Iraqis retreated, they set hundreds of oil wells on fire. The resulting pollution was the largest single environmental disaster in history.

- *Locate Iraq and Kuwait on a map of the world.*
- *What impact did this event have on the local environment?*
- *What impact might this event have on Michiganders?*

One way to find the location of a place is to look in a special book called an atlas.

Skill Builder

USING AN ATLAS

An atlas is a book that contains many different kinds of maps:

❖ **Physical Maps** show land features such as mountains or bodies of water and may even include the depths of oceans and lakes. The map on page 43 is an example of a physical map.

❖ **Political Maps** show the boundaries of countries or states—where one country or state ends and another begins. The map on page 19 is an example of a political map.

❖ **Theme Maps** usually deal with a single theme or topic. They are used to show rainfall, population, food production, highways, natural resources, land use or other special information. An example of a theme map is found on page 248.

A world atlas usually has maps showing every nation in the world. An atlas of the United States will usually have maps showing all 50 states. The maps in an atlas also often show where important cities are located.

WHERE WOULD YOU LOCATE YOUR BASKETBALL TEAM?

2F In this activity, you will apply your knowledge of geography to a specific purpose: choosing the best city for a new basketball team. Look for the following important words and phrases:

▶ Population Density   ▶ Almanac

▶ Per Capita Income   ▶ Index

Wow! It is hard to believe your good fortune over the last two weeks. First, an unknown uncle dies and leaves you $100 million. Then, you offer to buy a new women's basketball team in a league that is just being established. Your offer is accepted. At last your dream has come true. You are now the proud owner of a new team. There is just one problem. You must find a city in the Midwest in which to locate your team.

THINK ABOUT IT

1. In which city would you like to locate your women's basketball team?
2. Why would you want to locate the team in that city?

CHOOSING A CITY FOR A BASKETBALL TEAM

You decide to hire a panel of experts to help you with this important decision. They tell you that the location of your team requires a lot of thought and investigation. The final decision should depend on many factors. To start with, your experts have narrowed down the number of possible cities for

The Museum of Science and Industry makes Chicago an interesting place to locate your basketball team.

your team. They present you with the following list of major Midwestern cities to choose from:

❖ Detroit, Michigan   ❖ Madison, Wisconsin   ❖ Indianapolis, Indiana

❖ Chicago, Illinois   ❖ Cleveland, Ohio

Make a copy of the map on the right. Using an atlas, mark the location of each of these cities. Your map will let you see where your possible choices are located.

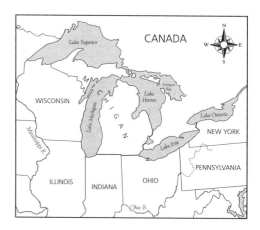

 ## LOOKING AT SOME IMPORTANT FACTORS

As the owner of a women's basketball team, you will need fans to attend the games in order to make money. Your experts now tell you to consider the following factors before deciding where to locate your team:

❖ **Population.** The city should have a population large enough to support a team.

❖ **Population Density** is the average number of people living within a given space. ◀ Think of population density as a measure of how crowded or empty an area is. The city for your team should have a high population density.

> To find the population density of a city, divide the number of people living in the city by the city's land area. For example, assume a city has a population of 6,000 people and an area of 30 square miles. To find the city's population density, divide the population by the number of square miles:
>
> $$\frac{200}{30)6{,}000}$$ The city has a population density of about 200 people per square mile.

❖ **Unemployment.** The city should have a low unemployment rate. This means that most people are working and can afford to attend some games each year or to buy products from advertisers who sponsor games.

❖ **Per Capita Income** is the average amount of money people earn. The city should ◀ have many people who earn enough money to spend on activities like attending a basketball game or buying advertisers' products.

❖ **Tourist Attractions.** The city should have interesting attractions that will encourage people in nearby areas to visit the city. While they are visiting, they may want to attend a basketball game. Interesting tourist attractions also make the town more inviting to skilled basketball players for your team.

You ask your experts, "Where can I find that kind of information about each city?" They tell you that this information is available in most almanacs (ôl' mə nakz).

ALMANAC

▶ An |almanac| is a book of facts. A new edition is published every year, so it is always up-to-date. An almanac covers a wide range of subjects such as art, astronomy, business, countries of the world, education, entertainment, farming, geography, history and religion. Almanacs also contain lists of movie stars, explorers, musicians, writers, Nobel Prize winners and athletes.

A variety of information can be found in an almanac. For example, you can find out which team won the football Super Bowl last year, or which city in Michigan has the largest population. Although there are many different almanacs, two of the best known are:

- The World Almanac and Book of Facts
- The Information Please Almanac

LEARNING HOW TO FIND INFORMATION IN AN ALMANAC

Almanacs are easy to use. The key is knowing where to look for things when using them. To locate the information you need, take the following steps:

❖ Get a copy of *The World Almanac and Book of Facts* or any other almanac.

▶ ❖ Open to the index of the almanac. An |index| is a tool that allows a reader of a book to find specific information quickly. It is usually located at the back of a book. However, in most almanacs the index appears at the beginning of the book. An index helps a reader to find *specific* topics by giving the page number where that topic is mentioned in the book.

❖ Look for "Cities, U.S." by turning to the appropriate pages in the index of your almanac. The box below shows you part of what you might see.

Cities, U.S.	**.686–95**
Area codes, telephone	.396–426
Buildings, tall	.696–702
Climate data	180–84, 195
Consumer price indexes	.113
Farthest east, north, south, west	.540
Housing prices	.727
Unemployment benefits	.142

❖ CONTINUED

There are several sources of information besides almanacs where facts about your cities can be found. You may also look in:

❖ **Encyclopedias.** Look under the headings for the states where these cities are located. For example, if you want information about Cleveland, look under the heading "Ohio."

❖ **State Travel and Tourism Agencies.** Most states have special agencies that provide information about cities in their state. Their telephone numbers are available in an almanac. Look under "States and Other Areas of the U.S." Once you find this section, look for *Tourist Information and Toll-Free Travel Information*.

❖ **City Travel and Tourism Departments.** Each city will probably have its own travel and tourism department. You can find the telephone numbers of these offices by calling the telephone "information" service for that city. Look in your phone book to find the area code of the city. When you speak to that city's travel department, ask for general tourism information.

USING SOURCES OF INFORMATION

While researching information about cities in the Midwest, you should fill in the following chart to help you keep track of the data you gather.

	Detroit, MI	Cleveland, OH	Chicago, IL	Madison, WI	Indianapolis, IN
Population	?	?	?	?	?
Population Density	?	?	?	?	?
Unemployment Rate	?	?	?	?	?
Per Capita Income	?	?	?	?	?
Major Tourist Attractions	?	?	?	?	?

MAKING A DECISION ABOUT WHERE TO LOCATE YOUR TEAM

After completing your chart, compare and contrast the information you have found. You must weigh the advantages and disadvantages of each city against the others.

MAKING YOUR DECISION

Remember, there is no "correct" answer. Each city will have its own advantages and disadvantages. After you consider all the information, answer the following questions:

❖ In which city would you locate your women's basketball team?

❖ Explain some of the factors that helped you reach your decision.

❖ Is this city different from the city you chose at the start of this activity? If so, what factors made you change your mind?

REACHING A CLASS CONSENSUS

After you have made your decision, compare your choice with those of your classmates. To do this, students who chose the same city should form a group. Students in each group should make an oral report to the class. Members of the group should give their reasons for selecting that particular city. Each group should have an opportunity to defend its choice.

After listening to the presentations, the class should try to reach a consensus about which city it thinks is best suited for locating a women's basketball team. A **consensus** is a general agreement about a topic or issue.

CREATING A NAME AND LOGO FOR YOUR TEAM

After agreeing on where to locate the team, you need to create a team name and logo. A team **logo** is a symbol used to identify a particular team. Your team will need a name and logo on its caps and shirts. The name and logo should serve as symbols of the city in which your team is located. For example, Detroit's basketball team uses a piston—a part of a car engine—for its name and symbol. On a copy of the basketball shirt, place your team's name and logo. Explain your choice for the name and what your logo stands for.

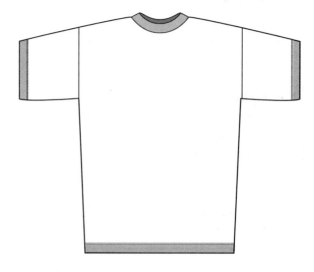

◆ STATES OF THE MIDWEST REGION ◆

STATE	POPULATION (1995)	AREA (in sq. miles)	WORLD WIDE WEB SITE
Michigan	9,549,353	96,705	http://www.migov.state.mi.us
Ohio	11,150,506	44,828	http://www.state.oh.us
Indiana	5,803,471	36,420	http://www.state.in.us
Illinois	11,829,940	57,918	http://www.state.il.us
Missouri	5,323,523	69,706	http://www.state.mo.us
Iowa	2,841,764	56,276	http://www.state.ia.us
Kansas	2,565,328	82,282	http://www.ink.org
Nebraska	1,637,112	77,358	http://www.state.ne.us
South Dakota	729,034	77,121	http://www.state.sd.us
North Dakota	641,367	70,704	http://www.state.nd.us
Minnesota	4,609,548	86,943	http://www.state.mn.us
Wisconsin	5,122,871	65,499	http://www.state.wi.us

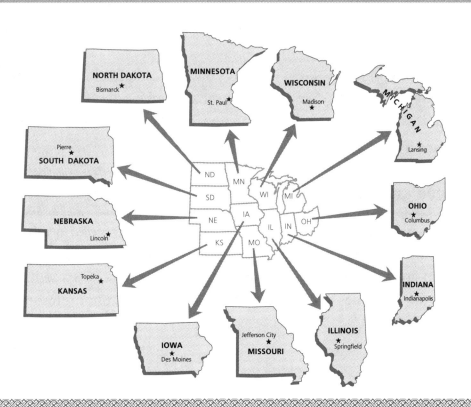

EXPANDING YOUR UNDERSTANDING

Creating Vocabulary Cards

Population Density
Define "population density."
Why might an owner of a business
be interested in knowing the
population density of an area?

Almanac
What is an "almanac"?
How can it be used?

Distinguishing Relevant From Irrelevant Information ─────────────

In this activity, you examined different data. One of the most important skills in examining data is the ability to tell the difference between **relevant** and **irrelevant** information.

RELEVANT AND IRRELEVANT INFORMATION

The same information can be relevant or irrelevant, depending upon what you need to find out or decide.

❖ **Relevant information** is connected to your topic. Relevant information is useful and appropriate and relates to what you are looking for. It helps you to decide whatever it is you must decide, or to know whatever it is you need to know.

❖ **Irrelevant information** is information not related or connected to your topic. It is either not useful for solving the problem you are working on, or it has no connection with whatever you are trying to find out about.

Imagine you wanted to identify the name of a state from certain information. You need to decide which clues would be relevant and which would be irrelevant. Look at the information provided on the following page. It provides clues about the name of a state. Examine the five clues to see how to separate relevant from irrelevant information.

A. **This state borders Michigan.** This information is relevant. It narrows your search from 50 states to the four states that border Michigan —(1) Wisconsin, (2) Illinois, (3) Indiana, and (4) Ohio.

B. **This state has a governor.** This information is correct, but irrelevant. Since every state has a governor, this information does not help you to identify the unknown state. The information is not useful.

C. **This state has more than seven letters in its name.** This information is relevant. Only two states that border Michigan have more than seven letters in their names: **W-i-s-c-o-n-s-i-n** and **I-l-l-i-n-o-i-s.** This information further narrows your search to either Wisconsin or Illinois. It is useful for your task of identifying the unknown state.

D. **This state has a state flag.** This information is correct, but irrelevant. Every state has a state flag. This clue does not help you to identify the unknown state.

E. **This state is the birthplace of a U.S. President.** This final clue is relevant. It rules out Wisconsin: no U.S. President was ever born in that state. However, Illinois was the birthplace of President Ronald Reagan. Therefore, the information was relevant because it helped you to complete your task.

Now that you understand the difference between relevant and irrelevant information, let's test that knowledge and skill. Use the information below to identify the "mystery city" from the following clues.

CAN YOU IDENTIFY THE MYSTERY CITY?

1. The city is located in Michigan.   Is clue #1 relevant? If so, why?

2. It is located in the Lower Peninsula.   Is clue #2 relevant? If so, why?

3. This city has a local newspaper.   Is clue #3 relevant? If so, why?

4. It is one of the state's ten largest cities.   Is clue #4 relevant? If so, why?

5. People in this city celebrate weddings.   Is clue #5 relevant? If so, why?

6. This is where the Motown sound began.   Is clue #6 relevant? If so, why?

?

The name of the mystery city is: _____

SUMMARIZING YOUR UNDERSTANDING

Directions: Make a copy of the following organizer. Then complete the blanks.

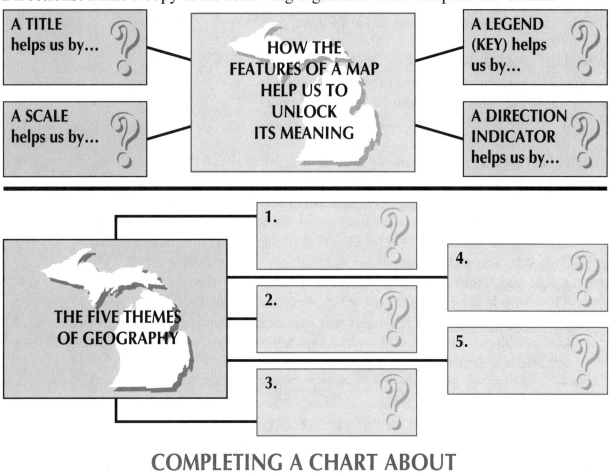

A TITLE
helps us by...

A SCALE
helps us by...

HOW THE
FEATURES OF A MAP
HELP US TO
UNLOCK
ITS MEANING

A LEGEND
(KEY) helps
us by...

A DIRECTION
INDICATOR
helps us by...

THE FIVE THEMES
OF GEOGRAPHY

1.

2.

3.

4.

5.

COMPLETING A CHART ABOUT MICHIGAN'S REGIONS

Each region of Michigan has unique characteristics. Make a large copy of the chart below and complete it to show the physical features of each region.

Major Characteristics	Upper Peninsula	Lower Peninsula
• Elevation	From 1,000 feet above sea level on the east to as much as 1,800 feet above sea level in the west	
• Main Rivers		
• Size		
• Topography		Level, with a lowland depression extending south from Saginaw Bay

AMERICAN HERITAGE

People first arrived in Michigan between 12,000 and 14,000 years ago.

Lewis Cass, Governor of Michigan Territory (1813–1831)

Michigan soldiers on Jefferson Avenue in Detroit march off to fight in the Civil War.

The term "American Heritage" refers to what we have gained from the past—our ideas, laws, type of government and customs. We enjoy the life-styles we lead today because of the struggles and accomplishments of those who lived before us. In this unit, you will learn about the history of your community, state and nation.

ÉTIENNE BRÛLÉ EXPLORES THE GREAT LAKES

It was a sunny morning in August 1622. A small band of Native Americans broke camp. They carried their canoes through the brush to the shore, where they would continue their long journey. The men laughed and joked as they walked. With them was a thirty-year-old Frenchman named **Étienne Brûlé**.

As they pushed off the shore in their canoes, the air was filled with the sweet smell of pine trees and flowers. Thick pine forests spread as far as their eyes could see. The men were back again on the crystal blue waters of Lake Huron. Brûlé looked around in wonder. No other European had seen this lake before. The Native Americans accompanying Brûlé spoke of an even larger lake ahead. They called the area Michigama, or "big lake."

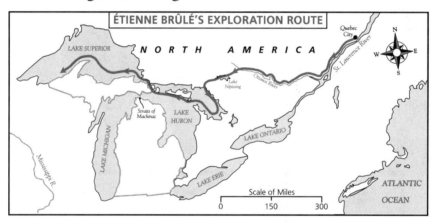

Brûlé had never seen lakes as large as these in France. Each lake seemed almost as large as the great ocean he had crossed on his journey from France to the "New World." Unlike the ocean, these lakes contained fresh water one could drink. They were filled with all types of fish. Berries, fruits and animals were plentiful in nearby forests. Surrounded by the overpowering beauty of these lakes and forests, it was no wonder that Brûlé loved his life outdoors and could imagine no other.

What events had brought Brûlé to this vast wilderness, thousands of miles from his homeland? The story really begins more than a hundred years earlier. Europeans had started exploring the world's oceans. Some people thought that the world was flat, like a tabletop. But many leading geographers believed that the world was round.

Christopher Columbus, the son of an Italian weaver, was one of those who believed the world was round. In 1492, he persuaded the King and Queen of Spain to provide him with ships and money for a voyage across the Atlantic Ocean to Asia. Instead, he found a "New World," unknown to anyone in Europe at that time.

Soon other European countries tried to find new routes to Asia. In 1534, the King of France sent **Jacques Cartier** to find an all-water route. Cartier crossed the Atlantic and landed at the mouth of the St. Lawrence River.

Sixty years later, **Samuel de Champlain** went back to the area Cartier had once explored. He sailed up the St. Lawrence River to a point where the river narrows. In 1608, he started the settlement of Quebec at this point. The settlement was built close to where the French could trade with Native Americans for furs.

Champlain exploring the Canadian wilderness.

Life in the new settlement of Quebec was hard. In the first few years, only a few of the settlers survived. One of the survivors was young Étienne Brûlé. He learned several Native American languages and became a great help to Champlain. As Brûlé grew older, he spent more and more time with the Native Americans. Because he understood several of their languages, Brûlé often went with Champlain on his explorations. In 1615, Brûlé and Champlain became the first Europeans to enter Lake Ontario.

That brings us to our starting point: August 1622. Brûlé had set out with a few Native American friends to explore the area beyond Lake Ontario. He became the first European to reach the western shores of Lake Huron. The men paddled their canoes towards the shores of the Upper Peninsula.

As he looked ahead, Brûlé wondered what he would find. Would he be the first person to find an all-water route to Asia? Would he discover new lands and riches? What impact would his travels have on France and on his newly adopted country? As you read this unit, you will find the answers to these and other questions you may have about the history of Michigan.

HOW WOULD YOU EDIT THIS ARTICLE?

3A In this activity, you will learn about the first people to live in the area we now call Michigan. Look for the following important words:

▶ Fact/Opinion   ▶ Wigwams   ▶ Longhouses   ▶ Hurons

▶ Ojibwa   ▶ Ottawa   ▶ Potawatomi   ▶ Menominee

A ▶ symbol appears in the margin where the **word** is first explained.

Imagine that your school will soon print its annual student magazine. This year's issue will focus on Native Americans who once lived in what is now Michigan. You have been given your first assignment by the Editor-in-Chief—the person who puts the magazine together. "Here is an article to read," the editor says. "It was written by one of your classmates. I would like you to make sure it contains only facts. I don't want any opinions in this article. Read it carefully and report back to me when you have finished. However, before you begin, you should read this comparison of facts and opinions."

Skill Builder

THE DIFFERENCE BETWEEN FACTS AND OPINIONS

▶ A statement of **fact** is something that can be checked for accuracy. Something is accurate if it is true. You can usually check a statement's accuracy by looking at other sources to see if they agree that it is correct.

Correct	*Incorrect*
Lansing is the capital of Michigan.	Marquette is the capital of Michigan.

▶ An **opinion** (ə pin' yən) is a statement of personal beliefs. It is not a statement that is true or false. An opinion *cannot* be checked for accuracy. There are two main types of opinion statements:

Opinions of personal taste express a person's feelings. For example, "Michigan is the best state to live in." People from another state might feel their state is better.

Opinions about the future make a prediction. For example, "When I grow up, I will go to college."

"Telling the difference between fact and opinion statements is only one part of your assignment," the editor continues. "I also need you to check the accuracy of factual statements, and to look for errors in punctuation, spelling and grammar. Lastly, I would like to know what you think is the most interesting thing in the article about the Native Americans of Michigan." Here is the article you are asked to read:

EDITOR'S INSTRUCTIONS: Read the following paragraphs and:
1. List the sentence numbers of all opinion statements.
2. Pick one of the sentences you just listed. Why do you think it is an opinion?
3. List the sentence number of one of the factual statements.
4. What sources might you check to see if this factual statement is accurate?

THE FIRST MICHIGANDERS: THE NATIVE AMERICANS

(1) At least 20,000 years ago, people from Asia crossed a narrow plain that once connected Alaska to Asia. (2) This new continent was very beautiful. (3) Hunters from Asia followed the animals as they moved into North and South America. (4) They hunted the animals with spears made from tree branches and tipped with pieces of stone. (5) They used the animals they killed for food and clothing.

(6) Gradually, more people arrived in the area around the Great Lakes. (7) About 3,000 years ago, these peoples learned to plant some crops. (8) Once they learned how to grow crops, they no longer had to travel from place to place in search of food. (9) This was the best lifestyle these people had ever had.

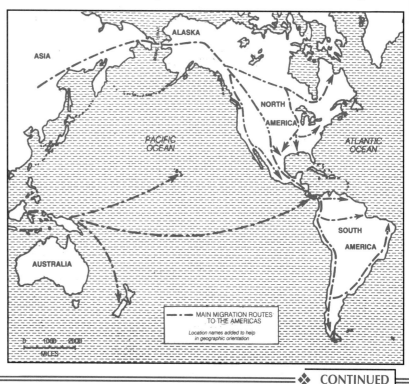

MAIN MIGRATION ROUTES TO THE AMERICAS

Location names added to help in geographic orientation

❖ CONTINUED

(10) For the next several thousand years, many different groups of Native Americans* lived in the Great Lakes region of what is now the United States. (11) Some of these peoples lived along the Grand Rapids River, the Muskegon River and the Saginaw River. (12) These people shared the custom of building large earth mounds to bury their dead. (13) Their earth mounds were quite beautiful. (14) Hundreds of years ago, these mound-building peoples suddenly disappeared. (15) **Archeologists** (*people who study past civilizations by examining artifacts*) are still not sure what happened to the mound-builders. (16) They believe a horrible disease or some other disaster may have struck these peoples.

*A NOTE ON NAMES

The native peoples of North and South America have been called by various names. When Christopher Columbus landed, he called them **Indians** because he thought he had landed in the islands of the East Indies. In the 1960s, the term **Native American** began to be used to show that these were the first people to live in the Americas. They have also been called **indigenous peoples**. *Indigenous* (in dij' ə nəhs) means native to a particular area.

FAMOUS PLACES: NORTON MOUND

Several mounds remain in the southern Lower Peninsula. The people now known as the Grand River Hopewells built over 45 mounds. One of the more famous mounds, the Norton Mound, is located outside Grand Rapids. Archeologists believe the mounds served a religious pur-

pose. They have found objects in them used in religious ceremonies. One mound had a pipe with the carving of an alligator. Since there were no alligators in this area, archeologists believe this shows the Hopewell people were active traders.

✎ YOUR NOTES ✐

1. Where did the first Native Americans come from?
2. What do you think happened to the mound builders?
3. List the numbers of all the opinion statements and the number of one factual statement.

EDITOR'S INSTRUCTIONS: You need to check the article's punctuation, especially the use of periods and question marks.
 • Periods (.) are used to end a statement.
 • Question marks (?) are used at the end of a question.
Continue to identify all opinion statements and to find one factual statement.

THE NATIVE AMERICAN TRIBES OF MICHIGAN

By the time the first European explorers began arriving—around 300 years ago—thousands of Native Americans lived in present-day Michigan. It was then possible to identify three main groups in this region: the Ojibwa, Ottawa and Potawatomi [./?] Although they were similar, each tribe had certain unique features.

THE OJIBWA (CHIPPEWA)

The **Ojibwa** were one of the largest Native American groups in Michigan. [./?] The Europeans used the name "**Chippewa**" to identify the Ojibwa.

In the summer, the Ojibwa tribe was able to stay together in one place. In the winter, each family left the tribe to live by itself. They separated because it was hard to find food in win-

Young Ojibwa boys.

ter. Tribe members feared that if the tribe remained together, people would starve.

❖ CONTINUED

The Ojibwa lived by the shores of the Great Lakes. They hunted, fished, planted crops and gathered fruits and nuts. The Ojibwa built houses known as **wigwams** . Some wigwams looked like soccer balls cut in half and placed on the ground. Other wigwams were cone-shaped. Men and women built them together. Branches were stuck into a circle in the ground. The tops of the branches were tied together with vines,

A village of cone-shape wigwams.
Why did these homes have an opening at the top?

roots or strips of bark. The frame was covered with birch bark and grass [./?] Animal skins were used for a door and to sleep on. A fire in the center of the wigwam was used for cooking and warmth. A hole at the top of the wigwam let smoke from the fire escape.

THE OTTAWA

Where does the name "Ottawa" come from [./?] It comes from the word *adawa*, which meant "to trade." The **Ottawa** lived in the western part of Michigan. They were related to the Ojibwa and followed many of their customs. They hunted, fished and farmed. They were also active traders. They traded woven mats and foods with other tribes for pottery and dyes. When the French came, they traded furs and food for guns, cooking utensils and liquor.

The Ottawa made their houses differently from the Ojibwa. Their houses were known as **longhouses** . A longhouse measured 50 to 100 feet long, and could be as much as 20 feet wide. As many as five or ten families might share one longhouse. Longhouses were made of branches covered with bark. Holes in the roof allowed smoke to escape. Benches along the sides of the longhouse were used for sit-

Interior of a Native American longhouse.

ting, eating and sleeping. [./?] Several longhouses were built near one another to form villages. People today live in much more comfortable houses.

THE POTAWATOMI

The **Potawatomi** lived in the southwestern part of the Lower Peninsula. They took their name from an Ojibwa phrase meaning "keepers of the fire." The Potawatomi

❖ CONTINUED

carried their fire from one settlement to another. Because it was warmer where the Potawatomi lived, they did more farming than the other tribes. They planted crops such as corn, beans, peas and sunflowers. Their homes were similar to the wigwams of the Ojibwa [./?]

OTHER TRIBES OF MICHIGAN

Other Native American tribes living in Michigan at this time included the Huron, Menominee and Miami.

Hurons in the early 19th century wearing European-style clothes.

The **Huron** (or Wyandot) lived near the waters that divide the Upper and Lower Peninsulas. They were chased from their original home in New York State by the Iroquois. The Iroquois and Huron were enemies even though both spoke similar languages, lived in longhouses and had similar appearances.

The **Menominee** lived in the western part of the Upper Peninsula near the Menominee River. The tribe took its name from the Ojibwa word for "wild rice people." They gathered rice from swampy areas. This food was a major part of their diet. Little is known about this tribe, except that their customs and lifestyles were similar to the Ojibwas.

NATIVE AMERICAN TRIBES OF MICHIGAN (1760's)

The **Miami** lived near the Kankakee River in the southwestern Lower Peninsula. The Miami settled in permanent villages in order to raise crops.

✎ YOUR NOTES ✐

1. How did life in a wigwam compare to life in a longhouse?

2. Which is the proper punctuation mark to use in these paragraphs?

◆ 1: (period/question mark)   ◆ 4: (period/question mark)

◆ 2: (period/question mark)   ◆ 5: (period/question mark)

◆ 3: (period/question mark)   ◆ 6: (period/question mark)

EDITOR'S INSTRUCTIONS: *You should also check a writer's grammar. One frequent error is using wrong verb forms: "He (singular) do (plural) what he wants." A similar mistake is to use a plural noun with a singular verb: "They (plural) eats (singular) their dinner early." A singular subject (he) requires a singular verb (does): "He does what he wants." A plural noun (they) requires a plural verb (eat): "They eat their dinner early." In this section, look for grammar problems and answer the questions at the end.*

TRIBAL LIFE-STYLES

Information

The tribes of the Great Lakes Region differed in the ways they made their homes, hunted and farmed. However, they all shared some customs and beliefs. The main tribes in Michigan spoke **Algonquian**. In addition to language, there [was/were] other similarities among many of these Native American groups.

OBTAINING FOOD

Most villages were built near rivers or lakes. Canoes were used both for transportation and to search for food. Usually, the men did the hunting, fishing and

COMPARING PICTURES

Ojibwas building a canoe (1780s)

Ojibwas building a canoe (1900s)

What similarities do you see between these two pictures?

❖ CONTINUED

making of canoes. They used natural materials, such as rocks and plant fibers, to make tools and weapons. They used spears, hooks and nets to fish in the waters of the Great Lakes. Bows and arrows, spears and clubs [was/were] used to kill deer, rabbits, moose, squirrels, beavers, ducks and turkeys. Some meat and fish were preserved by drying and then stored for use in winter.

Women gathered berries, nuts and other wild plants. Children helped gather berries and wild rice. Women [was/were] also in charge of growing corn, squash, beans, potatoes and other vegetables. Corn was a major food in their diet. Women crushed the corn in stone bowls to make flour for breads and stews. Men cleared the land by setting fire to the trees in an area. After the trees were burned down, ashes from the fire were mixed with the soil. Then the crops were planted, usually by the women. After 15 to 20 years, the soil became exhausted from continued planting. A village would then move to a new location.

APPEARANCE

The Native Americans of Michigan depended on the animals they hunted for their food and clothing. Most tribes made skirts, moccasins, leggings and clothes from the skins of deer and other animals in the area. They used sharp porcupine needles to create designs. Tribe members sometimes tattooed their faces and decorated themselves with feathers and shells. Tribes of the Great Lakes collected shells to make **wampum**. The wampum beads [was/were] strung together to make belts, ornaments and money. Today, we believe this was a silly practice!

A Native American family.
Can you identify any of the materials they are wearing?

Men usually wore their hair long. The men of some tribes shaved their heads, leaving a short strip on top. The Huron men cut off all of their hair, except for a narrow band down the middle of the head. This hairstyle looked so strange to the French that they called them *Huron*, meaning "hair of a wild pig." I think that we [has/have] a better sense of fashion today than the Hurons had.

❖ CONTINUED

THE ROLES OF WOMEN

In these societies children [was/were] more closely linked to their mother's relatives than to their father's. Children also took their names from the mother's family. Women were in charge of planting, cooking and raising children. When the men were out hunting, women ran the council house and made decisions for the entire village.

Ojibwa women weaving baskets.
What other tasks were the responsibility of Native American women?

✎ YOUR NOTES ✎

1. What kinds of foods did the Native Americans of the Great Lakes eat?
2. How did the roles of men and women differ?
3. Identify all opinion statements and one factual statement.
4. Which is the correct verb to use in paragraph:

- ◆ 1: (was/were)
- ◆ 2: (was/were)
- ◆ 3: (was/were)

- ◆ 4: (was/were)
- ◆ 5: (has/have)
- ◆ 6: (was/were)

EDITOR'S INSTRUCTIONS: List all opinion statements and one factual statement. Besides checking punctuation, editors also need to check spelling. In this section, use a dictionary to find the correct spelling for the words in [blue print].

Information

BELIEFS OF THE GREAT LAKES TRIBES

People in most societies share common ideals, customs and beliefs. The Native Americans of the Great Lakes region were no exception.

RELIGIOUS BELIEFS

Religion was important to the lives of Native Americans. They [worshiped/worshipped] a Great Spirit who was believed to be in all animals and objects. They

❖ CONTINUED

also believed in gods of the sky, woods and lakes. A tribal medicine man or woman helped people communicate with the spirit world. Because of their beliefs, the Native Americans only killed animals for [**subsistence/subsistance**]. Animals were killed when their bodies were needed for food, clothing or tools.

Native American man fishing.

WARFARE

Warfare was closely related to religion. A tribe would go to war if one of its members was killed by another tribe. It was believed that the spirit of the dead tribal member could not rest until revenge was taken. Members of the war party would [**bathe/bayth**] and fast (*not eat*) for several days to ensure their cleanliness. They would make a surprise attack on their enemy. They cut off the [**scalp/skalp**] of their victim's head as a way to prove to other tribal members and the spirit world that they had taken revenge.

Native American spears and arrowheads. Can you identify what these weapons are made of?

SENSE OF COMMUNITY / VALUES

Tribes of the Great Lakes believed people could not own the things of nature. They thought the land, forests and animals belonged to everyone [**equaly/equally**]. Everything was shared with members of the group. This was a much better way of living than we have today. Stealing and homelessness were rare. If members of the village did not work together to store food for winter, its members would face starvation. They believed all people were part of the Great Spirit, and that tribal leaders, called [**chiefs/cheefs**], should listen to everyone.

✏ YOUR NOTES ✏

1. What were some of the beliefs of the Native Americans living in Michigan?

2. What might lead one tribe to go to war with another tribe?

3. Identify all opinion statements and one factual statement from the reading.

4. Which is the correct spelling to use in these paragraphs?

- ◆ 1: (worshiped/worshipped)
- ◆ 1: (subsistence/subsistance)
- ◆ 2: (bathe/bayth)
- ◆ 2: (scalp/skalp)
- ◆ 3: (equaly/equally)
- ◆ 3: (chiefs/cheefs)

Closing

REVIEWING AND CHECKING THE ARTICLE

Now that you have finished reading the article, it is time to report back to the editor. You must tell her whether the article was completely factual or contained opinions. You must also discuss any errors that the article contained, and identify what was interesting for you.

Dear Editor-in-Chief,

I have reviewed the article. I found that the article contained (*some/many*) opinions. I found (*some/many*) sentences with errors. The most interesting thing that I learned about the Native Americans living in Michigan was ...

Sincerely,

_____
(*sign your name*)

Two days later you meet the editor again. She thanks you and asks you to do one more thing—to check the **accuracy** of the article. Remember, a factual statement is accurate if you can show that it is true and error-free. Since it would take too long to check every fact mentioned in the article, she suggests you choose any **two** factual statements to check. You can use a textbook, encyclopedia or almanac to check the accuracy of these statements.

Statements You Selected to Check	Source Used	The Statement is:
(1) ?	?	☐ Accurate ☐ Not Accurate
(2) ?	?	☐ Accurate ☐ Not Accurate

◆ THE NATIVE AMERICANS OF MICHIGAN TODAY ◆

In the 1800s, the national government began pushing Native American tribes from their homelands to **reservations** (*areas set aside by the government for Native Americans to live in*). In these years, many laws encouraged Native American children to attend non-tribal schools, and to use English instead of tribal languages.

Reservation life was often hard. Many tribal members left the reservation to find jobs elsewhere. Some became steelworkers, building bridges and tall buildings. But they also continued to search for ways to regain the lands they had lost, and the benefits they had once enjoyed as separate Native American nations.

Few Native Americans in Michigan today still live on reservations. Most live and work in Michigan's cities. Some of them, however, have remained on reservations and rebuilt them. Others returned to reservations as new job opportunities for mining, logging, fishing and gaming developed there.

MICHIGAN'S NATIVE AMERICAN RESERVATIONS

According to the government's last count, more than 55,000 Native Americans are now living in Michigan. This is less than one percent of the state's population. The largest number can be found in Wayne County. Other areas with many Native Americans include Bay Mills, Grand Traverse and Sault Ste. Marie.

Each year, Native Americans from around the state gather to socialize and celebrate their past at meetings called **powwows**. They dress in traditional clothing and perform ancient dances in a festive atmosphere. Participants take pride in their past as they move into the twenty-first century.

Michigan owes a great debt to its Native American peoples. Many cities, counties and rivers in Michigan bear Native American names. Many of Michigan's roadways, such as the I-75, I-94 and I-96, follow old trails once used by Native Americans hundreds of years ago.

◆ ◆ ◆ ◆ ◆ ◆

Kalamazoo, Muskegon, Cheboygan and Saginaw are counties in Michigan with Native American names. How many other places in Michigan can you identify with Native American names?

EXPANDING YOUR UNDERSTANDING

Creating Vocabulary Cards

Fact/Opinion
What is a statement of "fact"?
What is an "opinion"?
How is a statement of fact different from an opinion?

Wigwam
What is a "wigwam"?
How is it different from a longhouse?

Visiting a Museum

In this activity, you learned about different Native American tribes in Michigan. One way to learn more about these tribes is to visit a museum. Exhibits in local museums often trace the history of Native American groups that once lived in that area.

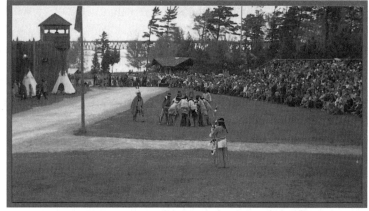

A re-enactment of a battle at Fort Michilimackinac. Today, the fort serves as a museum.

Before you visit a museum, let's first look at what a museum does. A **museum** is a place that stores, takes care of and exhibits (*puts on display*) special collections. Different museums collect almost anything you can imagine—from baseball cards to furniture. In many cases, a person's private collection becomes part of a museum's holdings.

When museums began over 500 years ago in Europe, they were the private art collections of rich and important people. Only a few people were allowed to see these collections. Today, museums are generally open to the public.

Not all museums are housed in large buildings. Some museum collections are in old factories or houses. In fact, the largest number of museums in the United States are historic homes, such as Fair Lane in Dearborn, the former home of Henry Ford.

Sometimes museums consist of several buildings and outdoor exhibits. Such museums can include farms, villages and forts. For example, Greenfield Village, in Dearborn, has many outdoor exhibits. Some of its buildings are restored. A **restored** building is one that has been fixed to look as it did in the past.

In later activities you will be asked to visit a museum. On any visit to a museum, select **one** object from their collection. Examine it closely. To guide you in what to look for, complete a copy of the worksheet below.

The Dossin Great Lakes Museum in Detroit is one of the many museums found in Michigan.
What is the name of the museum closest to where you live?

MUSEUM WORKSHEET

Name of the Object: _____

Description of the Object:

❖ Shape _____

❖ Colors _____

❖ How old is it? _____

❖ Design _____

❖ Made of _____

❖ Condition _____

What was the object used for? _____
_____
_____
_____
_____

Your Drawing or Photograph of the Object:

ARE YOU A GOOD HISTORIAN?

3B   In this activity, you will read about some of the exciting events from Michigan's early past. Look for the following words and phrases:

▶ Historians   ▶ Pontiac's War

▶ Northwest Passage   ▶ American Revolution

▶ French and Indian War   ▶ Declaration of Independence

History is the study of what happened in the past. People who study the past are known
▶ as **historians** (hi stōr' ē ənz). They study the past to understand how our modern society has come about. By understanding the past, we are better able to understand the present and to determine our future. This activity has reading passages about Michigan's early history. As you read, you will be asked to play the role of an amateur historian. Try to imagine what it would have been like to live in the past.

MICHIGAN UNDER FRENCH RULE

Although the native peoples of Michigan did not know it at the time, events were occurring many thousands of miles away that were going to affect their way of life. More than five hundred years ago, trade between Europe* and East Asia was very profitable. Traders used land routes that were long and dangerous. Some wanted to find a shorter and safer way. Several European nations sent out explorers to find an all-water route to the "Indies," the islands of East Asia.

⌒ *A Note on the Countries of Western Europe ⌒

Portugal, Spain, France and Great Britain were all active in early overseas exploration. Spain, France, and Portugal were kingdoms in Western Europe. Great Britain, an island west of Europe, consisted of three kingdoms with one ruler: England, Scotland and Wales. People from this island are often referred to as British. They can also be called English, Scottish or Welsh, depending on where in Britain they came from. The King of England also ruled over Ireland. Germany, then made up of many smaller states, was located in the center of Europe.

THE FIRST EUROPEANS EXPLORE MICHIGAN

> ***As you read, look for answers to the following questions:***
> **1.** Why did European explorers come to the area we now call Michigan?
> **2.** Why were explorers seeking a Northwest Passage?
> **3.** When did Étienne Brûlé and Jean Nicolet explore Michigan?

In 1492, **Christopher Columbus** sailed across the Atlantic Ocean to find a shorter route to the Indies. Columbus never landed in Michigan, but was the first European to find the Americas. On his return to Europe, he reported finding great wealth. Later, other Europeans sailed to what they called the "New World." They went in search of gold and other riches.

The idea that there was a water route to Asia encouraged other explorers to seek a passage by sea around North America. Some believed they could reach this route by sailing north through what they called the **Northwest Passage** . Searching for the Northwest Passage, French explorers sailed into the St. Lawrence River. In the early 1600s, they built a fort at Quebec.

Christopher Columbus.
What was he searching for on his voyage?

The first European to explore Michigan was the Frenchman **Étienne Brûlé**. As a young man, Brûlé was one of the first settlers in Quebec. In 1618, he traveled by canoe during winter and visited the area now known as Sault Ste. Marie.

Three years later, Brûlé returned to the St. Mary's River. He traveled by canoe into Lake Superior. In the eastern Upper Peninsula, he found Native Americans mining copper.

Later French explorers, such as **Jean Nicolet**, followed in the footsteps of Brûlé. Nicolet also believed in the existence of a Northwest Passage. He was convinced that he would eventually reach China. In 1634, Nicolet actually sailed through the Straits of Mackinac and discovered Lake Michigan. He eventually landed in Green Bay, Wisconsin. He carried a robe of silk to give to the Emperor of China. The native peoples who saw the robe and heard Nicolet fire his pistols were very impressed. Despite these efforts, Nicolet never found an all-water route to Asia.

THE AMATEUR HISTORIAN: RECREATING THE PAST ═══════

Tracing Historical Routes. On an outline map of Michigan, locate and mark some of the places French explorers reached. Use different colored pens or pencils to identify each explorer's "discovery." Add the routes of additional explorers as you continue to read the next section.

THE FRENCH COME TO MICHIGAN

As you read, look for answers to the following questions:
1. What was the main purpose of European missionaries in Michigan?
2. What role did missionaries play in Michigan's development?
3. Who were Father René Ménard, Claude Allouez and Father Marquette?

In the mid-1600s, a number of French missionaries arrived in Michigan. **Missionaries** are people who devote their lives to convincing others to follow their religion. French missionaries tried to convert (*change*) Native Americans to their religion, Roman Catholicism. One such missionary was Father **René Ménard**. In 1660, he canoed along the southern shore of Lake Superior. Ménard built a small settlement at Keweenaw Bay in the Upper Peninsula. The next year, he attempted to explore further westward. Ménard disappeared and was never heard from again.

Another missionary, **Claude Allouez**, set out to find Father Ménard in 1667. Although Allouez never found Ménard, he discovered copper in the Upper Peninsula. Allouez also found a great river to the west of Lake Superior: the Mississippi River.

Sault Ste. Marie was an important meeting place for Native Americans. Each summer, thousands gathered there to fish. In 1668, **Jacques Marquette**, a French missionary, arrived in Sault Ste. Marie and built a church there. The city of Marquette is the oldest city in Michigan today.

In 1669, **Adrien Jolliet** became the first explorer to visit the Lower Peninsula. In 1671, nearby St. Ignace was settled. In that same year, France claimed possession of what is today Michigan.

Father Marquette speaks to a group of Native Americans.
What do you think Marquette might be telling them?

The French King, **Louis XIV**, sent soldiers to the area to protect French control against the claims of other European countries. At that time, France and England were bitter rivals. Both countries wanted to control the region of the Great Lakes. Much of Michigan's early history was to be shaped by the conflict between these two European powers.

In 1679, **René-Robert Cavalier, Sieur de La Salle**, began building a series of forts around the Great Lakes to protect the French against Native Americans and the English. One of the forts was Fort Miami, located near present-day Saint Joseph. La Salle hoped to make a fortune by selling furs. He built a boat to ship furs through the Great Lakes and up the St. Lawrence. The boat, named the *Griffon*, was the first large ship to sail on the Great Lakes, but sank during its first year of operation.

La Salle supervising the loading of furs onto the *Griffon*.

In 1701, **Antoine de la Mothe Cadillac**, a French soldier, arrived at a place called *détroit*—"the strait." A **strait** is a narrow body of water connecting two larger bodies of water. Cadillac established Fort Pontchartrain on the straits connecting Lake Huron to Lake Erie. Today this location is known as **Detroit**.

In the 1600s and 1700s, people in Europe were willing to pay a great deal of money for furs to make clothing and hats. The beaver, one of the most prized animals for its fur, had

Antoine de la Mothe Cadillac meets the French King.

been nearly hunted out of existence in Europe. American beaver skins were therefore extremely valuable. The best fur hunters in North America were the Native Americans. Gradually, many tribes gave up their traditional way of life in order to sell furs to the French.

In all, fewer than 4,000 French people ever settled in the Michigan region. Most were traders and trappers. They traded weapons, ammunition, tools, liquor and trinkets to the Native Americans in exchange for animal skins. These traders and trappers shipped their animal skins to Montreal, a French stronghold in Canada, 500 miles to the east. From there, the skins were shipped to Europe.

Michigan changed little under French control. The French were mainly interested in converting native peoples to Christianity and in carrying on a profitable fur trade. Even so, the impact of French control on Michigan is still evident today. For example, places such as Detroit, Pointe La Barbe, Charleviox, Bois Blanc Island and Grand Marais all have French names.

THE AMATEUR HISTORIAN: RECREATING THE PAST

1. **Building a Model Fort**. Historians often need to "see" places from the past. Some-times a model helps us to imagine how a place actually looked. The illustration below shows Fort Michilimackinac. Built in 1715, the fort served as an important post for French soldiers and fur traders. Later it served as a fort for the British. Other French forts included Fort Miami and Fort Ponchartrain. Build your own model of Fort Michilimackinac based on the illustration. Make your model out of cardboard, paper, clay, paper maché or other materials. Alternatively, you might research what another fort in Michigan looked like and build a model of that fort.

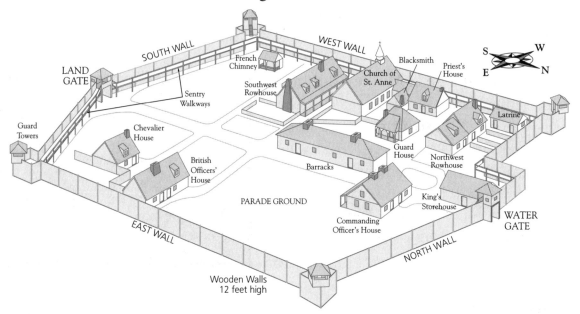

2. **Locating Historical Places**. On a map of Michigan, locate the areas once explored by the French. For example, find the waters of the Straits of Mackinac and Keweenaw Bay. See if you can find where the present-day cities of Sault Ste. Marie, Saint Joseph and Detroit are located.

THE BRITISH GAIN CONTROL OF MICHIGAN

A **colony** is an area where people from a foreign country settle. The settlers' original homeland becomes known as the "mother country." Although the colonists live far from the mother country, the mother country still governs them. In the later 1700s, France was growing rich from its colony in North America. This soon led to conflict with its rival, Great Britain, which had its own colonies along the Atlantic Coast.

MICHIGAN AND THE FRENCH AND INDIAN WAR

As you read, look for answers to the following questions:
1. Which factors led to conflict between the British and French?
2. Describe the events that happened during Pontiac's War.

By 1750, more than a million colonists lived in British North America. Many of them came in search of inexpensive land. As the area of settlement increased, some colonists began moving farther west. This brought the British and French settlers into conflict, since both powers claimed control of the Ohio River Valley. The British also believed the French were encouraging the Native Americans to attack their settlements.

View of Fort Michilimackinac today.

In 1754, a war broke out between Britain and France. For nine years, the two countries fought over control of North America. The Native Americans were caught in the middle of the conflict, known as the **French and Indian War**. Most tribes sided with the French. They feared the British settlers would take away their lands and destroy their way of life.

By 1763, the British had taken the forts around the Great Lakes from the French. Pontiac, an Ottawa chief, and other Native American chiefs worked together to fight against the British. During **Pontiac's War**, warriors massacred the British at Fort Michilimackinac. Soon they captured all the forts except Fort Ponchartrain in Detroit.

Pontiac came up with a plan to capture Detroit. His warriors were to set up camps around the fort. Pontiac and some of his chiefs, with guns hidden under their shoulder blankets, would enter the fort for a meeting with the commander. If the negotiations failed, the warriors would attack and capture the fort. Pontiac decided to call off his plan when the fort's commander learned of the plot.

Instead, Pontiac attacked the fort with 800 of his warriors. Pontiac's siege continued for five months. By the end of this period, the men in the fort had few supplies. There was almost nothing left to eat. But after 153 days, Pontiac's warriors were also getting anxious. They wanted to return to their families to prepare for the coming winter. Then Pontiac received news that the French had signed a peace treaty with England. Without French help, Pontiac gave up his attack and decided to return home.

Native Americans conduct a surprise attack on Fort Michilimackinac.

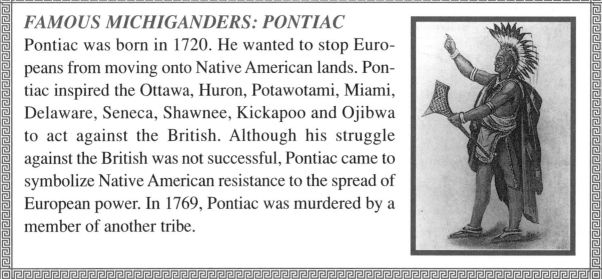

FAMOUS MICHIGANDERS: PONTIAC

Pontiac was born in 1720. He wanted to stop Europeans from moving onto Native American lands. Pontiac inspired the Ottawa, Huron, Potawotami, Miami, Delaware, Seneca, Shawnee, Kickapoo and Ojibwa to act against the British. Although his struggle against the British was not successful, Pontiac came to symbolize Native American resistance to the spread of European power. In 1769, Pontiac was murdered by a member of another tribe.

During the French and Indian War, the French won many of the early battles. But the British continued to send more troops to North America. In 1759, they captured the French fort at Quebec. The fort guarded the St. Lawrence River, the main waterway to the Great Lakes. After the French lost Quebec, they believed they could no longer protect Canada or lands further west. In 1763, France signed a treaty agreeing to give up their territories in North America. Michigan was now under British control.

THE AMATEUR HISTORIAN: RECREATING THE PAST

Considering Other Viewpoints. Imagine you are a Native American warrior living in Michigan during the 1750s. A war rages between France and Britain. Pretend you are visiting your family. Describe to them why you are fighting alongside the French against the British.

EVENTS LEADING TO THE AMERICAN REVOLUTION

> ### As you read, look for answers to the following questions:
> **A.** How did the end of the French and Indian War lead to problems between Great Britain and the colonists?
> **B.** Why were new British taxes so unpopular with the colonists?

The end of the French and Indian War promised to open western lands to British settlers. But the British government feared conflict between the settlers and Native Americans. To prevent trouble, the British announced in 1763 that settlers could not move west of the Appalachian Mountains. To keep the settlers out, British soldiers occupied Fort Detroit and Fort Michilimackinac. The new British policy greatly angered American colonists.

Soon other events upset the colonists still further. The British felt they had fought the French and Indian War to protect the colonists. The British government demanded that the American colonists help pay some of the war's costs. It placed a series of new taxes on the colonists. A **tax** is money collected by a government to pay its expenses.

The first of these taxes, announced in 1765, required the colonists to use specially stamped paper for newspapers and legal documents. This tax was so unpopular with the colonists that the British government finally gave it up.

In its place, the British passed new taxes on sugar, tea and other goods. None of the new taxes was discussed with the colonists or approved by a colonial assembly. The colonists believed this was

The Boston Tea Party: colonists, disguised as Native Americans, toss boxes of tea overboard to protest the British tax on tea.

unfair. They felt that the British government should have consulted with them before passing new taxes. The cry of "no taxation without representation" was heard throughout the colonies.

The American colonists were further angered when the British government passed the **Quebec Act** in 1774. This act changed the boundaries of Quebec Province. The province was extended south and west, making Michigan a part of Quebec Province. The American colonists in the 13 colonies were outraged at this move by the British government. They had hoped to settle in these western lands.

Protests over these events finally turned to bloodshed. In 1775, shots were fired between British soldiers and colonists in the colony of Massachusetts. Fighting quickly
▶ spread to the other colonies. The **American Revolution** had begun. A **revolution** is a change of government by force.

As the fighting continued, many colonists began to feel they would be better off without Great Britain as their mother country. Representatives from all thirteen colonies met in Philadelphia. After much discussion, they decided the colonies should break away from Great Britain and declare their independence.

Fighting in the American Revolution between British soldiers and colonists began in Massachusetts.

▶ The **Declaration of Independence** was issued on **July 4, 1776. Thomas Jefferson** was its main author. The Declaration explained to the world why the American colonists wanted independence. The first paragraph stated:

The Declaration of Independence

We hold these truths to be self-evident [obvious], that all men are created equal, that they are endowed [given] by their Creator [God] with certain unalienable [cannot be taken away] rights, that among these are life, liberty and the pursuit of happiness. That to secure [protect] these rights, governments are instituted [created] among Men, deriving [getting] their just powers from the consent of the governed, that whenever any form of government becomes destructive [harmful] of these ends, it is the right of the people to alter [change] or abolish [end] it, and to institute [create] new government …

✔ CHECKING YOUR UNDERSTANDING ✔

Sometimes, words written over 200 years ago are hard to understand. Let's see how well you understand this document by answering the following questions:

1. What do you think the writers meant by the following words or phrases?
 ❖ All men are created equal   ❖ Unalienable rights
 ❖ Liberty   ❖ Pursuit of happiness

2. The second sentence of the Declaration tells why governments are created.
 ❖ Can you explain this sentence in your own words? Do you agree?

The Declaration paved the way for the United States to become the first democratic nation in modern times.

THE AMATEUR HISTORIAN: RECREATING THE PAST ━━━━━━

1. **Role Playing.** Imagine that you and your classmates are colonial representatives meeting in Philadelphia. Hold an assembly session in your class in which you discuss: (1) the complaints of the colonists against Great Britain and (2) possible solutions.

2. **Writing an Editorial.** Newspaper editors often express their opinions on important issues. Pretend it is 1774. Write a short editorial giving your opinion about whether the British government was right in passing the Quebec Act.

MICHIGAN AND THE AMERICAN REVOLUTION

Most battles during the American Revolution happened outside of Michigan. However, Michigan did play an important role in the American Revolution.

THE REVOLUTIONARY WAR COMES TO MICHIGAN

> ***As you read, look for answers to the following questions:***
> 1. Whom did Native Americans side with during the American Revolution? Why?
> 2. Describe the struggles of George Rogers Clark against the British.
> 3. Name four nations that have flown their flags over Michigan.

When the Revolution began, the center of British government in Michigan was in Detroit, a small town with just over a thousand people. Detroit served as a base of operations for British soldiers fighting the American colonists in the Ohio River Valley and beyond.

Many Native Americans saw the American colonists as a threat and supported the British. The British encouraged the Native Americans, especially the Iroquois, to attack American settlers. The British believed that the help of the Iroquois would reduce the need for British soldiers in the area. The British provided the Native Americans with guns, ammunition and other supplies.

Settlers in Kentucky and Ohio lived in constant fear of attack. **George Rogers Clark**, a young backwoods settler, wanted to do something about it. He pleaded with Virginia for soldiers, but the governor would not spare any. Clark sought help from volunteers. About 175 men agreed to join him. In July 1778, Clark's army staged a surprise attack on the British fort at Kaskaskia, near St. Louis. The fort surrendered without a shot being fired. Next, Clark's army launched a successful attack on Fort Sackville in present-day Indiana.

Clark was now anxious to attack the British at Detroit. Virginia still refused his request for additional soldiers and supplies. Clark was forced to abandon his plans. Detroit remained under British control throughout the war.

In 1781, Spain decided to help the colonists against Great Britain. A group of Spanish soldiers from St. Louis made their way north up the Mississippi River. At Niles, in southwest Michigan, they attacked a nearly empty British fort. The Spanish were successful and raised their flag over the fort. They held the fort for only one day. Afterwards, they set it on fire. Niles is the only place in Michigan where the Spanish flag has ever flown. In all, four flags have flown over Michigan soil—the French, British, Spanish and American.

In the first years of the Revolutionary War, the colonial army faced one disaster after another. However, under the leadership of **General George Washington**, the colonists won important battles at Trenton, New Jersey (1776) and Saratoga, New York (1777). These victories helped persuade the French to assist the Americans.

George Washington.
How did Washington help to bring about an American victory?

In 1781, French and American forces trapped **General Cornwallis** and the British army on a swampy peninsula in Virginia. When General Cornwallis surrendered at Yorktown, Virginia, the American Revolutionary War was over. The British government recognized the independence of a new country, the United States, in the **Treaty of Paris of 1783**.

General Cornwallis surrenders at Yorktown.

THE AMATEUR HISTORIAN: RECREATING THE PAST

1. **Making Maps.** Create a map that shows the locations of the main forts during the Revolutionary War and the campaign of George Rogers Clark.

2. **Holding a History Pageant.** Create costumes that show how the people of Michigan might have dressed in colonial times. Then hold a pageant in which class members explain who they are supposed to be and what they are wearing.

◆ EARLY HOMES IN MICHIGAN ◆

When the first European and American settlers came to what is now Michigan, there were no homes waiting for them. To survive, they had to learn to meet their needs with local resources. The first question was usually where to build a home. Settlers looked for a site near water—a lake, stream or river. Water was needed for drinking, cooking, washing and watering crops.

Newcomers to Michigan did not hire anyone to help them. Instead, every family member had to help cut down trees, clear the fields of large stones and build the home. The tools they used were simple ones—an axe or a handsaw.

A pioneer family's first home was usually a log cabin. Logs were cut from the forests. With notched logs joined at the corners, a log cabin was relatively simple and fast to build. Logs from cleared land were hand-split into planks. Clay was used to make the houses weather-proof. Roofs were covered with tree bark or straw. Since nails were often unavailable, settlers used wooden wedges and clay to keep the house together.

Inside, pioneer homes often consisted of one large room with a single central fireplace. The fireplace was used for cooking, providing light in the evening and heating in the winter. The inside walls were bare or covered by wooden boards. Water was brought to the house in buckets. Floors were usually first made of dirt. In time, the floors were covered over with wooden planks. Windows were openings in the walls covered by shutters but

Inside an 18th century cabin.

without glass. Barns were later added to house animals. Toilets were outdoor "outhouses" because homes lacked running water.

Homes were rarely ever completely finished. Construction took place over a period of years. After the main home was constructed, improvements and additions were made. As the family grew in size, they added extra rooms.

◆ ◆ ◆ ◆ ◆ ◆

Early settlers in Michigan often built their homes near water. Water provided a means of transportation and a source of food. In what other ways did early settlers adapt to their environment?

EXPANDING YOUR UNDERSTANDING

Creating Vocabulary Cards

French and Indian War
Why was it begun?
Who won the war?

American Revolution
What was the American Revolution?
What role did Michigan play in the
American Revolution?

Learning to Use an Encyclopedia

One place to find information about the early history of Michigan is in a reference book. One very special reference book is an encyclopedia (en sī klə pē' dē ə).

ENCYCLOPEDIA

Encyclopedias provide information on a wide variety of subjects. You can find out about history, science, music and current events. They have articles about countries, states and famous people. Articles in an encyclopedia are arranged in alphabetical order. Encyclopedias usually consist of many volumes. The first volume starts with the letter "A." The last volume ends with the letter "Z." Each volume has guide words or letters on its spine to help you find the topics it contains.

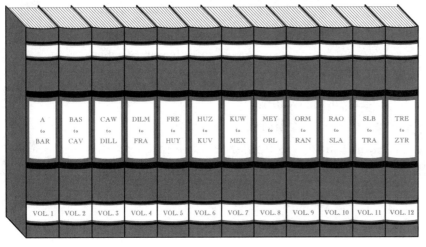

Which volume would you use to find information about:

1. the names of major rivers in Michigan?
2. the name of the first United States President?
3. the distance from the Earth to the Sun?

HOW GOOD A LISTENER ARE YOU?

3C In this activity, you will learn about Michigan in the years before statehood. Look for the following words and phrases:

▶ Articles of Confederation   ▶ War of 1812

▶ Northwest Ordinance   ▶ Cumberland Gap

▶ Bill of Rights   ▶ Erie Canal

▶ Battle of Fallen Timbers   ▶ Toledo Strip

Listening is an important part of our lives. We live in a society in which we often receive oral information. We listen to parents, friends, teachers, television and radio.

PLAYING THE TELEPHONE GAME

When we **listen**, we pay attention to what we hear. Just how good a listener are you? In this activity, you will have a chance to measure your listening ability by playing the "Telephone Game." Here are the rules:

❖ Your teacher will make up a sentence and whisper the sentence to a student.

❖ This student will whisper what he or she has heard from the teacher to another student. Once the first student has said the sentence to the second student, he or she should write the sentence down where no one else can see it.

❖ The second student should now whisper the sentence to a third student who writes it down. This procedure should continue until all the students in the class have participated in listening to the sentence.

❖ The last student will then announce to the class what he or she has heard as the sentence and write it on the chalkboard.

THINK ABOUT IT

Compare what the last student announces with what the teacher whispered to the first student.

◆ Were the two sentences the same?

◆ If not, what might explain the differences between the two sentences?

◆ Look at everyone's written sentences to see how the sentence has changed.

If your class is like most groups that play this game, the last sentence was different from the sentence first introduced by your teacher. Listening, speaking and communicating are key skills in modern society. This activity will help you improve these skills. Good listening requires you to take the following steps in preparation:

❖ **Get Ready to Listen.** Face the person who is about to speak. Remove anything that may block your seeing and hearing clearly. Focus on the speaker's message.

❖ **Determine your Purpose.** Know why you are about to listen. Are you listening to obtain information, to solve a problem or to provide feedback? If so, you should have your pen or pencil ready and your notebook open. If you are listening for enjoyment or appreciation, it is probably not necessary to take notes.

To practice these steps, the class should divide into groups. Each group can then use the reading passages in this activity to practice with. A different student in each group should read one of the passages aloud. The reader should begin with the title and questions that start the reading.

The other students in the group should listen without looking at the passages. They should also jot down any words or ideas they may want to discuss at the end of the reading. Use a copy of the following form when it is your turn to be a listener.

~   NOTES FOR DISCUSSION   ~

Notes during the reading:
1. What is the title of the reading?
2. List any words and ideas you want to discuss after the reading.

Notes after the reading:
1. How would you answer the questions you heard at the start of the reading?
2. Rate the reader on how well he or she read. Explain your rating.

━━━━ READING PASSAGE 1: ━━━━

THE NORTHWEST ORDINANCE

As this passage is being read, listen for answers to the following questions:
A. What were the Articles of Confederation?
B. What were the major provisions of the Northwest Ordinance?

After declaring independence, the former colonies became thirteen separate, independent states. They soon realized the need for some form of national government. After the experience of living under the British government, the former colonists feared making a central government that would be too powerful. The new states therefore created a weak national government in 1781, under an agreement known as the **Articles of Confederation** . ◀

One of the most important achievements of the new national government was to conclude a peace treaty with Great Britain. In the **Treaty of Paris**, the British government agreed to recognize the independence of the United States. The treaty also gave the **Northwest Territory** to the United States. The Northwest Territory stretched from the Appalachian Mountains to the Mississippi River, north of the Ohio River and south of the Great Lakes. It included present-day Michigan. The British continued to remain in control of Canada, north of the Great Lakes.

In 1787, the American government passed the **Northwest Ordinance** to regulate ◀ the Northwest Territory. The ordinance (*law*) divided the area into several smaller territories. The ordinance also established important procedures for eventually creating new states out of these territories.

Under the ordinance, Congress first appointed (*selected*) a territorial governor as leader for each territory. When a territory's population reached 60,000 adults, its citizens could write their own constitution and apply for admission as a state. Once the constitution was approved by Congress, the territory would be admitted as a new state, equal in all respects to the existing states. In passing this law, the new government established an important principle. The Northwest Ordinance promised the territories that someday they would be allowed to join the United States on equal terms as new states. In addition, the ordinance prohibited slavery, encouraged public education and guaranteed trial by jury and religious freedom throughout the Northwest Territory.

Which states were created out of the Northwest Territory?

At this point you should stop reading and hold a discussion with your group. The reader should act as the discussion leader. Ask group members for the title of the reading. Ask what words and ideas they wish to discuss. Then have students discuss the answers to the questions found in the box at the start of the reading.

READING PASSAGE 2:

AMERICANS CHANGE THEIR FORM OF GOVERNMENT

As this passage is being read, listen for answers to the following questions:
A. What problems existed with the Articles of Confederation?
B. How did the new constitution attempt to solve these problems?
C. Why was a bill of rights added to the constitution?

When they wrote the Articles of Confederation, Americans feared creating a national government that would be too powerful. Under the Articles of Confederation, the states kept the most important powers for themselves. Only the states could issue money, collect taxes and raise an army. This meant the national government could hardly defend itself. Trade between states became difficult when each state printed its own money. The country faced so many problems that many Americans demanded change.

In 1787, a convention met in Philadelphia, Pennsylvania, to write a new constitution. The members of the convention recommended a stronger national government with the power to collect taxes, issue money and raise its own army. It would also have a strong President, a Congress and a Supreme Court.

In this room the Constitutional Convention met in Philadelphia.

It was decided that before the Constitution would be accepted, nine states would have to **ratify** (*approve*) it. Special conventions were held in each state to ratify or reject the new Constitution of 1787. People in each state had strong opinions about whether the new system of government should be accepted or rejected. Some Americans feared

The signing of the U.S. Constitution.

the new national government would create harsh new taxes. Others argued that the new government might not respect people's rights. They demanded that a **Bill of Rights** be added ◀ to protect important liberties, such as the right to a fair trial and freedom of speech.

By 1788, eleven states voted to accept the Constitution. As a result, the new Constitution was approved. One year later, a Bill of Rights was added to the Constitution.

At this point you should stop reading and hold a discussion with your group. The reader should act as the discussion leader. Ask group members for the title of the reading. Ask what words and ideas they wish to discuss. Then have students discuss the answers to the questions found in the box at the start of the reading.

READING PASSAGE 3:

Information

TROUBLES WITH THE BRITISH CONTINUE

As this passage is being read, listen for answers to the following questions:
A. What happened at the Battle of Fallen Timbers?
B. What role did Michigan play in the War of 1812?

Despite the signing of the Treaty of Paris, the British continued to hold the forts of Detroit and Michilimackinac to protect their profitable fur trade. The British openly defied the United States, believing the Americans were too weak to force them out.

American pioneers suspected the British were also selling firearms to local Native American tribes and even secretly encouraging them to attack American settlers. As a result, few new settlers moved into the Northwest Territory. Many felt it was unsafe. In 1790, troops were sent to force the British out and to end Native American raids against settlers. In one battle, Native Americans killed 700 American soldiers.

In 1792, President George Washington sent General **Anthony Wayne** into the territory. In 1794, Wayne led a large and well-trained force against the Native Americans in northwest Ohio. In ▶ the **Battle of Fallen Timbers**, Wayne defeated the Native Americans. They agreed to leave most of what is now Ohio and the lands along the Detroit River and Straits of Mackinac. In exchange, the Native Americans received $20,000 in trade goods.

The Battle of Fallen Timbers.

Without the help of local Native Americans, the British realized they could not defeat General Wayne's army. They agreed to surrender Detroit and Michilimackinac. U.S. troops took over these forts, and Michigan at last came under the control of the United States.

This was not the end of troubles with the British. In 1806, a Shawnee chief named **Tecumseh** began uniting Native American tribes. Tecumseh encouraged them not to give up any more land to American settlers. Settlers in the Northwest Territory feared an attack by a mighty army of Native American warriors. Tecumseh received help from the British but was later defeated.

At the same time, the British were stopping American ships at sea to search for **deserters** (*people who had escaped from the military*) from the British navy. Sometimes the British stopped American ships and took American sailors off to serve on British ships. In 1812, Congress declared war on Great Britain.

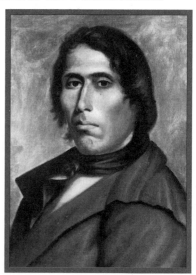

Tecumseh

▶ News of the **War of 1812** was slow to reach Michigan. The British acted quickly to send troops to the forts on the Great Lakes. On Lake Erie, the British had several warships. Commander **Oliver Perry** of the U.S. Navy was daring enough to surprise them. In a great naval battle Perry captured six ships. Perry's victory opened the way for American troops to retake Detroit in 1813. In 1815, the two sides agreed to make peace, bringing the war to an end.

During the Battle of Lake Erie, Oliver Perry leaves his sinking ship, the *Lawrence*.

At this point you should stop reading and hold a discussion with your group. The reader should act as the discussion leader. Ask group members for the title of the reading. Ask what words and ideas they wish to discuss. Then have students discuss the answers to the questions found in the box at the start of the reading.

READING PASSAGE 4:

THE POPULATION OF MICHIGAN GROWS

As this passage is being read, listen for answers to the following questions:
A. What were some of the accomplishments of Lewis Cass?
B. Why did many settlers avoid coming to Michigan until the late 1820s?

In 1813, **Lewis Cass** became the territorial governor of Michigan. Cass served for eighteen years, longer than any other person in Michigan history.

FAMOUS MICHIGANDERS: LEWIS CASS

Lewis Cass served as a colonel in the War of 1812. He established his fame as Michigan's territorial governor. Under his leadership, Michigan's population and wealth slowly began to grow. Cass encouraged settlers to come to Michigan. He persuaded the U.S. government to build new roads between Detroit and military outposts such as Fort Mackinac. Later, he was twice elected to the U.S. Senate. In 1848, Cass ran unsuccessfully for President. He also served as Secretary of War, Secretary of State, and Ambassador to France.

In 1810, there were only 4,762 settlers in Michigan. By 1820, the number had reached 9,000 people. That same year, Cass led an expedition to explore the Upper Peninsula. The expedition traveled 4,000 miles. Cass signed treaties with many tribes living in Michigan. He was able to persuade many tribes to give up their lands. Under Cass, Michigan began slowly changing into a land of farmers and settlers.

Despite Cass's efforts, early pioneers often avoided Michigan. Many settlers thought the land was undesirable. Winters were cold, and lands to the south were better suited for farming. Disease and mosquitoes made life in Michigan dangerous. The thick forests of Michigan also acted as a major barrier. Before a settler could plant

A traditional pioneer cabin.

crops, trees had to be removed and the land cleared. Most important of all, it was difficult to reach Michigan or to send goods from Michigan back east. The Appalachian Mountains were a barrier to travel and trade between the Atlantic coast and lands further west. The few roads that did exist were made of dirt and hard to pass when it rained. Most settlers preferred traveling by way of Kentucky through the ▶ **Cumberland Gap** or by water along the Ohio River. Both routes took settlers far south of Michigan.

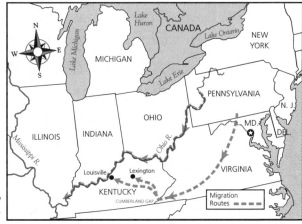

Through which states did the early settlers to the west usually pass?

For Michigan to become fully settled, it became important to establish a water route between the Atlantic Ocean and the Great Lakes, other than the St. Lawrence River in Canada. A **canal** (*a man-made ditch filled with water*) connecting the Great Lakes with the Northeast would make Michigan much easier to reach. Such a canal would also make it cheaper to ship goods by water instead of by land.

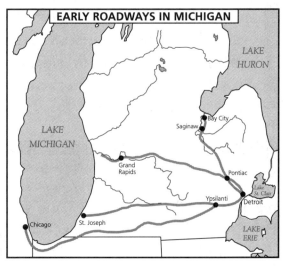

Where did most of Michigan's earliest major roads begin?

As it happened, in 1816 the Governor of New York proposed that a canal be built between the Hudson River and Lake Erie. Such a canal would allow people to travel from New York City to the Great Lakes entirely by water. Building the **Erie Canal** was a gigantic project, taking seven years to construct. Completed in 1825, the Erie Canal stretched 363 miles. The canal linked Buffalo on Lake Erie to Albany on the Hudson River.

Settlers now had a much easier way to get to Michigan with their belongings and livestock. They could take a steamboat up the Hudson River to Albany. Then it took about a week to travel the full length of the canal by flatboat. After they reached Lake Erie, settlers were carried on steamships across the Great Lakes. Ships usually docked in Detroit. From Detroit, settlers went into Michigan in all directions. Because of the Erie Canal, most immigrants to Michigan came from New York or New England. At the same time, the canal provided a convenient way for Michiganders to ship their goods to markets back east.

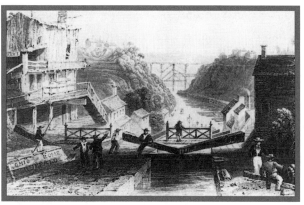

The opening of the Erie Canal.
How did the canal help Michigan's development?

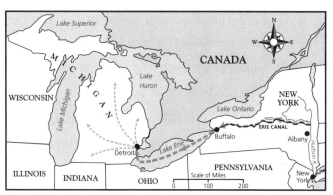

Describe the route taken by a person traveling from New York City to Michigan along the Erie Canal.

At this point you should stop reading and hold a discussion with your group. The reader should act as the discussion leader. Ask group members for the title of the reading. Ask what words and ideas they wish to discuss. Then have students discuss the answers to the questions found in the box at the start of the reading.

REPLAYING THE TELEPHONE GAME

You began this activity by participating in the "Telephone Game." Do you think your listening skills have now improved? To find out, replay the Telephone Game. Use the same rules as earlier. See if your message can be heard and repeated with less change than before.

◆ MICHIGAN'S ROAD TO STATEHOOD ◆

In this activity, you read about events before Michigan became a state. In this section, you will learn how Michigan finally became a state. Before starting this section, read the following *Skill Builder* about taking notes.

Skill Builder

USING NOTE CARDS

One way to keep track of information is by writing notes on index cards. The following shows how to organize information on a note card:

❖ **Key Word.** Use a key word or phrase that identifies the main topic of the note card. Group note cards together by their key words.

❖ **Source.** A source identifies where you found the information on the card. The source describes the name of the book and the author.

❖ **Notes.** Your notes on the note card should be **brief**.

The following example shows what information might be included on a note card based on Reading Passage 4—The Population of Michigan Grows.

> *Key Word: Population*
> *Source: Michigan: Its Land and Its People, pages 109-111.*
> *Authors: Killoran, Zimmer and Jarrett*
> *Notes: 1. At first, settlers passed by Michigan because the land was undesirable.*
> *2. Disease and forests acted as barriers against settlers.*
> *3. The few roads that existed were poor and hard to travel.*
> *4. The Erie Canal connected Lake Erie with the Atlantic Ocean.*
> *5. The Erie Canal made travel to Michigan much easier.*

When taking notes, remember these hints:

❖ finish reading the passage or section before beginning to take notes

❖ use abbreviations and symbols on your note cards to reduce note-taking

❖ focus on the main idea and a few supporting details

◆ ◆ ◆ ◆ ◆ ◆

Practice your note-taking skills on the following passage describing how Michigan became a state. Make your notes on index cards or pieces of paper.

MICHIGAN BECOMES A STATE

After the construction of the Erie Canal, Michigan's population grew rapidly. According to the Northwest Ordinance, a territory needed 60,000 people before it could apply for admission as a state. By 1835, Michigan had enough people to apply for statehood. Ohio, Indiana and Illinois had already been admitted as states.

Michiganders drew up a state constitution and applied for admission to the Union. Admission was delayed, however, because of a boundary dispute between Michigan and Ohio. Both claimed control of a small strip of land known as the **Toledo Strip**.

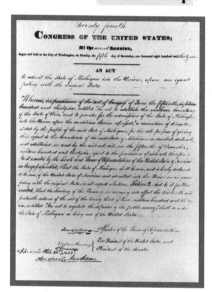

According to the Northwest Ordinance the strip was part of the Michigan Territory. However, Ohio was already a state, and had voting power in Congress. For a time, it appeared that Michigan and Ohio might go to war over the dispute. Congress settled the dispute by giving the Toledo Strip to Ohio. Michigan received the Upper Peninsula in exchange for giving up the strip.

With the dispute settled, the way was now cleared for Michigan to become a state. On **January 26, 1837**, Michigan became the 26th state in the United States. Detroit became the state's first capital.

Michigan soon grew rapidly. By 1840, its population was almost fifty times what it had been in 1800. In 1847, the state capital was moved from Detroit to a more central location at Lansing.

Act of Congress giving Michigan its statehood.

◆ ◆ ◆ ◆ ◆ ◆

Before completing your notecard, review the note-taking skills on page 112.

Key Word: Michigan's Statehood
Source: Michigan: Its Land and Its People, page 113.
Authors: Killoran, Zimmer and Jarrett
Notes: 1.
2.
3.
4.

EXPANDING YOUR UNDERSTANDING

Creating Vocabulary Cards

Northwest Ordinance
What was the "Northwest
Ordinance"?
Why was it important?

Toledo Strip
What was the "Toledo Strip"?
What role did it play in
Michigan history?

Continuing Your Role as an Amateur Historian

1. **Providing a Message.** Imagine that you are a citizen of Michigan and oppose giving the Toledo Strip to Ohio. Draw a poster, cartoon or advertisement that you think would persuade other Americans to support your view.

2. **Creating a Picture Gallery.** Some of Michigan's most important leaders lived in the period before Michigan was a state. What did these people look like? What roles did they play in Michigan's history? Create a picture gallery with some of these key people. Place a short account of the life and contributions of each individual beneath his or her picture.

FAMOUS MICHIGANDERS: STEVENS T. MASON

Stevens T. Mason was born in Virginia in 1811. His father was chosen as Secretary of the Michigan Territory in 1830. The next year, Mason was chosen to replace his father, who had moved to Texas. Mason was only 19 years old. When Mason sent troops to keep the Toledo Strip in Michigan, the President became angry with Mason. The President acted against Mason by sending a new secretary to the territory. But Michiganders did not forget Mason. When Michigan became a state, voters elected him as their first State Governor. Mason was only 24 years old. Because of his age, he is often referred to as the "Boy Governor."

HOW WOULD YOU DIAGRAM WHAT YOU READ?

3D In this activity, you will learn about Michigan from 1850 until after the Civil War. Look for the following important words and phrases:

▶ Main Idea

▶ Supporting Details

▶ Abolitionists

▶ Underground Railroad

▶ Civil War

▶ Confederate States of America

▶ Reading Map

▶ Appomattox Courthouse

Although you have already been reading for three or four years, have you ever thought about how complicated the act of reading is? Let's look more closely at what is involved in the process of reading.

> Describe what you do when you read something.

When you read, you try to understand the meaning of a group of words. To read well takes time and practice. You need to develop some special skills. The rest of this activity will help you to develop these skills.

Skill Builder

WHAT DOES IT MEAN TO READ SOMETHING?

A "reading passage" is a series of paragraphs that deal with the same topic or theme. Each paragraph contains one or more sentences. Together, the sentences of a paragraph usually focus on one idea, known as the **main idea**. The main ideas of all the paragraphs, in turn, relate to the theme of the reading passage. ◀

Usually one of the sentences in each paragraph tells the reader the paragraph's main idea. This sentence is called the **topic sentence**. The topic sentence is often at the beginning of the paragraph. However, sometimes a writer will put it in a different part of the paragraph.

The other sentences of the paragraph usually contain information about the topic sentence. They provide a description, an explanation, specific details or an illustration of the main topic. Because these sentences give details that support the main idea, they are called **supporting details**. ◀

The following reading passage is about Michigan's role in the events leading up to the Civil War. As you read each paragraph, look for its main idea and supporting details.

━━━ READING SELECTION 1: ━━━

MICHIGAN'S ROLE IN THE STRUGGLE AGAINST SLAVERY

Until the 1860s, slavery was legal in many parts of the United States. Under this system, one person could own another person as a piece of property. There were several ways Michiganders were active in the struggle against slavery. Slavery was never legal in Michigan. Some Michiganders tried to end it elsewhere.

First, many abolitionists were active in Michigan. **Abolitionists** were people who wanted to abolish slavery. They felt it was immoral. In 1832, **Elizabeth Chandler** started the Michigan Antislavery Society in Ann Arbor.

Second, Michigan played a key role in the **Underground Railroad** . This was not actually a railroad, but a way for slaves to escape to freedom. Slaves traveled secretly from place to place, hiding in homes along the way. They traveled on this "railroad" until they reached a place like Canada where slavery was illegal. Thousands of runaway slaves traveled through Michigan. Many of them stayed in Michigan to live as free people. Slave owners sometimes came to Michigan to look for their runaway slaves. They even had

Elizabeth Chandler started the first abolitionist society in Michigan.
What is an abolitionist?

Congress pass a law punishing anyone who helped a slave escape. In 1855, Michigan responded by prohibiting state and local officials from helping those trying to recapture ex-slaves.

Finally, a new political party started in Michigan which opposed the spread of slavery. Many people were unhappy with the way that the two political parties at the time were dealing with the slavery issue. In 1854, several thousand people met in Jackson, Michigan. They formed a new political party called the **Republican Party**. Republicans wanted to elect people to political office who would prevent the spread of slavery into the Western territories.

FAMOUS MICHIGANDERS: SOJOURNER TRUTH

One of Michigan's most famous abolitionists was Isabella Baumfree. She was born into slavery in New York, but was set free just before New York abolished slavery. Although unable to read or write, she gained a great knowledge of the Bible. In 1843, she traveled throughout the North speaking against the evils of slavery and in favor of women's rights. Baumfree took the name of **Sojourner Truth** because she believed her "sojourn" (*journey*) was a mission for God. In the 1850's, she settled in Battle Creek. During the Civil War she traveled around Michigan collecting food and clothing for African-American soldiers.

Let's look more closely at what you have just read. In this selection, the main idea appears in the first paragraph. It states that "there were several ways Michiganders were active in the struggle against slavery." The remaining sentences explain this statement in much greater detail. Notice how each paragraph in the passage focuses on another way that Michiganders worked against slavery. Within each paragraph, the topic sentence states what the paragraph is about. The other sentences give supporting details.

Sometimes, "seeing" ideas in the form of an image helps us to understand them better. Let's see what this first reading passage might look like if it were put in the form of a diagram.

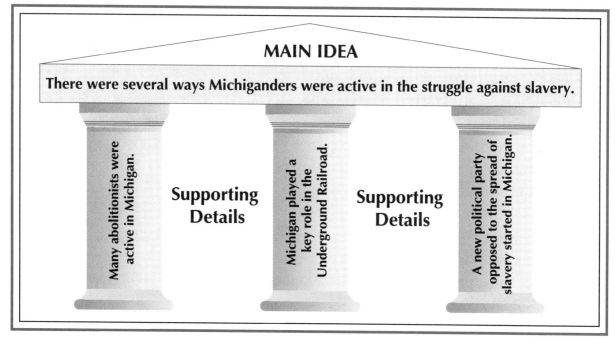

Notice how the sentences that provide details to support the main idea are shown as columns holding up the roof. The supporting sentences support the main idea, just like the columns of the building hold up its roof.

Now it is your turn. Read the following passage about the causes of the Civil War. After reading this passage, you should create a diagram showing the main idea and its supporting details.

▶ A **civil war** *is a war between people in the same country. The Civil War began when several Southern states seceded* (separated) *from the United States. These states formed their own country, the*
▶ **Confederate States of America**. *President Lincoln was determined that the United States would not be divided into two countries. When Confederate* (kən fed' ər it) *troops attacked* **Fort Sumter** *in Charleston harbor in April 1861, the Civil War began.*

Fort Sumter, South Carolina, in April, 1861.

READING SELECTION 2:

THE CAUSES OF THE CIVIL WAR

The Civil War was the most destructive war in U.S. history. More Americans were killed in the Civil War than in any other American war. Like most wars, the Civil War had several causes.

Many historians believe the most important cause of the Civil War was the existence of slavery. In the Southern states, plantation owners used slaves to grow cotton and other crops. In the North, the economy was based on free laborers who could work where they chose and received a wage. Slaves were not free, and did not receive wages. Many Northerners felt slavery was immoral. Slaveowners did not see themselves as evil. They pointed to slavery in the Bible and in other societies.

A slave auction.

❖ CONTINUED

A second reason for the Civil War was the breakdown of cooperation between the North and South. Northerners and Southerners disagreed over whether new states in the West should allow slavery. By the late 1850s, distrust between the North and South was growing. In 1860, **Abraham Lincoln** was elected President. Lincoln opposed the spread of slavery to new states. Many Southerners feared he might try to end slavery in the South.

A final cause of the war was a disagreement over **states' rights**. Some Americans believed each state had a right to secede from the United States. After Lincoln was elected, several Southern states decided to secede. President Lincoln believed their secession was illegal. He was willing to fight to preserve the Union.

This photograph from 1863 shows us Lincoln during the Civil War.

Now that you have finished reading the passage, complete the diagram below showing the main idea and its supporting details.

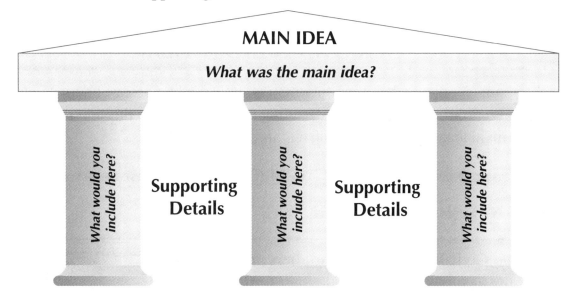

MAIN IDEA

What was the main idea?

What would you include here?

Supporting Details

What would you include here?

Supporting Details

What would you include here?

Your Task

COMPLETING A "READING MAP"

Another way to understand a reading is to create a "reading map." A **reading map** ◄ divides the main topic of the reading into smaller and smaller parts. It begins with the main idea in the center and surrounds this idea with supporting details. Let's see how this might look.

Reading Passage: Some scientists divide the foods we eat into four main groups. These groups are fruits and vegetables, dairy products, meat and grains. Hamburgers are made from meat. Most breakfast cereals are made of grains.

A "reading map" of this passage might look like this:

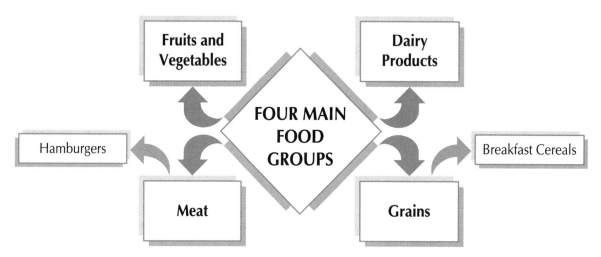

CREATING YOUR OWN "READING MAP"

Now that you understand what a reading map is, let's read a passage about Michigan during the Civil War and turn it into a "reading map." As you go through the passage, look for the main idea in each paragraph and its supporting details.

READING SELECTION 3:

MICHIGAN DURING THE CIVIL WAR

During the Civil War, Michigan soldiers fought in the Union army against the Confederate States. About 90,000 Michiganders volunteered for the army. Among them were the First Michigan Colored Infantry, made up entirely of African-American soldiers. Fort Wayne, on the Detroit River, was the main area where Michigan volunteers assembled.

Kinchen Artis, a soldier in Company H,
First Michigan Colored Infantry.

❖ CONTINUED

Michigan soldiers quickly established a reputation for courage and bravery. Soldiers from Michigan fought in most major battles of the Civil War, including Bull Run, Shiloh and Gettysburg. Under **General George Custer**, the Michigan Cavalry Brigade played a key role in helping the Union army win at Gettysburg.

At the time of the Civil War, women were not allowed to join the army. However, a few women from Michigan did take part in the war. **Sarah Emma Edmonds** disguised herself as a man and joined the army under the name of Franklin

George Armstrong Custer.

Thompson. She served for two years in the 2nd Michigan Infantry as a male nurse. Her true identity was revealed when she applied for a pension after the war.

In April 1865, the Civil War ended. The Confederate Army surrendered at **Appomattox Courthouse** in Virginia. On May 10,

The Sixth Michigan cavalry charge over Confederate lines in July, 1863.

1865, the Fourth Michigan Cavalry captured **Jefferson Davis**, the President of the Confederacy. By the time the Civil War ended, 14,000 soldiers from Michigan had died in battle or from disease during the war.

Now it's your turn. Make a copy of the reading map below. Use the reading passage about Michigan in the Civil War to complete your own "map."

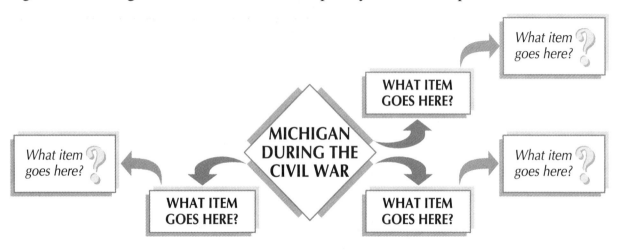

EXPANDING YOUR UNDERSTANDING

Creating Vocabulary Cards

Main Idea
What is the "main idea"?
What are "supporting details"?

Abolitionist
What was an "abolitionist"?
Name an abolitionist from
Michigan.

Reading a Book about the Civil War

One of the best ways to learn about the Civil War is to read a book. There are many excellent books that can help to bring the period of the Civil War alive. Select one of the following books, or read a book of your own choice about the Civil War. Then write a one-page book report.

- **A Picture Book of Sojourner Truth** by David A. Adler (Holiday House).
- **Nettie's Trip South** by Ann Turner (MacMillan).
- **Who Comes With Cannons** by Patricia Beatty (Murrow Junior).
- **Freedom Crossing** by Margaret Gott Clark (Scholastic)
- **Sweet Clara And The Freedom Quilt** by Deborah Hopkinson (Knopf)
- **If You Lived At The Time Of The Civil War** by Kay Moore (Scholastic)
- **Ghost Cadet** by Elaine Marie Alphin (Scholastic).

Michigan soldiers attack during the Civil War. *How can reading a book about the Civil War increase your understanding?*

Your book report should identify the book by its title and author. Then write two to three paragraphs summarizing the contents of the book. Conclude your report by saying whether or not you found the book worthwhile. Be sure to provide examples to support your conclusion.

HOW GOOD ARE YOU AT RECOGNIZING DIFFERENT TYPES OF READINGS?

3E In this activity, you will learn how many Michiganders earned their living in the years before and after the Civil War. Look for the following words and phrases:

▶ Geologist   ▶ Loggers
▶ Soo Locks   ▶ Bar Graphs

It would be hard to recognize other people if we didn't know the general pattern of the human face. Knowing this general pattern helps us to detect the slight differences in features that make a person's face unique—facial shape, hair color, nose, eyes and mouth. In many ways, it is the same with reading. We can better understand specific reading selections if we recognize their general patterns.

Skill Builder

THREE TYPES OF READINGS: PROBLEM-SOLUTION, SEQUENTIAL AND DESCRIPTIVE

Three common forms of reading passages are the problem-solution reading, the sequential (si kwen' shəl) reading and the descriptive reading.

TYPES OF READINGS		
Problem-Solution	**Sequential**	**Descriptive**
This type of reading identifies problems and describes solutions. Key words in this type include *problem, recommendation, solution* and *result*.	This type of reading presents events in chronological order. Chronological order is the order in which events occurred in time. Key words in this type of reading include *later, then, before, after, following* and *preceding*.	This type of reading *describes* a person, place or event. The main idea sentence often states what is being described. The rest of the selection provides the main characteristics of what is being described. Key words will usually focus on the *who, what, when* and *where* of what is being described.

In this activity, you will be presented with three reading passages. For each passage, you will need to identify the kind of reading it is and explain the reason for your choice. As you previously learned, it may help you to **first** create a diagram of the reading.

READING PASSAGE 1:

THE EMERGENCE OF MINING IN MICHIGAN

During the mid-1800s, new occupations appeared in Michigan. One of the most important of these was mining.

The first French explorers had noted the presence of copper in the Upper Peninsula. The discovery of copper in Michigan created new opportunities. **Copper** is a valuable mineral used to make coins, wire and machines. In the 1830s, **Douglass Houghton** found copper by the Ontonagon River. His discovery brought many miners into the Upper Peninsula. In the early 1840s, the first copper mining operations began. Soon Michigan led the nation in copper production.

FAMOUS MICHIGANDERS: DOUGLASS HOUGHTON

In 1830, Douglass Houghton (Hoo' tin) moved to Michigan. Houghton was a geologist. A **geologist** studies what rocks are made of. Around 1837, Houghton found a large boulder of copper. After Michigan became a state, Governor Mason hired Houghton to conduct a study of the state's mineral wealth. Houghton began his study in the Lower Peninsula, and later went to the Upper Peninsula. In 1841, he published his study, focusing on Michigan's large copper deposits. The study led to a mining rush, making Michigan the nation's leading copper producer.

In these same years, iron ore was also discovered in the Upper Peninsula. **William Burt**, a surveyor who worked with Houghton, surveyed land around Teal Lake. Burt located a vast amount of iron ore, hidden below the ground. Soon after, a rush of miners poured into the Upper Peninsula in search of iron. Iron mining began in the **Marquette Range** and spread to the Menominee and Gogebic Ranges.

Almost overnight, towns like Ironwood sprang up near iron mines.

❖ CONTINUED

In 1847, the first commercial iron ore operation began near Negaunee. Large ships carried the iron ore across the Great Lakes. The falls at Sault Ste. Marie, however, acted as a barrier. The ore had to be unloaded and carried by land to the other side of the falls. It was decided to build a canal that would allow ships to carry iron ore through the Great Lakes without having to unload.

In 1855, the **Soo Locks** were completed at Sault Ste. Marie. Shipping iron ore to places like Detroit and Chicago became much less expensive. Michigan's iron mining rapidly expanded. By 1860, 120,000 tons of iron ore were shipped, nearly ten times the amount carried only five years earlier. Michigan emerged as the nation's largest producer of iron ore.

Michigan's mining industry contributed to its large population growth. By the 1890s, Michigan had become the ninth most populated state in the nation.

COMPLETING YOUR FIRST DIAGRAM

Make a copy of the diagram below. Then complete each part of the diagram.

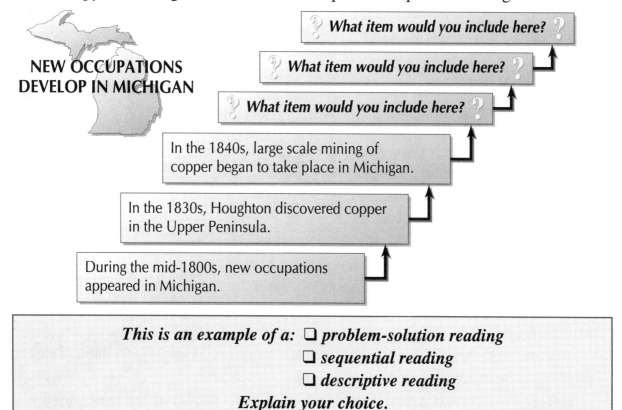

NEW OCCUPATIONS DEVELOP IN MICHIGAN

What item would you include here?

What item would you include here?

What item would you include here?

In the 1840s, large scale mining of copper began to take place in Michigan.

In the 1830s, Houghton discovered copper in the Upper Peninsula.

During the mid-1800s, new occupations appeared in Michigan.

This is an example of a: ❑ *problem-solution reading*
❑ *sequential reading*
❑ *descriptive reading*
Explain your choice.

After you read the next passage you will complete a diagram of the passage. You will be asked to identify the kind of reading it is and explain your choice.

READING SELECTION 2:

MICHIGAN'S LUMBER INDUSTRY GROWS

As the nation grew, the demand for lumber to build homes and furniture increased. Michigan's large number of trees were seen by logging companies as "green gold." **Loggers** are people who cut down trees. Thousands of them traveled to Michigan in search of work.

A group of loggers in the 1890s.
Why did they see trees as "green gold"?

Before the Civil War, cutting trees in Michigan was a small-scale operation. One of the greatest problems early loggers faced was getting timber from forests to sawmills. Logging companies relied on rivers to float the logs to sawmills. By 1849, there were 550 sawmills operating in such places as Muskegon, Menominee and Saginaw. Loggers usually cut the trees in winter and stored the logs near rivers until the spring or summer. When the weather became warmer, each logging company put its logs together to float down the river all at once, to save money.

Why were rivers used to transport logs to mills?

A solution to the problem of bringing more logs to sawmills was found in 1877. **Winfield Scott Gerrish** built a railroad through the forest with "narrow-gauge" tracks. These tracks were narrower than ordinary tracks, and allowed trains to go deeper into the forest. The new railroad helped loggers reach trees they were previously unable to remove. Soon other companies followed Gerrish's example. Lumber companies were no longer dependent on logging near rivers. Trees could be cut and shipped any time of the year. Any type of tree—including the most valuable ones—could now be cut and transported.

❖ CONTINUED

A new problem arose over how to turn all the logs suddenly available into lumber. Early sawmills made only one cut at time. A new type of saw was then invented, known as the "gang saw." The gang saw made several cuts into each log at the same time. Logs could now be cut into lumber much faster. By the 1890s, ten thousand people were employed in the lumber industry.

The growth of the lumber industry had an important effect on Michigan's forests. By the 1920s, half of Michigan's forests had been cut down by loggers or destroyed by forest fires. The soil in these areas was not able to support crops.

The Michigan legislature passed new laws to protect the forests. One of these laws required that a new seedling be planted to replace each tree that was cut down. Michigan's forests slowly began to grow back.

This man cuts a log using the single cut method.
How did the "gang saw" change the way lumber was milled?

Make a copy of the diagram below. Then complete each part of the diagram based on what you have just read about Michigan's lumber industry.

Michigan's Lumber Industry Grows

PROBLEMS

Logging companies could not transport many logs to sawmills.

Sawmills could not cut all the logs into lumber.

What would you put here?

PROBLEMS

SOLUTIONS

Logging companies began to use railroads with narrow-gauge tracks to carry logs.

What would you put here?

What would you put here?

SOLUTIONS

> *This is an example of a:* ❏ *problem-solution reading*
> ❏ *sequential reading*
> ❏ *descriptive reading*
> *Explain your choice.*

COMPLETING YOUR LAST DIAGRAM

Closing

After reading the following passage, complete the diagram. Then identify the kind of reading it is. Explain your choice.

━━━━ READING SELECTION 3: ━━━━

MICHIGAN BECOMES A MANUFACTURING STATE

The early twentieth century brought many important changes to Michigan. The basis of the state's economy moved away from agriculture, mining and logging to manufacturing. Factories sprang up almost everywhere. Michigan became one of the most highly industrialized states in the nation. It was a leader in manufacturing horse-drawn carriages, bicycles and railroad cars.

One of Michigan's best-known manufactured products was furniture. Grand Rapids became the center of the state's furniture-making industry. In 1836, the first furniture maker opened his doors in Grand Rapids. Other furniture manufacturers soon followed. Nearby forests provided the raw materials necessary for making furniture. Grand Rapids also had ample water power from its fast-flowing river.

Michigan's furniture-making industry received a boost at the Centennial Exposition held in Philadelphia in 1876. One of the exhibits displayed furniture made in Grand Rapids. The exhibit was such a success that orders soon poured into the city's workshops and factories.

A second important product made in Michigan was breakfast cereal. Two Michiganders, **Will Kellogg** and **Charles W. Post**, were early pioneers in the breakfast food industry. In the 1890s, Dr. John Kellogg ran a sanitarium to help people improve their health. At his sanitarium, he perfected a health food, which he served his patients.

Charles W. Post

❖ CONTINUED

In 1891, Charles W. Post visited the sanitarium as a patient. The following year, Post came up with the idea of selling a breakfast drink he called *Postum.* Soon afterwards, Post developed *Grape-Nuts,* a cereal made by baking wheat and malted barley.

Will Kellogg, the brother of Dr. Kellogg, desperately wanted to sell to the general public the cereals served to patients at the sanitarium. Dr. Kellogg at first refused to allow his name to be used in advertising these products. Will decided to go into business on his own. In 1906, he started a company selling a breakfast cereal he called Corn Flakes.

First office and plant of Post Cereals at Battle Creek.

By the early 1900s, Battle Creek had emerged as the cereal capital of the world. Will Kellogg's company became Kellogg's Cereals. Post's company eventually became General Foods. Both Kellogg's and General Foods grew into world-famous companies. Today, Battle Creek produces more breakfast cereal than any other city in the world.

Make a copy of the diagram below. Then complete the missing items in the diagram.

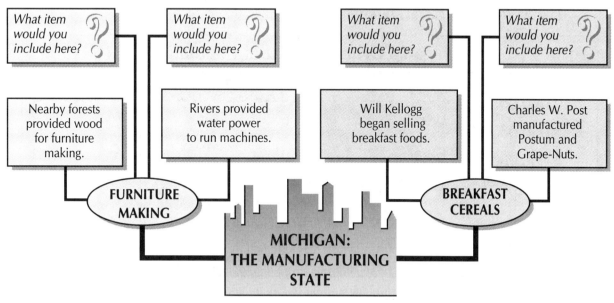

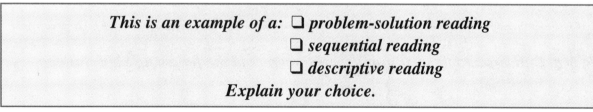

This is an example of a: ❑ *problem-solution reading*
❑ *sequential reading*
❑ *descriptive reading*
Explain your choice.

EXPANDING YOUR UNDERSTANDING

Creating Vocabulary Cards

Geologist
What is a "geologist"?
How did a geologist promote
mining in Michigan?

Soo Locks
Where are the Soo Locks located?
Why are they important
to Michigan's economy?

Creating Bar Graphs

In this activity, you learned how the basis of Michigan's economy changed from agriculture, mining and lumber to manufacturing. One of the most important effects of this change was a shift in the state's population. People from the countryside began moving to towns and cities to find jobs in factories. This change can be seen by examining the bar graph below. The graph shows the changes in Michigan's urban and rural populations between 1810 and 1990. Remember that **urban** (ur' ben) refers to towns and cities. The word **rural** (rur' al) refers to the countryside.

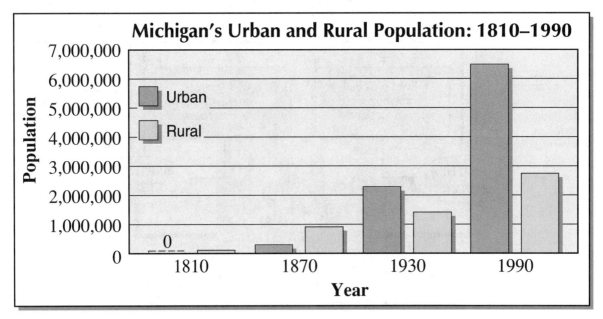

To better understand this bar graph, you should read the following Skill Builder.

Skill Builder

INTERPRETING BAR GRAPHS

What Is a Bar Graph?

A bar graph is a chart that shows parallel bars of different lengths. It is used to compare two or more items.

❖ What items are compared in this bar graph?

Keys to Understanding a Bar Graph

Bar graphs have a vertical axis, which runs from top to bottom, and a horizontal axis, which runs from left to right. Each axis has a title or explanation.

❖ In this graph, what does the vertical axis show?

❖ What does the horizontal axis show?

Interpreting a Bar Graph

Start by reading the title. It tells you what information is presented.

❖ What is the title of this bar graph?

To find specific information, look at the length of each bar in the graph. For example, how many people lived in rural areas in Michigan in 1870? To find the answer, slide your finger along the horizontal axis until you reach the "rural" bar for "1870." Next, run your finger to the top of that bar. If you look at the number scale along the vertical axis, you will see that the bar ends at about 940,000.

❖ Which year on the graph shows the least number of people living in cities in Michigan?

❖ How many people lived in urban areas in Michigan in 1990?

❖ How many lived in rural areas in 1990?

❖ What was the total population of Michigan in 1990?

One way to understand Michigan's changing population is to see how it compares with the rest of the nation. The table below presents information about the population of the United States. Use this information to create your own bar graph.

THE PERCENTAGES OF URBAN AND RURAL POPULATION OF THE UNITED STATES, 1810–1990				
	1810	**1870**	**1930**	**1990**
Urban	7%	25%	56%	75%
Rural	93%	75%	44%	25%

WHAT EFFECTS HAVE KEY EVENTS HAD ON MICHIGAN?

3F In this activity, you will read about the causes and effects of several key events in the history of Michigan. Look for the following important words and phrases:

▶ Cause and Effect   ▶ Great Depression

▶ World War I   ▶ New Deal

Have you ever seen the movie *Back To The Future?* In this film, the main character travels back in time. In doing so, he meets his mother while she is still a teenager. His sudden appearance in his mother's teenage life triggers effects that threaten to change events so that he will never be born. Such time travel into the past is not really possible. But part of the excitement of the film is that it reveals an important truth. If we could change even a single past event, we might change the entire course of history. Why is this so?

Skill Builder

UNDERSTANDING CAUSE-AND-EFFECT RELATIONSHIPS

Every event has some effects. Sometimes these effects can influence the entire future of a society. For example, a leader may decide that his or her nation should go to war. This decision can change the country's entire development. Historians often study the events of the past to better understand these cause-and-effect relationships.

▶ ❖ The cause of something is *what made it happen.* For example, turning on a light switch makes electricity flow to the bulb and lights it up. The *cause* of the light's going on was that someone turned on the switch.

▶ ❖ An effect is what happens *because* of a situation, action or event. For example, the light's going on was the *effect* of turning on the switch. Sometimes a single cause can start a whole chain of effects.

CAUSE		EFFECT
Someone turned on the switch.		The light went on.

In this activity, you will read about three events in Michigan's history. You will learn how each of them had both **causes** and **effects.** Read each selection. Then complete the diagram following each cause-and-effect reading.

THE BIRTH OF THE AUTOMOBILE INDUSTRY

Beginning in the 1890s, Michiganders saw the birth of a new industry. Until then, people either walked or took trains, boats or carriages to get around. Trains could only go where there were railroad tracks. The easiest way to get to most places was by horse and buggy. Then in the the 1890s young inventors began developing new gasoline-powered engines. By putting a gasoline engine into a buggy, these inventors created the "horseless carriage." Through their efforts, the automobile industry was born.

There were many reasons why Michigan became the center of the nation's automobile industry. First, several Michiganders were developing cars at the same time. People like **Ransom E. Olds**, **Henry Ford**, **Charles King**, **John Dodge**, **Henry Packard**, **William C. Durant** and **David Buick** were important in making Michigan an automobile center.

Two of the most important early pioneers in the auto industry were Ransom E. Olds and Henry Ford. Olds started producing cars in 1897. In the first year he sold 425 cars at a price of $650 each. Olds' success proved that there was big money to be made in selling automobiles. Ford put together a simple gasoline engine in 1893. He built his first car in 1896. It used four bicycle wheels and a two-cylinder engine. Ford then found people to invest money to form a new company while he continued to improve his model. Several years later, he began selling his first cars.

Will Durant

Ransom E. Olds

The earliest cars were very different from the automobiles we drive today. They looked like the carriages of the time, known as "buggies," but without horses. These first cars were simple, slow and made a lot of noise. They traveled on bumpy dirt roads, and often broke down. Because they were expensive, they were considered luxuries for the very rich.

❖ CONTINUED

Second, Michigan was already a key manufacturing center. Factories and skilled workers were available in Flint and Detroit. Third, Michigan had many of the raw materials needed for building cars. Iron ore and other resources were mined in the Upper Peninsula and could easily be shipped to Detroit and other manufacturing centers. Finally, the people

Henry Ford looks at his original "horseless carriage" alongside the ten-millionth car he produced.

who had made fortunes in the mining and lumber industries were willing to invest their money in the new auto industry.

Two milestones in the production of cars were achieved in 1908. Will Durant bought up several car-manufacturing companies and formed the **General Motors Corporation**. In the same year, Ford developed a simpler car known as the **Model T**. It was less than half the price of other cars and brought auto ownership within reach of the average American family. Over the next 19 years, Ford sold 15 million Model Ts in the United States. This automobile was the first truly mass-produced car in the world.

In 1914, Ford introduced the first moving **assembly line**. Before that

Early advertisements by the Ford Motor Company.

time, workers had carried parts from one part of the factory to another, or moved between different cars. Now a car was carried on a **conveyor belt**. Each worker would perform a few simple operations on the car, such as adding and tightening a bolt. Using this method, it took much less time to build a car. By 1927, Ford's factories were producing a new Model T every 24 seconds.

❖ CONTINUED

With these developments, the auto industry in Michigan grew. New factories were built, new jobs were created and entire industries sprang up just to serve the automobile. By 1914, four out of every five American cars were made in Michigan. New methods of production continued to change the industry and the country as a whole. General Motors introduced new styles and

A Ford assembly line in 1913.

other features, and soon surpassed Ford. In the early 1920s, the **Chrysler Company** was formed. It eventually became the third of the nation's "big three" automobile manufacturers.

The rise of the automobile industry has had many effects on Michigan and the world. Car manufacturing turned Michigan into a leading industrial state. Millions of jobs were created, and immigrants from all over the world came to Michigan. Detroit became one of the largest cities in the nation. Other cities in the state also grew because of the impact of the auto industry.

The Model A cost $395.
Ford sold almost 2 million of them in 1929 alone.

Because of cars, Michigan and other states built new roads and highways. The car let people travel wherever they wanted. Farms and small towns that could not be reached by boat or train were no longer isolated. Auto engines were used to build tractors, helping farmers to grow and harvest more crops. Gasoline-powered car engines also made possible the development of the tank, for use in warfare. Small gasoline engines, based on the car engine, were used to develop the first airplanes. The effect of the automobile has been great. It is hard to imagine life today without the work of such Michigan auto pioneers as Ransom E. Olds, Henry Ford and others.

◆ HENRY FORD: A CAR FOR ◆ THE GREAT MULTITUDE

The world was a very different place back when Henry Ford was born on July 30, 1863. Most Americans lived on farms. Roads were made of planks or dirt. People did not travel much. There were no electric lights or phones. As a young boy, Ford was fascinated by mechanical things, such as clocks and machines.

Henry Ford

In 1879, at age 16, Ford left his family's farm to become an apprentice in a Detroit machine shop. He wanted to learn everything there was to know about steam engines. To have more time to study steam engines, Ford later moved back to his family's farm in Dearborn. He took a job inspecting steam engines. One day, on a trip to Detroit, he saw his first gasoline engine. The gasoline engine had only been invented in the 1880s. Ford believed he could use this engine to create a carriage that moved on its own, without the aid of horses.

Ford next decided that he needed to learn more about electricity. Electricity was used to start gasoline engines. Ford took a job with the Edison Electrical Company, which made electricity for Detroit's new electric street lights. Ford was one of the engineers who looked after the steam engines that helped generate electricity. Soon he rose to the position of chief engineer.

Ford spent all his spare time developing a "horseless carriage." In late 1893, he completed his first gasoline engine. It took Ford two more years to complete his first car. Finally, at two o'clock in the morning of June 4, 1896, Ford finished his quadricycle. It was too large for the door of the shed, so he knocked out the door frame and several bricks for it to fit through. Then he tested it on the streets of Detroit, waking up all his neighbors. The new "horseless carriage" was noisy and scared the horses of other carriages. Many people looked at Ford's invention as a nuisance.

But Ford was greatly encouraged later that year. At a meeting of the Edison Company in New York, he met Thomas Edison, the inventor of the light bulb and many other devices. Edison encouraged Ford to keep working. Ford's idea was to make cars that all Americans could afford. "I will build a motorcar," he said "for the great multitude" (*large number of people*).

In 1903, Ford's company of 125 workers made 1,700 cars in three models. By 1906, Ford began planning the "Model T." The first Model T sold in 1908 for

$825. It was light and easy to drive. Ford kept reducing the price to increase sales. By 1912, the price had dropped to $575. By 1913, demand was so strong that Ford had to find new ways to make Model Ts faster. One day, Ford was visiting a meat-packing plant. He saw the bodies of dead calves hooked onto a conveyor belt. As they passed, butchers cut off individual pieces. Ford put this idea to work. In his automobile factory, the frame of the car moved on a conveyor belt from one

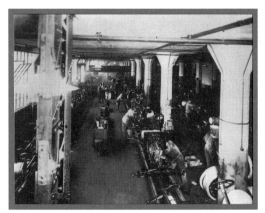

The Model T being assembled at Ford's Highland Park Plant (1914).

work station to the next, as workers added parts to the car. Workers no longer lost time moving from one work station to another.

In 1913, a Ford factory worker earned $2.38 for nine hours' work. The work was tiring, and there was a high turn-over rate. In 1914, Ford announced that he was more than doubling his workers' wages to $5 a day and would reduce their workday to 8 hours. Ford called his plan "one of the finest cost-cutting moves we ever made." Workers were happier, and fewer of them quit their jobs. It also meant workers could afford to buy cars, increasing Ford's own sales.

Ford's business continued to grow. In the 1920s, Americans were enjoying good times and many of them bought Model Ts. Ford began building the largest automobile plant in the world at River Rouge, outside of Detroit. Ford had complete control over every part of his operation. The new factory produced cars out of raw materials from Ford iron and coal mines. The iron ore and coal were shipped through the Great Lakes on Ford ships.

By the late 1920s, Ford faced new competition from General Motors. Their Chevrolet cars were also affordable and had features that the Model T lacked— like an electric starter, new styles and several colors. Ford's son, Edsel, tried to persuade his father to start new models, but Henry Ford refused to listen. In 1926, Ford finally agreed to follow his son's advice. The Ford factory was closed for six months in 1927 while Ford re-tooled for the new Model A.

When Henry Ford died in 1947, he left a fortune valued at one billion dollars. Much of his fortune went to the Ford Foundation. It became the largest private foundation in the world devoted to charitable, artistic and educational purposes. But Ford's greatest contribution can be found in the automobiles, trucks and tractors that make our lives what they are today.

COMPLETING A
CAUSE-AND-EFFECT DIAGRAM

If we put the information on page 133 to 135 into a graphic organizer, it might look something like this:

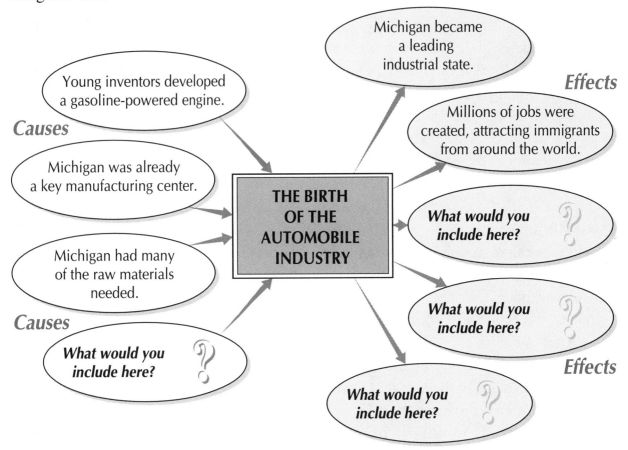

Now that you have had some practice with a cause-and-effect reading, let's try converting the following reading about World War I into a graphic organizer.

WORLD WAR I

World War I began in Europe in 1914. The assassination (*killing*) of a member of Austria-Hungary's ruling family was the spark that started the war. Within a few weeks, almost all of Europe was drawn into the conflict. World War I quickly turned into a new kind of war, with machine guns, airplanes, submarines, poison gas and tanks.

At first, the United States kept out of the fighting. However, Americans kept shipping goods to Britain and France. This angered Germany. When German submarines began to attack and sink American ships, the United States entered the war in 1917.

❖ CONTINUED

World War I brought many changes to Michigan. The war stirred patriotic spirits. Flags were displayed in factories and homes. Thousands of men volunteered for the army. One in four Michiganders bought "liberty bonds" to help pay for the war.

Michigan soldiers in World War I.

Michigan played an important role in helping to win the war. The state's factories were soon producing more war goods than any other state. The Ford Motor Company built 60 ships. Many American military planes were also built in Michigan. Women worked in factories in place of men who went off to fight in the war. Michigan's farmers grew more food so that they could feed American, French and British soldiers. Other Michiganders ate less meat and other foods to save more for the military. A large military base, Camp Custer, was built near Battle Creek, where thousands of soldiers were trained. Before the war was over, 175,000 Michiganders had served in the military. About 5,000 of them were killed and more than 15,000 were wounded in the war.

The end of the war had further effects on Michigan. The state emerged from the war as a leading industrial giant. Michiganders paid more in taxes than ever before. The **Nineteenth Amendment** to the U.S. Constitution gave women the right to vote. Michiganders and other Americans turned against future involvement with foreign nations. They did not want to risk being drawn into a war again.

Your Task

COMPLETING ANOTHER
CAUSE-AND-EFFECT DIAGRAM

Now let's try converting this reading passage into a cause-and-effect graphic organizer.

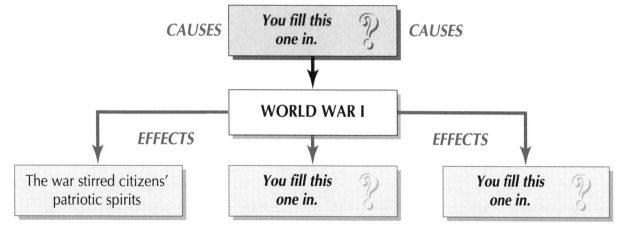

Let's turn one more cause-and-effect reading into a graphic organizer. First read the introduction that follows. Then read about the Great Depression and create a graphic organizer of your own.

In the 1920s, most Michiganders enjoyed a period of good times known as the "Roaring Twenties." During this period, many people began buying automobiles. The state prospered as the major supplier of the nation's automobiles. The number and size of towns and industries continued to grow. This growth produced new wealth for Michigan. However, this period of prosperity was cut short in 1929.

THE GREAT DEPRESSION

In the New York Stock Exchange, people buy and sell shares (or *stocks*) in most of the nation's large corporations. On **October 29, 1929**, the price of stocks began to fall when many people started to sell their stocks. Soon people began to panic, afraid that their stocks would lose all their value. By the end of the day, stock prices had dropped greatly. Hundreds of thousands of Americans lost all of their savings.

The **Stock Market Crash** had many effects in Michigan and the nation. Companies could no longer sell stocks easily to raise money. Banks that had invested in stocks faced hard times. Many people tried to take their savings out of the bank at the same time. This caused many banks to fail. People stopped spending money except for necessities. Many businesses shut down. As businesses closed, people were thrown out of work. Soon the nation was in a deep economic **depression**. In a depression, many businesses close and millions of people are unemployed.

One immediate effect of the **Great Depression** was on banks. In Michigan, many banks went out of business between 1930 and 1933. People who had money in these banks lost their life savings.

A mother holds her child in front of their "home" during the Great Depression.

❖ CONTINUED

The automobile industry was also greatly affected. In 1929, more than four million cars were sold in the United States. In 1931, less than half as many cars were sold. Tens of thousands of workers in automobile factories in Michigan lost their jobs. Soon, other industrialists also had to lay off workers when the demand for auto parts, tires and raw materials decreased. Local governments had no money to pay teachers and other employees. By 1933, more than half of Michigan's industrial workers had lost their jobs. Even those who kept their jobs were paid lower wages.

As the Depression worsened, people ran out of money to pay back loans on their houses and farms. Others could not pay taxes to the government on their property. Thousands of people lost their homes and farms.

During these years, many people had nowhere to live and little to eat. Some went to live with relatives, but often they had no money either. Many city and county governments across Michigan provided needy citizens with hot meals and places to sleep. Volunteer agencies also provided some relief. **Mayor Frank Murphy** of Detroit turned an abandoned warehouse into a shelter for the homeless.

Mayor Frank Murphy (*seated*) went on to become Governor of Michigan.

One of the most important effects of the Great Depression was the New Deal. In 1933, **Franklin D. Roosevelt** (roo' ze velt) became President of the United States. Roosevelt promised Americans a **New Deal** . Under this program, many new government agencies were created to help deal with the Depression.

President Franklin Roosevelt (*seated*) signs a New Deal program into law.

❖ CONTINUED

New Deal agencies provided work to needy Michiganders. The **Civilian Conservation Corps** gave work to over 100,000 single men between the ages of 17 and 25. They lived in camps and wore uniforms. Members planted trees, made trails in forests, reclaimed eroded land and performed many other outdoor tasks

These Michigan workers were glad to find employment during the Depression.

Other New Deal programs built schools, post offices, parks and roads. The **Works Progress Administration** put people back to work constructing buildings, digging sewers and completing other large projects. The program also employed artists and writers. Many murals in post offices, for example, were painted by these artists. More than 200,000 Michiganders worked at one time under this program.

The New Deal also encouraged workers to join together in unions. One of the most important unions was in the auto industry. Automobile manufacturers had opposed labor unions and strikes. The

Members of the United Auto Workers demonstrate against Ford Motors and Governor Frank Murphy for refusing their demands.

New Deal supported workers who wanted to organize into labor unions. After a bitter strike, General Motors recognized the **United Auto Workers** in 1937. This union helped win better conditions for its workers.

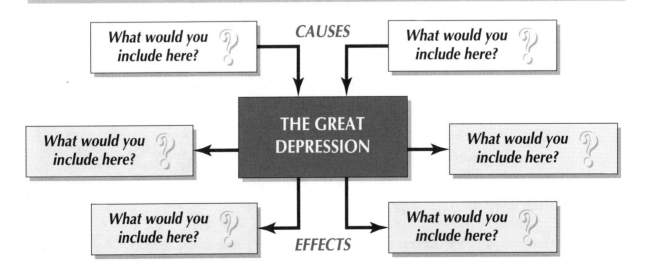

EXPANDING YOUR UNDERSTANDING

Creating Vocabulary Cards

Cause
What is a "cause"?
Name an event and identify one of its causes.

Effect
What is an "effect"?
Name an event and identify one of its effects.

Identifying a Community Statue or Monument

Key events in a state's history, such as the production of the Model T or the outbreak of World War I, usually have significance for many citizens. Communities often honor such events and the people involved in them.

Sometimes communities build a **statue** honoring a person involved in these events. Other communities mark events or personal achievements with some other type of **monument**.

How familiar are you with the important events or people honored by a statue or monument in your community? Locate **one** such statue or monument. Then complete the following:

❖ **Where.** Identify where the statue or monument is located.

❖ **Who/What.** Identify the person or event honored by the statue or monument.

❖ **Why.** Explain what the person accomplished or why the community built the statue or monument.

❖ **Photo.** Provide a picture or photograph showing the statue or monument.

Statue of Joe Louis, the boxer, in Cobo Hall, Detroit.

WHAT WAS IT LIKE
TO LIVE THROUGH WORLD WAR II?

3G   In this activity, you will learn about Michigan's role in World War II. Look for the following important words and phrases:

▶ Primary Source   ▶ Oral History

▶ Secondary Source   ▶ Narrative Writing

A good historian is like a detective. A detective arrives after a crime has taken place. The detective then tries to figure out who committed the crime by looking for clues. He or she may interview witnesses, examine evidence and check facts. From these clues, the detective tries to put together the story of what really happened.

Skill Builder

DISTINGUISHING BETWEEN
PRIMARY AND SECONDARY SOURCES

Historians are not involved in solving crimes, but they do try to figure out what took place in the past. Both detectives and historians look through many sources for clues to tell them what really happened. In this section, you will be asked to act as a historian by looking at several sources. Historians rely on two types of sources.

PRIMARY SOURCES

▶ | Primary sources | are the original records of an event. They include eyewitness reports, records written at the time of the event, letters sent by people involved in the event, speeches, diaries, photographs and audio and video tapes. Most of the facts we know about past events come from primary sources.

SECONDARY SOURCES

▶ | Secondary sources | are writings and viewpoints about an event by historians and other authors who did not directly experience the event. The author of a secondary source does not have firsthand experience of the event. Secondary sources, such as textbooks and magazine articles, provide summaries of the information found in primary sources. Historians often read these writings to learn about other historians' ideas.

✔ CHECKING YOUR UNDERSTANDING ✔

Can you think of some other examples of primary and secondary sources?

A **diary** is a daily record of a person's experiences and feelings. This diary contains many interesting entries from the World War II period. Read each of the entries in this diary.

September 12, 1941. Two days ago a German submarine attacked a U.S. destroyer off the coast of Ireland. In a speech to Americans, President Franklin D. Roosevelt compared Hitler to a rattlesnake. The President has ordered U.S. naval ships to escort all trading ships across the Atlantic Ocean, and ordered U.S. ships to "shoot on sight" any German submarines they find. I fear our nation is moving closer to war with Germany.

December 8, 1941. Japan attacked Pearl Harbor yesterday. In less than two hours, 10 warships were sunk or damaged and thousands of U.S. servicemen were killed. President Roosevelt has called a special meeting of the U.S. Congress to ask them to declare war on Japan. This will surely bring the United States into war with Germany, since they have promised to fight together with Japan.

May 9, 1942. President Roosevelt has ordered 112,000 Japanese Americans living on the West Coast to move to isolated "camps." The government fears they will try to help Japan win the war. However, there is no evidence to show they are disloyal. In fact, more than 71,000 of them were born in the United States. Dad has joined the navy and is somewhere in the Pacific. Mom is now working in a factory where they build aircraft engines.

January 13, 1944. Newspapers are reporting that Hitler is attempting to murder the entire Jewish population of Europe. There are stories about concentration camps in German-controlled Europe. It is said that in these camps innocent people are killed with poison gas and their bodies are burned. Witnesses report millions of Jews, Poles and others are being killed. Here at home, we have no gasoline, sugar, copper, rubber or many other goods. Times are hard, but everyone is doing their part to win the war.

June 6, 1944. We have received no letters from Dad for two months. Mom is very worried. General Dwight Eisenhower, who commands all American troops in Europe, has begun an invasion against Hitler. Today is being called **D-Day**. The radio has said that almost three million soldiers are invading France. I pray this attempt at freeing Europe will be successful and the war will be over.

November 4, 1944. President Roosevelt's bid for re-election has been successful. Roosevelt is the first President to be elected four times. We have received a letter from Dad that he is well.

✔ CHECKING YOUR UNDERSTANDING ✔

1. Is this diary a primary or secondary source? Explain.
2. What does the diary tell you about life during World War II?
3. What does the diary tell you about the writer's concerns and feelings?

The following page appeared in a history book about the United States during World War II.

MICHIGAN'S ROLE IN WORLD WAR II

Michigan played a vital role in helping the United States win the war. It led all other states in producing war materials. Michigan's factories made airplanes, tanks, ships, armor plate, gas masks, radios and other war goods. Detroit earned the title of the "Arsenal of Democracy" for its wartime production. The automobile industry played an especially key role in producing wartime goods.

By 1941, the production of automobiles had reached record levels. When the war began, civilian production of passenger cars stopped. Automobile manufacturers turned their industrial strength to winning the war. Chrysler opened a plant in Warren Township. During the war, this plant turned out more than 25,000 tanks. Another tank plant, operated by Fisher Body, produced Sherman tanks and tank destroyers. Oldsmobile began making shells for the army, while Chrysler produced anti-aircraft guns. Studebaker was involved in making aircraft engines.

One of the most spectacular operations of the war took place at Ford's Willow Run Plant. Ford applied its assembly line techniques used in auto production to build B-24 bombers. Workers from Detroit, Ann Arbor, Ypsilanti and other nearby towns flocked to Willow Run. By March 1944, Willow Run was making one bomber every hour.

The demand for workers brought thousands of men and women to Michigan. This put a

Women assemble the tail section of a bomber.

strain on available housing. Temporary buildings were constructed by the government to house workers at Detroit, Muskegon, Saginaw and Pontiac. During the war there was a shortage of men to work in the factories. Nearly a third of the workers were women. They worked as typists, riveters and welders.

Besides manufacturing, Michigan contributed to the war in other ways. More than 600,000 Michiganders served in the armed forces. Some of Michigan's university professors worked in laboratories on secret government projects, such as developing the atomic bomb.

✔ CHECKING YOUR UNDERSTANDING ✔

Is this textbook page a primary or a secondary source? How can you tell?

BECOMING AN ORAL HISTORIAN

One of the best ways to learn about an important event like World War II is to speak to people who actually lived at that time. You might interview a family member who lived through an important event in history such as World War II. If you were to record this family member's story, you would be participating in a special process. Historians call ▶ this **oral history** —collecting memories of the past through interviews of eyewitnesses.

THE IMPORTANCE OF ORAL HISTORY

People seem to have less time today than in the past for keeping diaries or writing journals. As a result, there is a growing need to preserve the personal side of history for future generations. Fortunately, people are living longer. Many provide a rich resource for historians because they actually experienced the past events that historians are now interested in.

In this section, you will have an opportunity to become an oral historian. Remember that your interview will only record a person's memories of the past. A person's memories are often not the whole story, and only give that person's point of view. An individual's memory of events sometimes changes over time and may not be accurate.

HOW TO BE AN ORAL HISTORIAN

Acting as an oral historian involves more than just turning on a tape recorder or video camera and letting someone talk. Careful planning and research are needed to conduct a successful interview.

SELECTING AN ORAL HISTORY PROJECT
The first step is to decide **whom** to interview and **why**. The most common type of oral history involves interviewing a family member or friend. You might interview a grandparent or senior citizen. Your interview should focus on learning about important events that person has experienced during his or her lifetime.

DEVELOPING A QUESTIONNAIRE
Start by creating a questionnaire. A **questionnaire** (kwes' che nahr) is an outline of topics you want to cover during your interview. You should use "leading" words—such as **describe**, **explain** and **discuss**. Remember, you want to "open up" the

❖ CONTINUED

memory of the person you are interviewing. To ask someone about a particular topic like World War II, you would first do some background research to help you think of good questions. Here is a sample questionnaire.

SAMPLE QUESTIONNAIRE

- **Describe** what it was like to be living in Michigan during World War II.
- **Discuss** what your relatives were doing during the war.
- What is your most vivid memory from that period?
  Explain your answer.

CONDUCTING THE INTERVIEW

A successful interview will depend in large part on how you behave during the interview itself. Here are some helpful hints to keep in mind:

❖ **Make an Appointment.** Make an appointment several days in advance. Allow at least 30 minutes for the interview. Bring along a good tape recorder. Be sure to practice using it before going to the interview.

❖ **The Start of the Interview.** It might be helpful to start by chatting informally with the person being interviewed, to put yourselves at ease. Start recording the interview with a short introduction, such as:

This interview is being conducted with Mrs. Celeste Smith at her home. It is Thursday, April 3, 1998. It is 4:30 in the afternoon.

Begin the interview with easy questions. Your questionnaire will help you to ask questions that call for descriptive answers.

❖ **Closing the Interview.** End the interview by thanking your interviewee. If you feel the interview has gone on too long, arrange another time for a follow-up interview. For example, you might say:

I would like to end the interview now. However, this was so interesting I would like to come back and talk more about other things you remember about growing up in Michigan. Would that be all right with you?

❖ CONTINUED

CREATING A COVER SHEET FOR THE TAPES

Use the guide below to create a cover sheet that explains what was discussed.

COVER SHEET FOR THE TAPED INTERVIEW

Interview Topic: _____

Person Interviewed: _____

Signature Granting Permission: _____

RUNNING TIME AND IDEAS COVERED

Minutes: 1–4 General background information

Minutes: 5–8 Memories of life in Michigan during World War II

Minutes: 9–15 How life has changed in Michigan since the war

Closing

WRITING ABOUT YOUR INTERVIEWEE'S EXPERIENCE

Now that you have concluded the interview, write a narrative essay describing what life was like during World War II. Before you begin writing your essay, read the following Skill Builder.

Skill Builder

HOW TO WRITE A NARRATIVE ESSAY

What Is a "Narrative"?

Narrative writing is used to *narrate,* or "tell about," an event or a series of related events. In a narrative, you describe each event or situation as it developed.

When Is Narrative Writing Used?

Narrative writing is used to tell a story as events unfold. You might use a narrative to tell about an event like World War II or even an interesting day at your school.

Helpful Hints

Start at the beginning and move step-by-step through the story. Stay on the point of the story and try to be specific. You don't need to write every single detail that happened. Instead, focus on things that contribute to your theme.

EXPANDING YOUR UNDERSTANDING

Creating Vocabulary Cards

Primary Source
What is a "primary" source?
Give an example of a primary
source.

Secondary Source
What is a "secondary" source?
Give an example of a secondary
source.

Presenting a "Show and Tell"

Family members often own objects that are memories or keepsakes of past experiences. For example, your parent, grandfather or uncle might have a medal, photograph, uniform or document from World War II. Select one object from your home to take to school. Discuss with your parent which objects you are allowed to take. Bring the object or a photograph of the object to class for a **show and tell**. A "show and tell" means that you:

❖ **show** the object to the other members of your class.

❖ **tell** the members of your class about the object. Discuss any interesting stories you know about it—for example, how it came into your family's possession, where it originally came from or who made it.

Skill Builder

PRESENTING ORAL INFORMATION

An oral report is one way to share information with others. Here are some tips for delivering the "tell" part of your presentation:

❖ **Prepare.** Prepare for what you are going to say. Make a list of your main points. Review the information you are going to present and be sure you understand it.

❖ **Practice.** Practice giving your report in front of a mirror or to a parent, neighbor or friend. The more you practice, the less nervous you will be.

❖ **Presentation.** Avoid reading directly from your note cards or paper. Highlight a few key words to use as reminders to trigger your memory about what you want to say. Stay within any time limit you are given. Stand up straight and speak loudly and clearly. Try to maintain eye contact with your audience.

HOW WOULD YOU OUTLINE THIS READING?

3H In this activity, you will learn about some important developments that have occurred in Michigan since World War II. You will also learn the skill of outlining. Look for the following important words and phrases:

▶ Outline
▶ Civil Rights Movement

▶ Segregation
▶ Discrimination

▶ An **outline** is a brief plan in which a topic is divided into different parts. The purpose of an outline is to show how a topic and its parts are related. An outline can also serve as a blueprint to help guide you through a reading.

HOW OUTLINES ARE ORGANIZED

Outlines begin with general topics and then provide details. The major topics are numbered with **Roman numerals** (I, II, III). If the topic listed by a Roman numeral needs to be further divided, its sub-topics are identified by **capital letters** (A, B, C). If these sub-topics need to be divided even further, each smaller topic is given an **Arabic numeral** (1, 2, 3).

Let's look at how this process of outlining works. Assume you want to create an outline about your own life. Here is how you start:

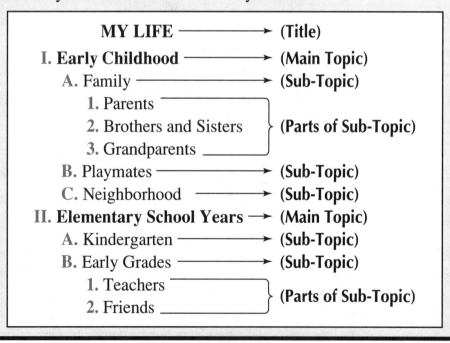

Notice how in this example each smaller part helps us to understand a larger idea. For example, the information you put under "Teachers" and "Friends" would help explain the sub-topic "Early Grades." Knowing what you fill in about "Kindergarten" and "Early Grades" would explain the larger topic "Elementary School Years." This larger topic is one of the two main parts that make up the general theme of "My Life."

Now read about the history of Michigan in the years following World War II. One of the biggest areas of change, Civil Rights, is dealt with in a separate reading. After reading the passage, complete the outline that follows.

MICHIGAN AFTER WORLD WAR II

The years following World War II brought many changes and opportunities to Michigan. The state experienced rapid economic growth. Many citizens became involved in world affairs and reformed their state government.

Just after World War II, veterans were given money by the federal government to go to college. Michigan's colleges and universities experienced large increases in enrollment. Michigan also began to increase the number of its community colleges.

In 1948, **G. Mennen Williams** was first elected Governor. He was elected Governor for a total of six two-year terms. This was more than any other person in state history. As Governor, Williams oversaw the building of the Mackinac Bridge. He also faced many problems. Michigan's state government often did not have enough money to pay its workers or to support many of its social programs. Williams wanted to pass a state income tax, but failed to gain enough support to do so. Michigan did not pass its first state income tax until 1967.

Dodge Motor Company, Hamtramck (1950).
After the war many Michiganders
returned to jobs in the
automobile industry.

In the late 1950s and 1960s, a new trend developed. Suburbs around Michigan's cities began to grow. A suburb is a community outside of a city where many people live who work in the city. A wave of suburban home building began just outside many of the state's large cities. Areas like Warren, Allen Park, Livonia, East Grand Rapids and East Lansing emerged as important new suburbs.

❖ CONTINUED

In 1954, the nation's first shopping mall, Northland, was built near the suburb of Southfield. A shopping mall is a group of stores under one roof. As many people moved to the suburbs, businesses followed. Auto manufacturers began building new plants in the suburbs, where their workers lived.

The growth of suburbs took businesses and people away from Michigan's largest cities. City income from taxes was reduced, causing problems in providing public services. Detroit's Renaissance Center was built to attract business back.

After the war, America's increased role in world affairs also affected Michiganders. Arthur Vandenberg, U.S. Senator for Michigan, helped win support for the United Nations. Detroit-born Ralph Bunche became U.S. Ambassador to the

The Renaissance Center stands as a symbol of Detroit's future.

United Nations. He helped settle differences between Arabs and Israelis, and was awarded the Nobel Peace Prize in 1950. In the early 1950s, the United States became involved in a war in Korea, a country in East Asia. Michiganders were again called on to fight for their country. The Korean War lasted for three years.

Twenty years later, the United States became involved in another war in Asia, this time in Vietnam. More than 360,000 Michiganders served in this war. At home, the war was unpopular. Many college students participated in anti-war demonstrations. Some universities in Michigan closed for a time because of student protests. The war finally ended when American troops left Vietnam in 1975.

In the 1970s, the auto industry faced new competition from foreign-made cars. The price of gasoline increased when world oil prices went up. Buyers wanted smaller foreign cars, instead of larger "gas guzzlers" made in Detroit. Some buyers began to feel that foreign-made cars were of better quality. As auto sales declined, factories laid off workers and unemployment increased. For a time, Michigan had the nation's highest unemployment rate. Chrysler Corporation was saved from going out of business when the federal government agreed to guarantee payment of its loans.

In the 1980s, many Michiganders still faced hard times. But business, union and government leaders began working together to improve conditions. In the late 1980s and 1990s, auto manufacturers began making better cars. Improvements in technology led to increased production. Auto sales began to improve, and unemployment declined. New industries made Michigan less dependent on auto sales.

1. How did the growth of suburbs affect Michigan's cities?
2. Why did American car-makers face problems in the 1970s?
3. How did the conditions in Michigan change in the 1980s and 1990s?
4. Would you have liked to have lived during any part of this period? Explain.

Your Task

COMPLETING AN OUTLINE

Below is an example of an outline of this reading. Some items have been left out. Make a copy of the outline. Then complete the items that have been omitted.

MICHIGAN AFTER WORLD WAR II

I. Michigan Just After the War:

    A. Veterans were given money to go to college.
    B. Michigan increased the number of its community colleges.
    C. G. Mennen Williams was elected Governor for six terms.
    D. *What do you think goes here?*

II. The Growth of Suburbs in the 1950s and 1960s

    A. Suburbs began to develop in Michigan.
    B. _____?_____

III. Michigan's Cities Face New Problems in the 1950s and 1960s

    A. People and businesses began to move away from the cities.
    B. _____?_____
    C. _____?_____

IV. *What do you think goes here?*

    A. _____?_____
    B. _____?_____
    C. _____?_____

V. Michigan in the 1970s

    A. _____?_____
    B. _____?_____
    C. _____?_____

VI. *What do you think goes here?*

    A. _____?_____
    B. _____?_____
    C. _____?_____

Closing

CREATING YOUR OWN OUTLINE

Let's practice your newly-learned skill of outlining. Read the following passage. Then put the information it contains into outline form.

THE CIVIL RIGHTS MOVEMENT IN MICHIGAN

A segregated movie theatre.
How can you tell this movie theatre is segregated?

► The Civil Rights Movement of the 1950s and 1960s aimed at providing equal rights to citizens of all races.

After Reconstruction (1865–1877), many Southern states established separate schools, beaches and restrooms for white and black citizens. This separation of citizens was known as ► segregation (seg' rə gā shən). African Americans were also kept from voting, serving on juries or participating in public life.

In Northern states like Michigan, African Americans also faced many problems. They faced **prejudice** (prej' ə dis), a negative view formed beforehand without ► knowing the facts. In addition, they also faced discrimination (di skrim ə nā' shun), treating someone differently on the basis of race. Some employers refused to hire African Americans. In some communities, homeowners refused to sell their homes to them. African Americans were also prevented from joining many sports clubs and other activities.

On a hot night in June 1943, an argument broke out in Belle Isle Park in Detroit. African Americans and whites started fighting. Soon the fighting spread beyond the park. For two nights, people fought and rioted. Thirty-four people were killed and hundreds were injured. State and federal troops finally had to be called in to restore order.

Soldiers attempting to restore order in Detroit.

❖ CONTINUED

In 1954, the U.S. Supreme Court ruled that segregated public schools were unlawful. The court ordered schools to **integrate** (*bring people of different races together*) as soon as possible. African Americans and others now organized a Civil Rights Movement. They fought against segregation not only in schools but in all areas of public life. In the South, African Americans and their supporters took **freedom rides** on public trains and buses. They sat where African Americans were banned from sitting by local laws. They held **sit-ins** at public lunch counters, where only whites were supposed to sit. Some of these brave demonstrators were volunteers from Northern states, like Michigan.

Thurgood Marshall was the chief lawyer who argued the case against public school segregation. Marshall later became the first African American to be appointed to the U.S. Supreme Court.

In 1963, African Americans and other Americans from across the nation gathered in Washington, D.C. for a **March on Washington**. The march was organized by **Dr. Martin Luther King, Jr.** and other Civil Rights leaders.

Soon after, the Civil Rights Act of 1964 was passed. The act made it a crime for restaurants, hotels, stores, bus companies and other public services to discriminate against someone because of their race. It also prohibited discrimination in employment on the basis of sex, and threatened to cut off Federal money to school districts with segregated schools.

Many African Americans were still unhappy with the slow pace of change. In Michigan and other Northern states, African Americans often felt trapped in their own sections of the city, known as **ghettos.** Frequently, they could not get jobs that paid well.

Many African American workers were barred from well-paid jobs.

Many African Americans in Michigan were demanding change. Some of their leaders, like **Malcolm X**, who grew up in Lansing, felt that African Americans should use force to protect themselves.

❖ CONTINUED

In 1967, a small group of Detroit residents began rioting. The rioters caused damage and death. Peace was finally restored after a week of violence.

Since 1967, many strides have been made in Civil Rights. Civil Rights laws and special programs like **Affirmative Action** have helped African Americans to help themselves. These programs have increased the number of minority

Forty-three people died in the riots of 1967.

students in colleges and minority members in professions like the law and medicine. Progress in ending the racial discrimination of the past has been achieved in large part because of the Civil Rights Movement. Today, we live in a **multicultural society**. Racial discrimination is illegal. Americans of all races are found in all walks of life.

The outline below has already been started for you. Copy it into your notebook and complete any items that have been omitted.

THE CIVIL RIGHTS MOVEMENT IN MICHIGAN

I. The Old System of Racial Segregation
>   A. Segregation was practiced in many Southern States.
>   B. *What do you think goes here?*
>   C. *What do you think goes here?*

II. The U.S. Supreme Court Orders Schools to Integrate
>   A. African Americans and others organize a Civil Rights Movement.
>   B. _____?_____
>   C. _____?_____
>   D. _____?_____

III. The Struggle for Equality in Michigan's Civil Rights Movement
>   A. _____?_____
>   B. _____?_____
>   C. _____?_____
>   D. _____?_____

◆ THE MUSEUM OF AFRICAN-AMERICAN HISTORY ◆

The idea of a Museum of African-American History was born in 1965. Dr. Charles Wright, a Detroit doctor, visited a memorial celebrating Danish heroes in World War II. Inspired by his visit, Dr. Wright decided to create a similar memorial to the achievements of African Americans. The first museum opened in a private home. In 1987, the museum moved to a larger building.

In April 1997, the city of Detroit opened the largest and most costly African-American history museum in the world. The building's design is unique. The museum is designed to look like an African hut. It has a 100-foot-diameter dome, representing the shapes of African huts. The dome is a typical African structure.

Visitors to the museum take a journey through four centuries of black history. At the museum's center is a model slave ship. Life-sized figures of African slaves are shown chained in the ship's hold. Teenagers from the Detroit area were used as models for these statues. Surrounding the slave ship model are exhibits about the Civil Rights Movement. For example, one exhibit deals with the first sit-in at a lunch counter in Greensboro, North Carolina.

Many exhibits focus on the contributions to society made by African Americans. There is an exhibit of well-known inventions by African Africans. Items such as the stoplight and the gas mask are displayed there. The museum also has Dr. Mae Jemison's flight suit. She is the nation's first African-American female astronaut.

The museum is very student-friendly. For example, you can turn large plastic panels to find a question on top and the answer on the bottom. To illustrate African-American language contributions, one panel shows a stack of $100 bills. The question asks: "How did we get moolah?" The answer is: "It came from the Bantu word *mulambo*, meaning 'a lot of money.'"

EXPANDING YOUR UNDERSTANDING

Creating Vocabulary Cards

Outline
What is an "outline"?
What is it used for?

Civil Rights Movement
What was the "Civil Rights Movement"?
Why was it important?

Creating a Collage about the Motown Sound

During the 1950s, **Berry Gordy** worked on an assembly line at the Ford Motor Company. Gordy loved music. A friend suggested he start a record company. In 1959, Gordy borrowed $800 to start **Motown Records**. He named his company after shortening two words often associated with Detroit—motor town.

Motown's first hit record was "Shop Around," by his friend "Smokey" Robinson. Under Gordy's leadership, Motown Records grew quickly. Gordy hired others to make records. Michael Jackson, Stevie Wonder, the Temptations, the Four Tops, and Gladys Knight and the Pips were all soon releasing top songs. Among Motown's most successful singers were **Diana Ross and the Supremes**.

Soon records made at Gordy's small studio were dominating the record charts as the #1 songs in America. Before long Gordy's business became the nation's biggest African-American-owned business. In the 1970s and 1980s, things changed at Motown. Diana Ross left the Supremes and Stevie Wonder left Motown. In 1972, Berry Gordy himself moved to Los Angeles to begin making movies. In 1988, MCA records bought Motown for $61 million.

Esther Edwards, Gordy's sister, continued to hold on to Motown's office. When fans still showed up on their doorstep, she got the idea of developing a museum. Presently, the Motown Museum has been restored and enlarged. It draws visitors from around the world.

> Motown has had a great impact on American music. Using pictures of artists or Motown-associated events, create a collage about the Motown sound. Search old newspapers and magazines or write to the Motown Museum for photographs and brochures.

WHICH EVENTS WOULD YOU PLACE ON THE TIMELINE?

31 In this activity, you will learn how to make a timeline, using key events in history. Look for the following important words and phrases:

▶ Timeline   ▶ Decade   ▶ B.C.
▶ Chronological Order   ▶ Century   ▶ A.D.

Reading about history allows your imagination to wander back in time. It is exciting to read about the people and events of the past. Often, while important events were taking place in one part of the world, equally important events were happening somewhere else. In order to see these connections, historians often use a timeline.

Skill Builder

TIMELINES AND THEIR MAIN PARTS

A timeline is a type of graph. It shows a group of events arranged along a line in ◀
chronological order . "Chronological order" means the order in which the events ◀
actually happened. A timeline can cover anything from a very short period to several thousand years. Its main purpose is to show a sequence of events. To understand a timeline, look at its main parts—its title, the events and the dates.

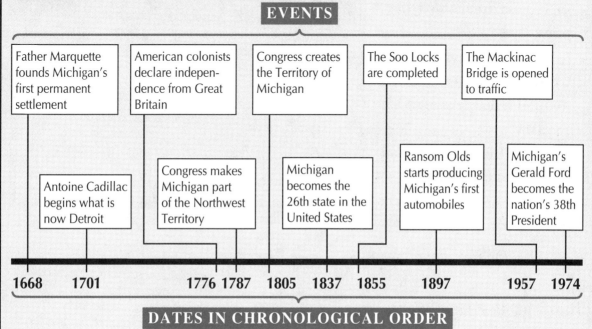

TITLE ▶ **MAJOR EVENTS IN THE HISTORY OF MICHIGAN**

EVENTS

Father Marquette founds Michigan's first permanent settlement

American colonists declare independence from Great Britain

Congress creates the Territory of Michigan

The Soo Locks are completed

The Mackinac Bridge is opened to traffic

Antoine Cadillac begins what is now Detroit

Congress makes Michigan part of the Northwest Territory

Michigan becomes the 26th state in the United States

Ransom Olds starts producing Michigan's first automobiles

Michigan's Gerald Ford becomes the nation's 38th President

1668   1701   1776 1787   1805   1837 1855   1897   1957   1974

DATES IN CHRONOLOGICAL ORDER

✔ CHECKING YOUR UNDERSTANDING ✔

This timeline has 10 important events in the history of Michigan.

- Select **two** events on the timeline and explain why you think they are important enough to appear on a timeline of key events in the history of Michigan.
- Select **two** events from the history of Michigan that are not found on this timeline. For each event selected, explain why you think the event is important to Michigan's history and should be added to the timeline.

TITLE

The title tells you the overall topic of the timeline. In the timeline on the previous page, the title means that the items listed are major events in the history of Michigan.

✔ CHECKING YOUR UNDERSTANDING ✔

Selecting a title. A series of events is listed below. What title would you give a timeline that had these events?

- In 1908, Will Durant forms **General Motors Company**.
- In 1909, **Ford Motor Company** produces its first Model T car.
- In 1911, **Chevrolet Company** is begun.
- In 1914, **Ford Motor Company** establishes a minimum daily wage of $5.
- In 1935, Michigan auto workers form the **United Automobile Workers**.
- In 1942, car factories turn to making war materials.

Henry Ford about to ride in his first "horseless carriage."

- In 1980, the U.S. government helps save **Chrysler** with a loan.

Your Timeline Title: _____?_____

TIMELINE DESIGN

On a timeline, the earliest event appears on the far left. The rest of the events are placed to the right of it in the order in which they occurred.

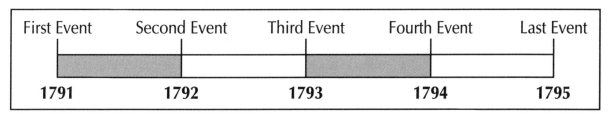

Sometimes timelines are drawn up and down (*vertically*) instead of left to right (*horizontally*). In that case, the earliest event is usually placed at the bottom of the timeline. The rest of the events are placed above the first event in the order in which they occurred.

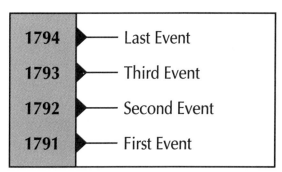

PERIODS OF TIME

To fully understand timelines, you must also know about time periods. For short periods of time, you can divide a timeline into one-year intervals. For example:

For longer periods of time, you can divide a timeline into decades. A **decade** is a period ◄ of ten years. For example, the following timeline shows six decades of time:

An even longer period of time is a century. A **century** is a period of 100 years. For ◄ example, the following timeline shows six centuries of time.

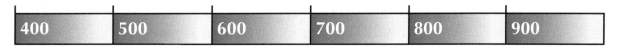

Now you try it. Make a copy of the timeline below and put in the years from 1300 to 1800, by centuries:

How we identify centuries may seem confusing at first. The "20th century" means the 100 years from 1901 to 2000. The 1990s, therefore, belong to the 20th century. Let's see why.

1–100	First Century	201–300	Third Century
101–200	Second Century	301–400	Fourth Century

✔ CHECKING YOUR UNDERSTANDING ✔

1. Which century was 701–800?

2. Which century was 1501–1600?

3. What is the present century, 1901–2000?

4. What will the next century be called?

THE DIVISION OF TIME

In most of the world today, dates are based on when it is believed Jesus Christ was born. These dates are divided into two groups: B.C. and A.D. The dividing point is the birth of Christ.

▶ **B.C.** (Before Christ) refers to any time before his birth. Sometimes B.C. is referred to as B.C.E.—Before the Common Era.

▶ **A.D.** refers to the time after the birth of Christ. A.D. stands for the Latin phrase *Anno Domini*—"in the year of our Lord." Sometimes A.D. appears as C.E.—meaning in the Common Era.

Writers always add B.C. or B.C.E. to a date before the birth of Christ. However, we usually do not bother to write A.D. or C.E. if the date is *after* the birth of Christ. For example, if the year is 1998, we generally write 1998—not 1998 A.D.

MEASURING THE PASSAGE OF TIME

To measure the number of years from one date to another, just subtract the smaller date from the larger date. Assume the year is 1997. How long ago was 1500? By subtracting 1500 from 1997, we arrive at 497 years ago.

1997	(1997 years since the birth of Jesus)
− 1500	(1500 years since the birth of Jesus)
497	years ago

· ✔ CHECKING YOUR UNDERSTANDING ✔

In 1622, Étienne Brûlé became the first European to enter Lake Huron and visit the Upper Peninsula. How many years ago was that?

EVENTS

Each event on a timeline should be related to the timeline's title. For instance, if a timeline has the title "The European Exploration of the Great Lakes," Étiénne Brûlé's travels might appear as an event. Christopher Columbus' voyages should not appear, since Columbus never explored the Great Lakes.

SELECTING EVENTS FOR A TIMELINE

Let's practice the skill of selecting appropriate events by choosing events for a timeline titled: "Key Events in the History of Michigan." **Hint:** Look for events that are related to the title. In the following list of events, you will notice that **not every event** is related to the history of Michigan. Decide **which** events you think are related to the title of the timeline. Then, on a separate sheet of paper, make a timeline of these events in chronological order.

EVENTS IN THE HISTORY OF MICHIGAN

- ❖ 1973   The Detroit Renaissance Center opens.
- ❖ 1996   The Summer Olympics are held in Atlanta, Georgia.
- ❖ 1865   President Abraham Lincoln is killed by an assassin in Washington, D.C.
- ❖ 1791   The Bill of Rights is added to the U.S. Constitution.
- ❖ 1967   Michigan's state legislature approves a state lottery.
- ❖ 1991   John Engler is elected Michigan's 46th governor.
- ❖ 1964   A new state constitution is adopted for Michigan.
- ❖ 1992   Bill Clinton is elected President of the United States
- ❖ 1776   The Declaration of Independence is issued.
- ❖ 1974   President Nixon resigns as President.
- ❖ 1911   A fire at New York's Triangle Shirtwaist Factory kills many workers.
- ❖ 1980   For the first time, more cars are made in Japan than in the United States.

Note: Often you will have to list a date that falls *between* two dates on a timeline. For example, 1903 is between 1900 and 1910. Since 1903 is closer to 1900 (3 years) than it is to 1910 (7 years), put it closer to 1900 than to 1910 on the timeline.

EXPANDING YOUR UNDERSTANDING

Creating Vocabulary Cards

Timeline
What is a "timeline"?
How are timelines used?

Chronological Order
What is "chronological order"?
Arrange the following dates in
chronological order: 1903, 1864,
1987, 1542 and 1745.

Making a Timeline About Your Life

Often, a number of events happening during a person's lifetime stand out. For example, your parents may remember what they were doing in July 1969 when Neil Armstrong and Buzz Aldrin first stepped onto the moon. In this section, you will look at several important events that happened in your lifetime. Choose the **five** most important events of your life and put them on the timeline. Make the first year the one in which you were born.

IMPORTANT EVENTS IN MY LIFE

Birth Year

Ask your parent or guardian for **three** important events that happened to them in the last ten years. Add those events to your timeline.

WHAT DOES THE FUTURE HOLD FOR MICHIGAN?

3J In this activity, you will look at the future direction that Michigan is taking. Look for the following important words and phrases.

▶ Futurologist ▶ Prediction Chain ▶ Internet

Introduction

THE ROLE OF A FUTUROLOGIST

Now that you have studied Michigan's past, you might be tempted to wonder about its future. What will Michigan be like ten or twenty years from now? How is the state likely to change by the time you are grown up?

THINK ABOUT IT

1. What do you think are some of the biggest changes your parents and grandparents have seen during their lifetimes?
2. What are some of the changes that you expect to see in Michigan while you are growing up?

There is no way to know for sure what the future will be like. It is, however, fun to guess. People who predict the future are called **futurologists**. In this activity, you will ◀ have an opportunity to play the role of an amateur futurologist. A futurologist makes predictions about the future by looking at the present and thinking about changes that will probably occur. Then the futurologist considers the effects that these changes may have.

Skill Builder

MAKING A PREDICTION CHAIN

Futurologists often put their information into the form of a diagram called a prediction chain. A **prediction chain** is used to forecast events before they actually ◀ happen. In a prediction chain you take the following steps:

❖ Begin by writing down the effect you expect from an event or development. It sometimes helps to put the effect in the form of a "what if" question.

❖ Carefully examine each expected effect. Try to think about what further developments will take place if that effect comes about.

❖ **CONTINUED**

❖ Finally, think about what else might happen if these further developments take place. Put these additional effects in a separate box next to the first set of effects.

Here is an example of a prediction chain dealing with a possible event taking place tomorrow.

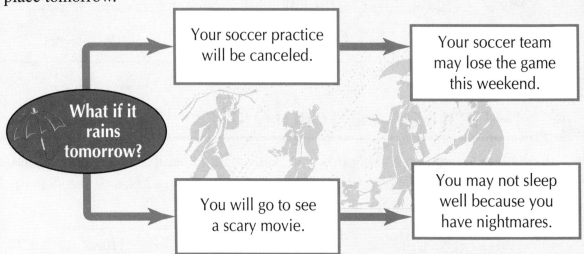

What if it rains tomorrow?

Your soccer practice will be canceled.

Your soccer team may lose the game this weekend.

You will go to see a scary movie.

You may not sleep well because you have nightmares.

When making a prediction chain, think carefully about the effects of each possible event. Then think about further developments that may result from these. By using this method, futurologists are able to slowly piece together what might happen in the future. Like any chain, a prediction chain is only as strong as its weakest link. Your final predictions are only as good as the earlier predictions they are based on.

Information

TRANSPORTATION AND COMMUNICATION

Now it's your turn to make some predictions about Michigan's future. Two of the most important areas in which recent changes have occurred are transportation and communication.

TRANSPORTATION

In transportation, Michigan has built many new highways criss-crossing the state. These highways now allow people to drive automobiles and trucks to almost any part of the state.

Michigan has many modern highways that criss-cross the state.

The completion of the St. Lawrence Seaway allows ports in Michigan to receive large ocean-going ships with containers. A **container** is a large metal box the size of a truck. Containers are loaded with goods and stacked on top of each other on ships. This method of packing goods makes them easier to handle and less expensive to transport. The use of trucks, ships and containers allows people to ship goods easily anywhere in the world.

Ships such as this one carry goods in containers. *How does using containers make loading and unloading a ship faster?*

What are some of the effects of these developments in transportation? What further changes do you expect to see in the future? To help decide, complete a copy of the following prediction chain:

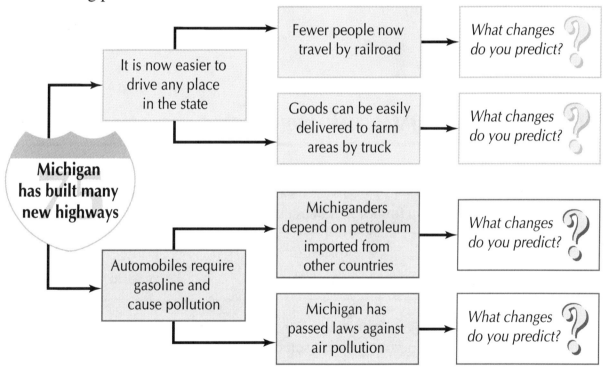

Michigan has built many new highways

It is now easier to drive any place in the state

- Fewer people now travel by railroad → *What changes do you predict?*
- Goods can be easily delivered to farm areas by truck → *What changes do you predict?*

Automobiles require gasoline and cause pollution

- Michiganders depend on petroleum imported from other countries → *What changes do you predict?*
- Michigan has passed laws against air pollution → *What changes do you predict?*

COMMUNICATIONS

In communications, people have come to rely on receiving information from books, magazines, newspapers, telephones, radio and television. One important new development in communications is the **Internet** —a system that links computers around the ◄ world. People use telephone lines to connect their computer with the Internet. Through the Internet, they can send electronic messages (e-mail) to other computer users.

What effects do you think these developments will have on Michigan? For example, how might the Internet change the shopping habits of Michiganders?

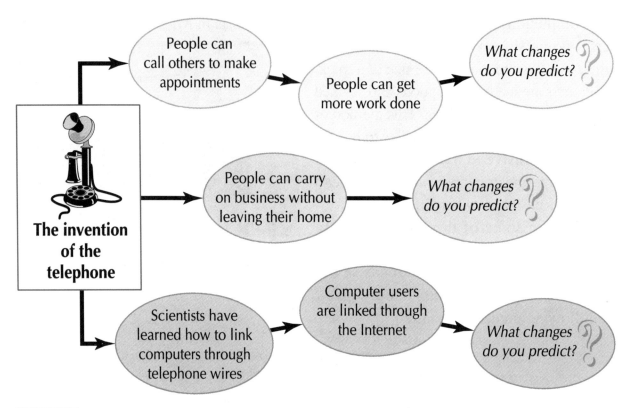

CREATING YOUR OWN PREDICTION CHAIN

Now you are ready make your own set of predictions. Your teacher should divide your class into groups. Choose one of the following fields. Make a prediction chain based on what changes your group thinks will happen in that area.

❖ health care	❖ pollution	❖ population growth
❖ education	❖ auto industry	❖ types of jobs

To help prepare your prediction chain, talk to your parents and grandparents about what changes they expect in your group's selected area. Look at newspaper and magazine stories to see what changes are expected. Then discuss what effects the group should put into its prediction chain. When the groups have completed their predictions, they should discuss and compare their results with each other.

THINK ABOUT IT

1. What are some of the changes you now expect to occur in your state?
2. How do you think these changes might affect you?

EXPANDING YOUR UNDERSTANDING

Creating Vocabulary Cards

Futurologist
What is a "futurologist"?
Why is it helpful to know what
might develop in the future?

Prediction Chain
What is a "prediction chain"?
Why is it helpful to use a
prediction chain?

Using the Internet for Research

As you read in this activity, one of the most important developments that will affect the future of communications is the Internet. The Internet began in the 1960s. Today, the Internet uses a common language allowing all types of computers to communicate. Anyone with a computer and modem can use the Internet. A **modem** converts data to information that can be sent over a telephone line. With an e-mail address on the Internet, a computer can send and receive messages.

Some agencies and companies make information available on the Internet. The following Internet-sites are about Michigan. Locate **one** site and write a summary of the information that can be found there.

- ❖ httl://kalamazoo.inetmi.com/mihmpg.htm
- ❖ http://www.travel-michigan.state.mi.us/
- ❖ http://mic1.dmb.state.mi.us/michome/educ/sddb.htm

FAMOUS PLACES: MICHIGAN STATE UNIVERSITY

In the 1850s, the state government built an independent college of scientific agriculture. In 1855, the school opened as the first college of agriculture in the nation. The school is dedicated to its mission of teaching, research and public service. In 1955, the school changed its name from Michigan State College to Michigan State University. Today, M.S.U. is one of the nation's leading academic institutions. It is also one of the largest single-campus universities in the United States.

Monument at the entrance to Michigan State University

AN INTRODUCTION TO THE CORE DEMOCRATIC VALUES

In this unit, you learned about what Michiganders did in the past. History is especially concerned with the issues people faced and the choices they made. For example

❖ Should the colonies have become an independent nation?

❖ Should Americans have abolished slavery?

❖ Should Americans have entered wars overseas?

In making a choice, an individual or a group of people usually begins by thinking about what things are possible. Then they decide which choice is "best."

In making decisions such as this, Americans apply a set of common values. A **value** is something we consider important and worthwhile. We refer to the basic values of our democratic society as the **core democratic values**. The idea that every person has worth and dignity is one of the most important of these. American society is based on the belief that the importance of every person should be recognized and respected by others.

Our core democratic values are found mainly in two key documents: the **Declaration of Independence** and the **U.S. Constitution.** These documents can be thought of as two mighty pillars supporting our society.

In the Declaration of Independence, Americans declared their freedom from Great Britain. The declaration also announced that there were certain basic truths that all governments should recognize. One of these truths was that the purpose of every government should be to protect the "life, liberty and ... happiness" of its citizens.

The U.S. Constitution established the basic system of American government. It also guaranteed Americans many individual rights.

Our core democratic values can be divided into two groups:

❖ the rights of individuals

❖ the principles or general rules of government

Let's take a closer look at the first of these—the rights of individuals. We will look at the second, the principles of government, in a later unit. In the United States, each of us has the following rights:

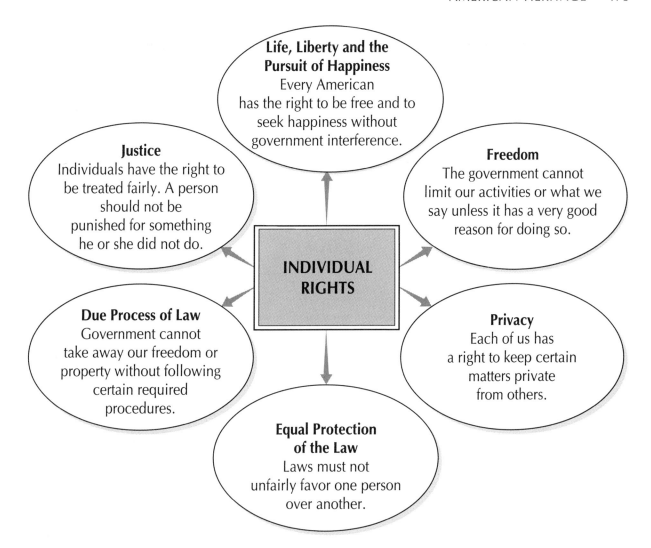

It's not always easy to protect individual rights. Often a balance is needed between protecting an individual's rights and meeting the demands of society. For example, a town government may want to build a new highway. Unfortunately, there is no way to avoid having the new roadway cut across farmer Tom's property. He does not want to sell his property to the town. In deciding what to do, it is important for the town to consider Tom's right to own private property. The town must also meet the needs of its other citizens for a highway. However, the town cannot simply take away Tom's land. In solving the problem the town must also obey certain rules. It must hold a hearing in which Tom can present his views. If the town still decides to take Tom's land, it must pay him a fair price. The town has based its actions, paying for Tom's land, on a core democratic value—people have a right to private property.

SUMMARIZING YOUR UNDERSTANDING

Directions: Fill in the blanks in the following graphic organizers.

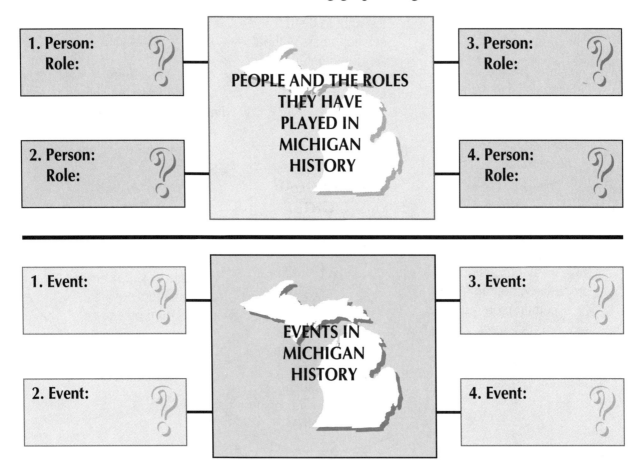

FINDING INFORMATION IN DIFFERENT REFERENCE SOURCES

A reference tool is helpful in finding different kinds of information. See if you know when to use an **almanac**, **atlas** or **encyclopedia**.

Where would you find information about…

1. _____ the results of the last election for the Governor of Michigan?
2. _____ the life of Henry Ford?
3. _____ the location of the Au Sable River in Michigan?
4. _____ the current population of Michigan?
5. _____ last year's win-loss record for the Detroit Lions, a football team?
6. _____ the names of Michigan's Representatives in the U.S. Congress?
7. _____ the lifestyles of the early settlers in Michigan?
8. _____ the towns of Michigan's Upper Peninsula?

PEOPLE IN SOCIETY

William McKinley School, Traverse City, in 1900.

Diana Ross and the Supremes.

School children visit Meridian Historical Village in Lansing.

D o you like pizza, tacos or egg rolls? Each of these foods was brought to Michigan by a different ethnic group. An **ethnic group** is a group of people who share traditions, customs, beliefs and ancestors. Michigan's many ethnic groups have created a mixture of cultures that make Michigan an exciting place to live. In this unit, you will learn about the different ethnic groups of your state. This unit will help you to appreciate how each group has contributed something special and unique to Michigan.

A VISIT TO EUROPE

ou are studying the word "hello" in many different languages for your big trip. You and your family are going on a vacation to Europe. You are excited about the start of your voyage. This will be your first time in a jet airplane. You can hardly wait to get started.

Before you know it, you and your family are at the airport, ready to board the plane. You check in at the departure gate and slowly make your way onto the plane. After you settle in, the flight attendant announces what to do in case of an emergency. Soon your plane is climbing high above the clouds. In only a few hours, you will be in a place thousands of miles from home where people speak different languages and follow different customs. You realize that the way you speak and dress may seem out of place.

A few hours into your flight the attendant serves dinner. You are too excited to think about eating. Soon you doze off, exhausted by the day's events. You are awakened by the flight attendant asking passengers to fasten their seat belts and prepare for landing. It is time for your first stop: Warsaw, Poland.

Warsaw is a large city in central Poland, built along the Vistula River. Although Warsaw is over seven hundred years old, most of the city was destroyed in World War II. You check into a modern hotel in the center of town. After resting from your flight, your parents take you to the *Stare Miasto* (Old Town) where the white and brown brick buildings have been rebuilt to look like they did hundreds of years ago.

You stop to eat at a restaurant overlooking the large town square. Your parents order some unusual dishes—including stuffed cabbage, kielbasa (*Polish sausages*) and a stew of pork, cabbage and sauerkraut called *bigos*. You are also served potatoes and Polish bread.

As night falls, you walk in the direction of the royal castle. Some people are strolling through the streets. Others are carrying their shopping. There are also many tourists. Almost everyone seems to be talking in strange languages you cannot understand. The cars that drive by look quite different. Most are smaller than American cars, although they race quickly through Warsaw's streets.

After several days of traveling through Poland, the Czech Republic and Austria, you fly to the city of Munich in Germany. Munich is located near forests and mountain areas. You travel through beautiful villages with churches that are more than five hundred years old. Some of these ancient towns seem to have a church on every corner.

Like the Poles, Germans speak a language you cannot understand at all. In the countryside you can sometimes see men wearing the traditional folk costume: *lederhosen* (*short leather pants*), a white shirt, suspenders and a green hat with a red feather. You and your family stop to eat at a large outdoor garden. Here you are served sausages. Instead of eating these sausages on soft hot dog rolls, you eat them on small, round rolls called "brotchen." After the meal you think how strange it is that these Germans are serving one of your favorite foods—sausages.

After a few weeks, it is time to fly home. On the return flight you think about all the wonderful countries you have visited. The world is indeed a very special place. There are so many different climates, land forms and customs. The people in each place seem to have developed their own way of life. Social scientists call these ways of life "culture." Culture includes the language, customs, dress, foods, attitudes and beliefs of a people.

You now realize that Michigan has been influenced by cultures from around the world. You wonder how these different cultures reached Michigan. What role did these cultures play in the state's development? The answers to these and other questions await you in this unit.

HOW WOULD YOU CATEGORIZE YOURSELF?

4A In this activity, you will learn how people often identify with groups based on their race, nationality, ethnicity and religion. Look for the following important words and phrases:

▶ Concept   ▶ Pie Chart   ▶ Ethnic Group

▶ Race   ▶ Nationality   ▶ Religion

A ▶ symbol appears in the margin where the **word** or **phrase** is first explained.

One of the things that makes the United States very special is its people. Each American is unique. Yet each one of us also has something in common with others. For example, many people wear similar clothes and eat similar foods. The characteristics that people share sometimes lead them to identify themselves as part of a special group.

HOW ARE PEOPLE OFTEN GROUPED?

In this activity, you will learn some of the ways Americans identify themselves. However, before you look at other groups, let's first see how you might "group" yourself:

❖ What is your race?   ❖ What is your ethnic group?

❖ What is your nationality?   ❖ What is your religion?

Did you group yourself correctly? The answer really depends on how you define these words. Each of these—race, nationality, ethnicity and religion—is a concept. A ▶ **concept** gives a name to things that, although different, have something in common. For example, the idea of a "bird" is a concept. It applies to many different creatures: eagles, blue jays, ducks and chickens. However, all these animals share a common characteristic—they have feathers.

duck

blue jay

eagle

chicken

You have probably heard people use the words *race, nationality, ethnic group* and *religion.* How well can you define these concepts? Let's take a look at each of them.

RACE

Over the course of time, human beings in different parts of the world developed slight physical differences. For example, some people have a light skin color; others have a darker skin color. Sometimes these differences are used to identify different groups of people.

A **race** is a group of people who are identified by the color of their skin and other ◀ physical characteristics. The U.S. Census Bureau currently lists six groups that classify Americans by race:

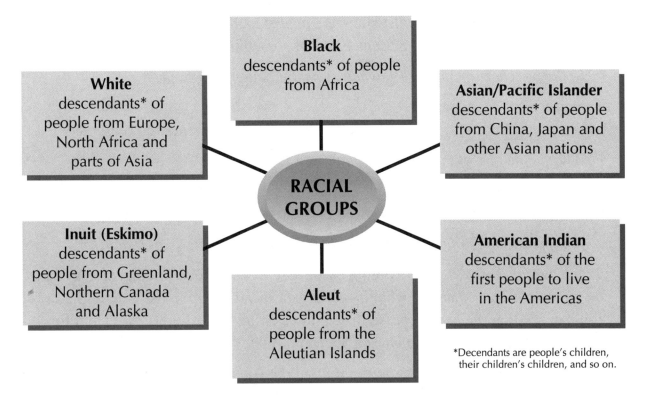

Black
descendants* of people from Africa

White
descendants* of people from Europe, North Africa and parts of Asia

Asian/Pacific Islander
descendants* of people from China, Japan and other Asian nations

RACIAL GROUPS

Inuit (Eskimo)
descendants* of people from Greenland, Northern Canada and Alaska

Aleut
descendants* of people from the Aleutian Islands

American Indian
descendants* of the first people to live in the Americas

*Decendants are people's children, their children's children, and so on.

People from each of these racial groups have ancestors who came from different places. Many people have mixed racial backgrounds.

—————————————— THINK ABOUT IT

Which racial group (or groups) do you now think you belong to?

The United States is a **multi-racial society**, made up of people of many different races. The pie chart to the right shows the racial makeup of the United States in 1990, when the last national census (*count*) was taken.

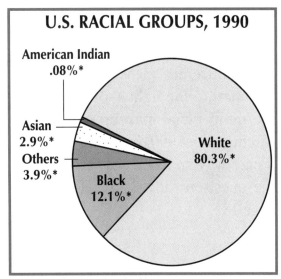

U.S. RACIAL GROUPS, 1990

American Indian .08%*

Asian 2.9%*

Others 3.9%*

Black 12.1%*

White 80.3%*

*percent (%) means hundredths

If you are having trouble interpreting the information in this pie chart, you should read the following Skill Builder.

INTERPRETING PIE CHARTS

What Is a Pie Chart?

A pie chart (or *circle graph*) is a circle, divided into different size slices. Its main function is to show how the slices are related to the whole "pie." If you add all of the slices together, they represent 100% of something.

❖ *In the pie chart on page 179, what items are being compared?*

Interpreting a Pie Chart

Look at the title. It will give you an overall idea of the information presented.

❖ *What is the title of the pie chart on page 179?*

Then look at the slices of the pie. Notice how each slice is related to the other slices and to the whole pie. Each slice gives the percentage of a racial group.

❖ *What percentage of people in the United States are "American Indian"?*

A pie chart also allows you to compare the size of each slice to other slices or to the whole pie. For example, what is the largest racial group in the United States? You can see that the slice representing whites is the largest—80.3%. Therefore, the largest racial group in the United States is white.

❖ *What is the second largest racial group in the United States?*

Like the rest of the United States, Michigan is also made up of people from many different races. The pie chart to the right shows the multi-racial makeup of Michigan in 1990. Examine it carefully and then answer the questions at the top of page 181.

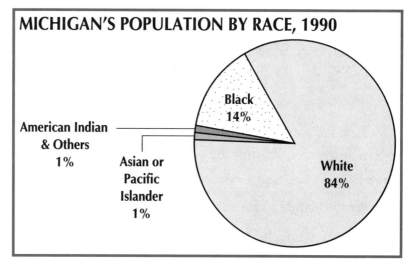

MICHIGAN'S POPULATION BY RACE, 1990

✔ **CHECKING YOUR UNDERSTANDING** ✔

1. What is the title of this pie chart?
2. In this pie chart, what items are compared?
3. What percentage of Michiganders are white?

NATIONALITY

The word **nationality** refers to the country in which a person is a citizen. Therefore, ◀
if you were born in the United States or became a U.S. citizen, your nationality is
American.

National origin refers to the country where your parents, grandparents or ancestors
came from. **Ancestors** are members of your family who lived a long time ago, such
as your great-grandparents. Most Americans have ancestors from other countries. For
example, the national origin of one of your friends might be German. A German American is an American whose family (*parents, grandparents* or *ancestors*) originally came
from Germany.

THINK ABOUT IT

When you go home, ask your parents where your family's ancestors came from.
What do you think they will say?

✔ **CHECKING YOUR UNDERSTANDING** ✔

What percentage of Michiganders trace their ancestry back to Germany?

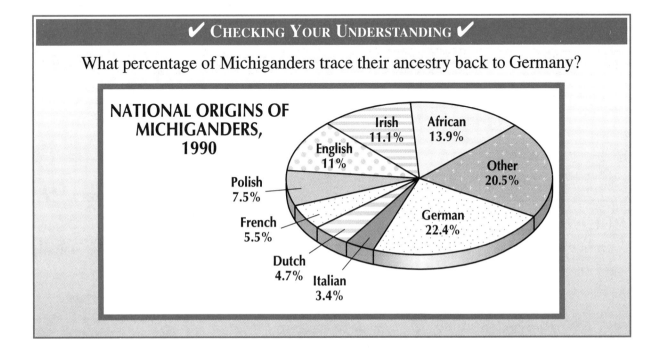

NATIONAL ORIGINS OF MICHIGANDERS, 1990

Irish 11.1%
African 13.9%
English 11%
Other 20.5%
Polish 7.5%
German 22.4%
French 5.5%
Dutch 4.7%
Italian 3.4%

ETHNICITY

▶ **Ethnic groups** are made up of people who share similar traits or characteristics. These traits vary. Some of the most common are national origin, language or race. For example, African Americans are of the same race. In the United States, people's national origin often forms the basis of their ethnic identity. For instance, people who trace their ancestors back to Ireland belong to an ethnic group known as Irish Americans.

There are many areas of ethnic diversity in Michigan. Dearborn and Detroit have large groups of Arab Americans. Frankenmuth is a center for people of German ancestry. Grand Rapids and Holland have many Dutch Americans, while the Upper Peninsula is home to many people with ancestors from Finland. A few years ago, the University of Michigan studied ethnic groups in Michigan. They found that Michigan had more than 100 different ethnic groups.

This German immigrant family came to live in Michigan in 1855.
In what part of Michigan did many German immigrants settle?

Knowing someone's ethnic group may tell us something about that person's way of life. It may tell us what foods the person prefers. We may also be able to guess something about that person's other habits and customs. However, we have to avoid the dangers of **stereotyping** (ster' ē ə tīp ing)—assuming that all people from one ethnic group are the same. Individual differences are just as important as ethnic identity.

✔ CHECKING YOUR UNDERSTANDING ✔

Name **two** ethnic foods popular with Michiganders:

Food	This food comes from .....
❖ _____?_____	❖ _____?_____
❖ _____?_____	❖ _____?_____

RELIGION

▶ Another way that people often group themselves is by religion. Most **religions** usually have the following characteristics:

a belief in God or several gods	a set of customs and practices	an organization, such as a church or mosque, that provides leadership

Religion has played a key role in Michigan since its earliest history. Some of the early explorers of Michigan were missionaries. They tried to convert Native Americans to Christianity. The French who settled the region were mainly Roman Catholic. Many later immigrants to Michigan also came from Catholic countries.

In the early 1800s, people from the Northeast United States began coming to Michigan. Most were Protestants, such as Congregationalists, Methodists and Baptists. Germans and Scandinavians brought Lutheranism to Michigan. Today, more than half of all Michiganders are Protestant. Jews and Muslims make up the largest non-Christian groups.

A Muslim house of worship in Dearborn.
Can you name some of the houses of worship in your neighborhood?

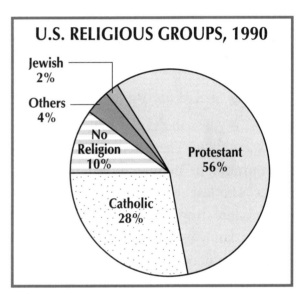

U.S. RELIGIOUS GROUPS, 1990

Jewish 2%
Others 4%
No Religion 10%
Catholic 28%
Protestant 56%

✔ CHECKING YOUR UNDERSTANDING ✔

1. Name two major religious groups in Michigan.
2. Which religious group in the United States has the largest percentage?

Closing

REVIEWING HOW YOU IDENTIFIED YOURSELF

At the start of this activity you were asked to "group" yourself. Review the start of this activity to check what you wrote. How would you *now* group yourself?

- ❖ What is your race?
- ❖ What is your nationality?
- ❖ What is your ethnic group?
- ❖ What is your religion?

EXPANDING YOUR UNDERSTANDING

Creating Vocabulary Cards

Race
Define "race."
Give an example of a racial group.

Ethnic Group
Define "ethnic group."
Give an example of an ethnic group.

Creating an Ethnic Pie Chart

Every 10 years the U.S. Census Bureau conducts a **census**. The census attempts to count the number of people living in the United States. The last census, taken in 1990, showed some interesting data about American ethnic groups, such as African Americans. About 12% of the people living in the United States were African American. In comparison, about 14% of Michiganders are African American.

There are many ways of looking at figures supplied by the Census Bureau. The table shows where African Americans live. About nine out of every 100 African Americans lived in the West in 1990. Converting such information from a table to a pie chart often makes it easier to understand.

Make a copy of the circle to the right. Then take each item in the table and mark its share of the "pie." Use the markings around the outer edge of the circle to help you to divide the "pie." Each space between the marks represents 1% of the whole "pie." The West has already been done for you. When you are finished, give your pie chart a title.

AFRICAN AMERICANS BY LOCATION: 1990	
West	9%
Midwest	19%
Northeast	19%
South	53%

Title: _____

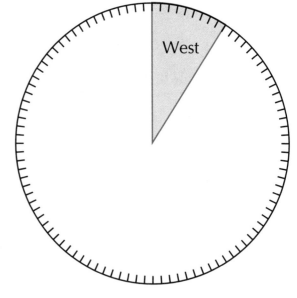

West

WHAT GENERALIZATIONS CAN YOU MAKE ABOUT ETHNIC GROUPS IN MICHIGAN?

4B

In this activity, you will learn about some of the ethnic groups that have made Michigan their home. Look for the following important words:

▶ Generalization   ▶ Slavery

▶ Hispanic   ▶ Segregation

Generalizations (jen' ər ə li zā' shənz) are powerful organizing tools. They allow us to summarize large amounts of information. In this activity, you will examine how generalizations are formed. You will also practice making your own generalizations.

WHAT IS A GENERALIZATION?

Let's begin by examining the following list:

❖ **Detroit** is located on the **Detroit River.**

❖ **Harrisville** is located on the shore of **Lake Huron.**

❖ **Marquette** is located on the shore of **Lake Superior.**

❖ **Manistee** is on the shore of **Lake Michigan.**

It may be hard to remember all of these facts. But if you look at them as a group, you might see a pattern. These four facts about cities in Michigan have something in common. This pattern may actually be more important than any one specific fact.

The Detroit River.
What does Detroit have in common with Harrisville, Marquette and Manistee?

THINK ABOUT IT

What do these four facts about cities in Michigan have in common?

HOW GENERALIZATIONS ARE FORMED

The list shows that these *cities are located near large bodies of water*. This general statement describes what all of the specific examples have in common. When a general statement identifies a common pattern, it is called a ⬛**generalization**⬛. Let's see how this generalization might be presented in a diagram.

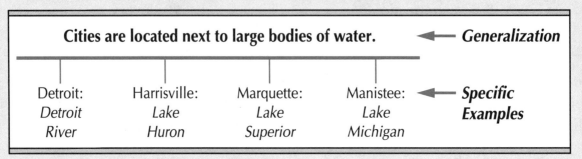

A generalization shows what several facts have in common. A generalization can also help us to make predictions. Each of the earlier examples showed a city next to a large body of water. We might now guess that if we look at any city, it will also be located next to a large body of water.

Although generalizations are useful tools, we must be careful in applying them. For example, is our generalization really true for all cities? Suppose we applied it to Cadillac, another city in Michigan. A map will show that Cadillac is **not** located next to a large body of water. This means we must change our original generalization. Based on the facts we now have, we can say that *many,* but not all, cities are located next to large bodies of water.

When you are asked if a generalization is true, you must find specific examples and facts to support it. Remember, generalizations are always subject to change as new information is learned. Now let's see how this changed generalization might look in a diagram:

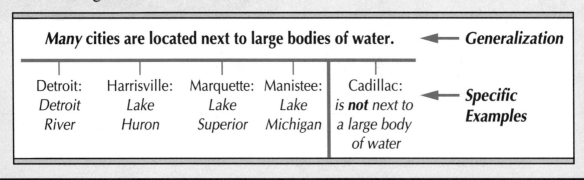

You have just learned how a generalization is formed and changed. How good are you at forming your own generalizations? Let's apply what you have just learned to see if you can make generalizations about different ethnic groups in Michigan. For example, think about whether the following generalization is accurate:

Most ethnic groups in Michigan faced similar problems when they first arrived.

GERMAN AMERICANS

WHY THEY CAME

Germany is a country in the center of Europe. Before 1871, Germany was made up of many smaller states. Despite this lack of political unity, Germans shared a common culture and language. Starting in the 1840s, many Germans began to migrate to the United States.

Advertisement in the 1850s, encouraging Germans to migrate to Michigan.

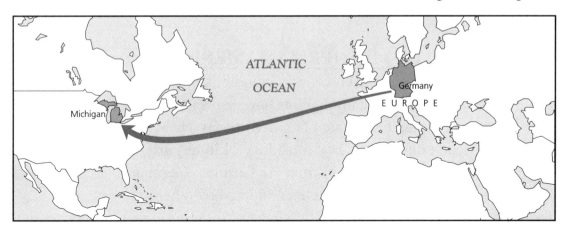

Most German **immigrants** left their homeland because they faced great political and economic hardships. In the 1840s, growing poverty led to violence throughout the German states. Many Germans also faced starvation when their potato crop was destroyed by disease. Faced with such problems, many Germans saw America as a land of opportunity. Many German immigrants came to Michigan after first arriving on the East Coast. By this time, boats were able to bring great numbers of people from New York and New England to Michigan by way of the Erie Canal and Lake Erie.

This marker tells the story of Michigan's first German immigrants.

WHERE THEY SETTLED

Thousands of German immigrants settled in the Detroit area. Others were actually headed to Wisconsin and other Midwestern states, but decided to settle in the towns and farmlands of Washtenaw, Saginaw and Clinton counties instead. Towns such as **Frankenmuth** and **Westphalia** were founded by German immigrants. These areas still have a strong German character today.

Frankenmuth is famous for its many restaurants serving German food.

THE PROBLEMS THEY FACED

German immigrants faced many difficulties when they first arrived. One problem was that most of them spoke only German. They had a hard time communicating with their English-speaking neighbors. Those Germans who moved to rural counties to become farmers faced the huge task of making their own homes and farms. Those who settled in big cities faced different problems. They lived in houses that were often overcrowded. Most of these immigrants worked hard so that they and their children could lead better lives.

CONTRIBUTIONS OF THE GERMAN AMERICANS

From the 1840s until the early 20th century, hundreds of thousands of German immigrants settled in Michigan. These immigrants have had a great influence on the state. For example, German communities created hundreds of private schools that influenced the system of American education. They introduced kindergarten to the United States. *Kindergarten* means a "garden of children" in German. Germans also placed a heavy emphasis on sports programs that were later adopted by other schools.

German workers brought many skills with them from Europe. They were particularly talented in carpentry and baking, and were famous for brewing good beer. In the last years of the 19th century, German workers and professionals played an active and important role in helping organize labor unions. These unions tried to improve conditions for people who worked for big companies.

German immigrants made many cultural contributions to Michigan. They had a great love of music and organized bands, orchestras and singing societies. In fact, the first formal concert ever held in Detroit was given by a touring German singer in 1833. German immigrants later formed a brass band and a Detroit Harmony society to promote choral music. Beginning in the 1850s, a German theater group performed plays throughout Michigan.

Much of German-American culture is celebrated today during German-day festivals. At these events, people wear traditional costumes such as *lederhosen* (*men's leather shorts with suspenders*) and *dirndl* (*women's full skirts*). Throughout Michigan, it's always possible to find typical German cooking, with its famous sausages and sauerkraut.

✔ CHECKING YOUR UNDERSTANDING ✔

1. Why did German immigrants come to America?
2. Where in Michigan did many of the German immigrants settle?
3. What was life like for the first German settlers in Michigan?

POLISH AMERICANS

WHY THEY CAME

Polish immigrants came to Michigan from Poland, a country located in eastern Europe.

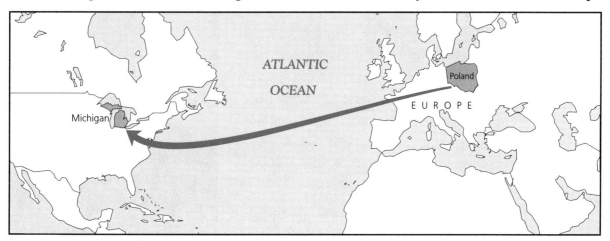

Some Poles came to Michigan as early as the 1850s. They started small farming communities such as Parisville in Huron County. Larger numbers of Poles began arriving in the 1880s. Many Poles were poor farmers forced off their lands by their foreign rulers. Other Poles wanted to escape military duty and the conditions that kept them in poverty.

By the late 1800s, many Poles began to hear of job opportunities in America. Jobs that took only hours to learn were plentiful in the factories of America's manufacturing centers. In addition, new shipping companies offered faster and safer ships, and a chance to be transported directly to inland cities such as Detroit. These advances made the trip much easier than just a few years earlier. They encouraged many more people from Poland to make the journey.

WHERE THEY SETTLED

Most Poles came to Michigan to have their own land to farm. However, by the end of the century, little land suitable for farming was still for sale. After 1900, most Poles settled in industrial cities such as Detroit, Lansing, Saginaw and Grand Rapids. By 1900, 15% of the people in Detroit were Polish-born. In 1902, the suburb of Hamtramck was a small community of German farmers. By 1920, the arrival of 50,000 new immigrants turned the area into a Polish neighborhood.

Many Polish immigrants worked on farms; others settled in industrial cities.

THE PROBLEMS THEY FACED

Polish immigrants faced many difficulties when they came to Michigan. Most of them spoke only Polish. It was hard for them to communicate with their English neighbors. As a result, many lived in exclusively Polish communities when they first arrived. Poles were also Catholic, a religion that the Protestant majority of Michigan considered strange. Because of these cultural differences, Poles often faced prejudice from others.

Difficult working conditions created another problem for many Poles. While factory jobs were plentiful, they often required working 10 hours a day at low wages. Although conditions improved in later years, many Polish workers continued to struggle just to make enough money to support their families. Many of these immigrants were also forced to live in overcrowded and unhealthy tenements.

Polish immigrant children.

CONTRIBUTIONS OF POLISH AMERICANS

Polish Americans played a major role in the industrialization of Michigan. They served as an important source of labor in such industries as automobiles, steel, clothing and food processing. They also played a vital part in the formation of labor unions such as the United Automobile Workers, which worked hard to improve the living and working conditions of all workers.

Polish Americans created a rich community life that served as a model for all Americans. They built neighborhoods of brick houses and started churches, newspapers and schools. These contributed to the cultural life of the cities in which they lived. Polish-American Michiganders have also made significant contributions in fields ranging from business to science and sports.

✔ CHECKING YOUR UNDERSTANDING ✔

1. Why did Polish immigrants come to America?
2. Where in Michigan did many of the Polish immigrants settle?
3. What was life like for the first Polish settlers in Michigan?

MEXICAN AMERICANS

WHY THEY CAME

Mexico is a Spanish-speaking country located south of the United States. For the past century, many Mexicans have had trouble finding enough work in their country to support their families. Since the United States and Mexico share a common border, millions of Mexicans have migrated north to find work. Most of the Mexicans who originally came here hoped to escape the poverty they faced in their homeland.

A few Mexicans arrived in Michigan as early as the 1920s. Many more came in the years following World War II. In the beginning, most worked on farms to help harvest such crops as navy beans, asparagus, sugar beets and cherries.

Mexican Americans are the largest group of Spanish-speaking people in Michigan. However, Michigan has immigrants from other parts of Latin America. People have come to Michigan from Cuba, Puerto Rico and the countries of Central America. People who come from Spanish-speaking countries in the Western Hemisphere are often referred to as **Hispanic**. As a group, they share many cultural similarities, such as the ◀ Spanish language and the Catholic religion.

WHERE THEY SETTLED

At first, Mexicans settled in the farm communities of southeastern Michigan, especially in Wayne, Oakland, Ingham and Genesee counties. In later years, many Mexicans moved to the larger cities of Michigan. This move took place when machines began to replace the manual labor Mexicans once supplied to farms. Today, there are sizable Mexican-American communities in Detroit, Lansing and Grand Rapids.

THE PROBLEMS THEY FACED

When Mexicans arrived in Michigan, many were poor and had little education. It was difficult to find well-paying jobs. At first, most could not speak English, which added to their problems. The jobs they could get, particularly in farming, required exhausting work in orchards and fields. These jobs demanded long hours of work at low pay. Farm workers often found themselves isolated in the countryside, far from the conveniences of modern life. Many lived in poor housing and had little or no professional health care.

Mexicans, often found work in Michigan's farm areas.

Mexican Americans who moved into large cities also faced economic problems. Like other immigrants, they often found themselves in overcrowded neighborhoods with run-down housing. Many could only find work in the lowest-paid jobs offered by factories or small businesses, such as restaurants. Mexican Americans also faced ethnic prejudice. Gradually, Mexican Americans began creating prosperous lives for themselves throughout Michigan.

CONTRIBUTIONS OF MEXICAN AMERICANS

For many years, Mexican Americans performed much of the work on Michigan's farms. More recently, Mexican-American communities have enriched the culture of the state's cities. Mexican Americans have opened up many small businesses, including restaurants. Mexican food, with its tacos, burritos and enchiladas, has added to the diversity of foods that Michiganders now enjoy. Mexican and other Latino music, such as Salsa, is now part of the state's cultural mix.

SELECT LOCATIONS OF MICHIGAN'S MAJOR ETHNIC GROUPS

- British
- German
- Scandinavian
- Dutch
- Polish
- Irish
- African
- Middle Eastern
- Asian
- Hispanic

FAMOUS PLACES: DETROIT INSTITUTE OF ART

Diego Rivera was a painter born in Mexico in 1886. In the 1930s, he created a series of murals (*large wall paintings*) for public buildings. Rivera's murals showed the hardships of life faced by America's industrial workers. One of his murals, *Detroit Industry*, was completed for the Detroit Institute of Art. The painting created a controversy because it appeared to criticize the treatment of workers. A similar Rivera mural, painted for New York City's Rockefeller Center, was destroyed when it, too, came under heavy criticism.

Most Mexican Americans place a high value on the importance of family. They often have worked to create safe and friendly neighborhoods for their children. Mexican Americans have also played a growing role in local enterprises, schools and churches. These activities help to make Michigan a better place for all who live here.

✔ CHECKING YOUR UNDERSTANDING ✔

1. Why did Mexican immigrants come to the United States?
2. Where in Michigan did many of the Mexican immigrants settle?
3. What was life like for the first Mexican immigrants in Michigan?

ARAB AMERICANS

WHY THEY CAME

Arabs are people who come from several countries in the Middle East and North Africa. Among the best-known Arab nations are Egypt, Jordan, Syria and Iraq. Arabs from these different countries share a common culture. They speak the Arabic language. Most Arab people follow the Islamic faith, a religion founded by Mohammed in the 7th century.

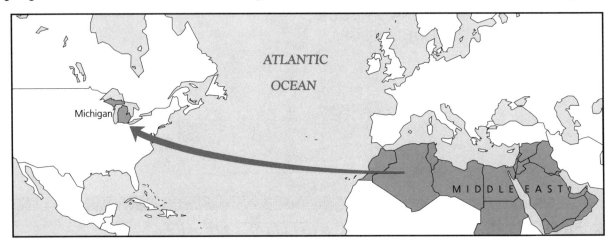

The first Arabs arrived in Michigan in the late 1800s. Many came to earn enough money to buy land back in their home countries. They often worked as traveling peddlers (*people selling goods they carry*). They sold jewelry, cloth and housewares to farmers and housewives throughout Michigan. With the skills they learned as peddlers, many Arab Americans later opened dry goods and grocery stores in major cities. In the early 1900s, other Arab Americans took jobs in car factories and industrial plants in the Detroit area.

Great numbers of Arab Americans arrived in the years following World War II. They came to escape political troubles and wars. The new Arab immigrants of the 1960s included many students who wanted a university education. There were also many wealthy professionals, as well as poor peasants who lost their land in various wars. Many Arabs came to Michigan because they had relatives here or knew that the state's large Arab-American community could help them adjust to American life.

WHERE THEY SETTLED

Although Arab Americans live throughout Michigan, most of them settled in the Detroit area. More Arab Americans live in Detroit than in any other city of the United States. The state's first mosque (*Islamic house of worship*) was built in Highland Park in 1919.

When Ford opened an auto plant in Dearborn, many Arab immigrants moved there. Soon Dearborn had a large Arab community. More recent Arab immigrants continue to settle there. Today, so many Arabs live in Dearborn that it is sometimes called "Little Syria."

THE PROBLEMS THEY FACED

The first Arab Americans faced many difficulties. When they arrived from the Middle East, they found themselves in a culture very different from their own. Their language and writing were totally unrelated to English. Their religion was also quite different. Their unusual dress made many of them stand out. One time in Grand Rapids, several Syrian men were arrested after complaints that they were wearing "nightgowns" in public. In fact, they had been wearing traditional Arab clothing.

This family is dressed in traditional Arabic clothing.

Arab Americans continue to face prejudice. Some Americans unfairly associate violence in the Middle East with Arab Americans. A war between the United States and Iraq in 1991 made it especially difficult for Arab Americans to escape such prejudice.

CONTRIBUTIONS OF ARAB AMERICANS

Arab Americans have made many contributions to Michigan's rich ethnic mix. They have introduced new music, literature, foods and clothing styles to Michigan. Arab Americans have opened up grocery stores, hotels and retail shops, adding variety to the neighborhoods in which they live. Among the best known Arab Americans is **Helen Thomas**, a White House journalist. She has reported on every President from John F. Kennedy to Bill Clinton. She is the daughter of Syrian immigrants who settled in Detroit. Another well-known Arab American is **Casey Kasem**, a Detroit-born disk jockey who hosts "America's Top 40" radio show. The show has introduced his listeners to many new rock n' roll stars.

✔ CHECKING YOUR UNDERSTANDING ✔

1. Why did Arab immigrants come to America?
2. Where in Michigan did many Arab immigrants settle?
3. What was life like for the first Arab immigrants in Michigan?

◆ DUTCH AMERICANS IN MICHIGAN ◆

The Netherlands, (also called Holland), is a small country in western Europe whose people are known as the "Dutch." In the 1840s, sixty Dutch immigrants came to Michigan to find a better way of life. They settled in an area by the Black River near Lake Michigan.

The settlers built a Dutch outpost and named it Holland, after their former homeland. Soon a second group of 800 Dutch immigrants arrived. The settlers were discouraged by what they found—swamps and insect-infested forests.

The following winter brought milder weather. This allowed the pioneers to build homes and a church. They decided to buy a large ship to bring supplies and other goods to the settlement. But first a channel between Lake Michigan and Black Lake had to be dug. When Michigan's state government delayed providing the money, the settlers took up picks and shovels and dug the channel by themselves.

By 1871, Holland, Michigan, was firmly established. However, a fire in October of that year destroyed most of the town. Though they had little money and few possessions, the residents decided to rebuild. Even a fire could not destroy the spirit of these people. Holland has continued to grow ever since.

In 1927, members of a women's club suggested planting flowers around the city. Since the town had ties to the Netherlands, they suggested the town adopt the tulip as its flower. Soon after, 100,000 tulip bulbs from the Netherlands were planted. Thousands of Michiganders came to Holland to see the tulips in bloom. The event proved so popular that **Tulip Time** became an annual event.

In 1933, a group of students began performing dances wearing "klompen" (*Dutch wooden shoes*). They called themselves the **Klompen Dancers**. Currently, there are more than 1,400 klompen dancers in Michigan. Tulip Time has grown to be one of Michigan's most popular and important festivals. The festival emphasizes traditional Dutch costumes, dances and foods. Today, Dutch Americans are one of the largest ethnic

Klompen dancers during a parade in Holland. *Have you ever witnessed Tulip Time?*

groups in Michigan. They make up about six percent of the state's population.

CREATING A GENERALIZATION

Can you think of a general statement that is true for all of the ethnic groups you have just read about? You might recall that each of them faced problems in adjusting to life in Michigan. This kind of statement is a generalization.

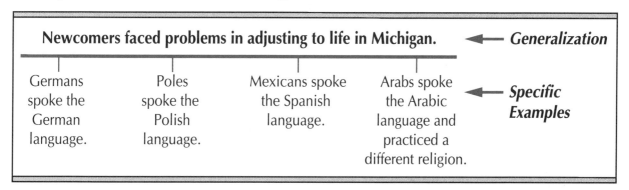

Newcomers faced problems in adjusting to life in Michigan. ← *Generalization*

| Germans spoke the German language. | Poles spoke the Polish language. | Mexicans spoke the Spanish language. | Arabs spoke the Arabic language and practiced a different religion. |

← *Specific Examples*

✔ CHECKING YOUR UNDERSTANDING ✔

Can you make **one** other generalization about all four groups? Think about all the similarities that you can among these groups. Make a copy of the guide below. Then write out your generalization and a specific example for each group.

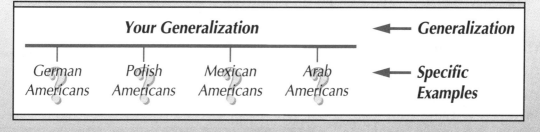

Your Generalization ← *Generalization*

German Americans   Polish Americans   Mexican Americans   Arab Americans   ← *Specific Examples*

REVISING YOUR GENERALIZATION: AFRICAN AMERICANS

WHY THEY CAME

Unlike other groups, most people from Africa did not choose to come to North America. They were brought here by force as slaves. **Slavery** was a system where one person ◄ claimed to "own" another person. Slaves worked without pay and only received whatever food, clothing and shelter the owner provided.

Slaves were first brought to North America by sea captains. These sea captains traded with local African tribes to obtain their prisoners as slaves. The slaves were then chained together on very crowded ships for the long voyage across the Atlantic Ocean. Many of them died while making the crossing. Once in the Americas, the survivors were sold as slaves at auctions.

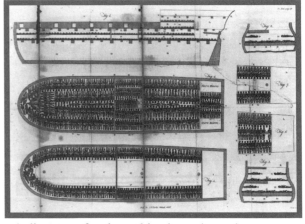

A diagram of a slave ship shows how slaves were crammed aboard like cargo.

African American slavery lasted over two hundred years. In the United States, slavery was ended by the Civil War. Even after 1865, African Americans continued to face many difficulties. Until the 1900s most lived in the South. They received little education and were often the targets of violence. Most Southern states ▶ enforced a policy of **segregation** (*separation of the races*), in which blacks were forced to use separate schools and other public facilities. In general, African Americans lived in poor conditions with little hope of economic advancement.

African Americans have lived in Michigan since pioneer days. Large numbers of African Americans started arriving in Michigan during World War I. With the outbreak of war, Michigan's factories became busier than ever. At the same time, the war cut off immigration from Europe. Businessmen encouraged workers, especially African Americans, to move to Michigan. After the war, new laws kept immigration from Europe low. This created a continuing need for workers. Thousands of African Americans moved from the South to Michigan in search of a better life.

How does this picture illustrate the kind of discrimination faced by African Americans in the South?

Many African Americans left their homes in the South and headed to Northern cities.
What factors attracted these workers to Michigan?

WHERE THEY SETTLED

Most African Americans settled in the industrial cities of the Lower Peninsula. The Detroit area, as the center of the auto industry, was the most popular destination. In 1910, there were fewer than 6,000 African Americans living in Wayne County, where Detroit is located. By 1930, that number had jumped to 120,000. African Americans also headed to such cities as Grand Rapids, Saginaw and Flint.

The black population of Michigan kept on rising throughout the 20th century. World War II and expanded industrial growth brought new job opportunities. Today, African Americans make up about 14 percent of the state's population. Many African-American Michiganders continue to live around Detroit. African Americans also reside in smaller manufacturing cities in the southern half of the state.

THE PROBLEMS THEY FACED

African Americans often faced serious problems on their arrival in Michigan. They discovered that racial discrimination in Michigan was sometimes almost as bad as in the South. African Americans were forced to live in overcrowded neighborhoods with poor housing. Some employers refused to hire them. Many schools in Michigan were racially segregated and refused to admit African-American students.

On a few occasions, tensions between blacks and whites turned into violence. In 1943, some whites protested African-American residents moving into a housing complex in a white neighborhood of Detroit. A riot broke out in which 34 people were killed. In 1967, another riot destroyed many African-American homes and stores in Detroit. Since the 1960s,

A car is set on fire during a 1943 riot in Detroit.

however, great progress has been made. This progress has been the result of the Civil Rights Movement, which has made most racial discrimination illegal. Today, Michiganders are moving together towards a more prosperous and peaceful society.

CONTRIBUTIONS OF AFRICAN AMERICANS

African Americans have made many contributions to life in Michigan. Their labor helped support the state's industrial factories, especially during the two World Wars. They often worked hard at low-paying factory jobs with dedication and pride.

African Americans also played a major role in the Civil Rights Movement of the 1950s and 1960s. In 1955, Michigan was one of the first states to officially outlaw job discrimination. By the 1960s, African-American politicians and other Civil Rights leaders began to have great influence throughout the state. In 1968, racial discrimination in housing was outlawed. These advances also helped end discrimination against women, Hispanics, Asians, Native Americans, senior citizens and people with disabilities.

At this Woolworth lunch counter, four African Americans were once refused service at a "Whites-only" section in Greensboro, N.C. (1960). The "sit-in" set off a challenge to segregation throughout the South.

The cultural contributions of Michigan's African Americans have been especially significant. African-American singers created the "Motown Sound," and made Detroit a center of musical talent. African-American athletes have dominated Michigan's professional sports teams. Many people consider **Joe Louis** to have been the greatest boxer of all time. Other

Joe Louis speaks to a group of youngsters.
Why is Joe Louis famous?

prominent African-American Michiganders include **Ralph Bunche**, a statesman who helped to set up the United Nations, and **Malcolm X**, a Civil Rights leader.

✔ CHECKING YOUR UNDERSTANDING ✔

1. How were most Africans first brought to America?
2. Where in Michigan did many African Americans settle?
3. What was life like for African Americans in Michigan before the Civil Rights Movement?

FAMOUS MICHIGANDERS: ROSA PARKS

In the 1950s, African Americans began to speak out against racial discrimination. Rosa Parks was a seamstress living in Montgomery, Alabama. On December 1, 1955, she refused to give up her seat in the front of the bus to a white bus rider. Parks' action went against Southern rules requiring African Americans to sit in the back seats of buses. Her arrest began a black boycott of the city's buses. After a year, the boycott ended with a victory for African Americans. Two years later, fearing for her safety, Rosa Parks moved to Detroit. There is now a street named in her honor.

Rosa Parks wearing the Medal of Freedom.

Closing

UPDATING YOUR GENERALIZATION

Let's return to the generalization found on page 197. Is this generalization also true for African Americans? If not, how would you change the generalization?

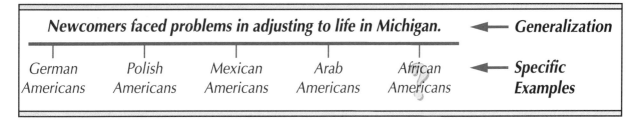

Newcomers faced problems in adjusting to life in Michigan.	← *Generalization*
German Americans Polish Americans Mexican Americans Arab Americans African Americans	← *Specific Examples*

EXPANDING YOUR UNDERSTANDING

Creating Vocabulary Cards

Generalization
What is a "generalization"?
Give an example of a generalization.

African Americans
What problems did African Americans face in moving to Michigan?
What contributions have they made?

Holding a Multicultural Fair

In this activity, you learned about the experiences of several ethnic groups in Michigan. What else can you learn about these and other ethnic groups? In order to find out, let's hold a **Multicultural Fair**.

Your teacher should divide your class into teams. Each team will represent a different cultural group in your community. Try not to choose your own ethnic group. Each team will be assigned a section of the classroom in which to create a booth for the multicultural fair. Booths should be decorated to reflect the cultures they represent. Each team should collect or make the items listed below. Teams will be awarded points for each item they can find, make or create:

❖ **Foods (20 points).**

Display recipes and pictures of typical ethnic foods. They should be the foods for which the group is best known.

> **NOTE:** *For each student who prepares food for other students to sample, the team will receive a bonus of 10 points.*

❖ **Customs and Traditions (20 points).**

Display posters or pictures showing some of the unique customs and practices of the group they represent.

❖ **Music (15 points).**

Bring tapes of music popular among members of the group they represent.

❖ **Dance (15 points).**

Perform traditional dances popular with members of the group they chose.

❖ **Holidays (15 points).**

Display articles or make pictures illustrating the holidays the group celebrates.

❖ **Costumes (15 points).**

Display pictures, drawings or photographs of people dressed in traditional costumes of the group.

> **NOTE:** *For each student who wears a traditional costume on the day of the fair, the team will receive a bonus of 10 points.*

On the day of the fair, students should visit each team's booth.

WHO WOULD YOU NOMINATE TO THE MICHIGAN HALL OF FAME?

4C   In this activity, you will learn about people who have contributed to the greatness of Michigan. Look for the following important words and phrases:

▶ Criteria   ▶ Autobiography   ▶ Thesaurus

▶ Biography   ▶ Descriptive Writing   ▶ Table of Contents

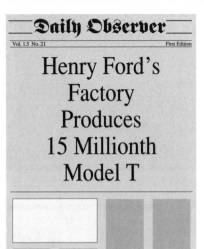

Daily Observer

Vol. 1.5 No. 21   First Edition

Henry Ford's Factory Produces 15 Millionth Model T

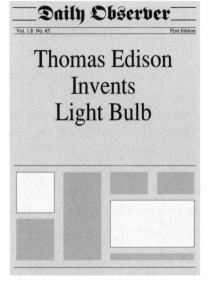

Daily Observer

Vol. 1.8 No. 45   First Edition

Thomas Edison Invents Light Bulb

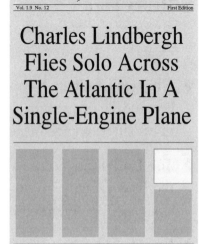

Daily Observer

Vol. 1.9 No. 12   First Edition

Charles Lindbergh Flies Solo Across The Atlantic In A Single-Engine Plane

Daily Observer

Vol. 1.9 No. 24   First Edition

Joe Louis Wins World's Heavyweight Boxing Championship

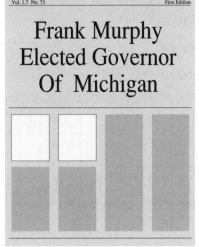

Daily Observer

Vol. 1.7 No. 73   First Edition

Frank Murphy Elected Governor Of Michigan

Daily Observer

Vol. 1.4 No. 81   First Edition

Diana Ross Wins Music Award

THINK ABOUT IT

What do you think all these newspaper headlines have in common?

WHO ARE THESE PEOPLE?

You may have heard the names of some of these people before. Each of them is famous for a special reason:

❖ **Thomas Edison** moved to Port Huron in 1854 with his family. He became America's greatest inventor. His inventions include the light bulb, sound recordings and moving pictures.

❖ **Henry Ford** was born in 1863 in Dearborn. Ford changed the nation by producing cars the average American was able to afford.

❖ **Charles Lindbergh** was born in Detroit. In 1927, he became the first person to fly across the Atlantic Ocean, in his single-engine plane, *The Spirit of St. Louis.*

Thomas Edison and his phonograph.

❖ **Joe Louis** moved to Michigan at age 12. In 1937, he won the heavyweight boxing championship of the world. Louis successfully defended his title more than 25 times.

❖ **Frank Murphy** was born in Harbor Beach in 1890. During his career, Murphy served Michigan as a judge, mayor and governor. He served the nation as Attorney General and became a U.S. Supreme Court Justice.

❖ **Diana Ross** was born in Detroit. Her singing group, the Supremes, became the trio most closely associated with the Motown Sound. In 1970, she left the group to perform on her own.

Charles Lindbergh

QUALIFICATIONS FOR THE MICHIGAN HALL OF FAME

The gender (*male or female*), religion and ethnic background of the people above are varied. However, they all have one thing in common—each one was either born in or grew up in Michigan.

Many sports honor their best players in a Hall of Fame. For example, the Baseball Hall of Fame is located in Cooperstown, New York. Michigan has its own Hall of Fame for women in Lansing. However, Michigan does not have an official Hall of Fame to honor all of its famous citizens.

Can you imagine what it would be like if your state did have its own Hall of Fame? Whom might it honor? Whom would you recommend to include? In this activity, your class will be divided into groups. Each group will nominate **one** person to an imaginary Michigan Hall of Fame. Here are the qualifications for admission:

QUALIFICATIONS FOR THE MICHIGAN HALL OF FAME

❖ Each nominee must have been born in Michigan or have lived part of his or her life here.

❖ A nominee can come from any field. For example, he or she may be an athlete scientist, inventor, politician, president or corporate executive.

❖ A nominee can be someone alive today or a historical figure from the past.

❖ A nominee must have done something that would be considered "great."

WHAT MAKES SOMEONE GREAT?

Notice the last qualification—having done something considered "great." What does "great" actually mean? To answer this, you should create a list of **criteria** (*standards* ◄ *used to judge something*). For example, you might decide that someone who has done something "great" must be well-known. If the person is not well-known, he or she would not meet your criteria for "greatness." Let's begin by creating criteria for "greatness." Complete the first criterion by indicating your choice. Then add other criteria of your own.

✔ CRITERIA FOR GREATNESS ✔

The "great" person should be known throughout:

   (a) the nation   (b) the State of Michigan   (c) my community

A "great" person is someone who _____?_____ and _____?_____.

RESEARCHING YOUR NOMINEE

Before you begin your task, let's review how to research your nominee. You and the other members of your group can find this information in a number of sources:

REFERENCE BOOKS

Reference books are special books that contain information on many topics. Most people do not read an entire reference book. Instead, they read only the information they are searching for. There are many kinds of reference books—encyclopedias, dictionaries, almanacs and atlases. Reference books are found in a special "Reference" section of a library. Most libraries do not allow these books to be taken out.

Some reference books that might help you to find information about noted Michiganders are the following:

- **Michigan Women Firsts and Founders,** by Rachel B. Harley and Betty Mac-Dowell (Michigan Women's Studies Association, Inc.)
- **Michigan Governors Growing Up,** by Willah Weddon (NOG Press)
- **Historic Women of Michigan,** Edited by Rosalie Riegele Troester (Michigan Women's Studies Association)

All of these books contain biographies of famous Michiganders.

ENCYCLOPEDIA

Encyclopedias have articles about many well-known people. You will recall that these articles are arranged in alphabetical order. An encyclopedia has guide words or letters on the spine of each volume. The guide words help you to locate the idea or name of the person you are looking for. Recently, many encyclopedias have become available on computers with CD-ROM disks.

BIOGRAPHY

▶ A **biography** (bi og' rə fē) is a book about a person's life. A biography can be an excellent source of detailed information. Some well-known people have had biographies written about them by several authors.

Dr. John Harvey Kellogg ran a sanitarium where people came to relax and to learn about eating proper foods. In 1876, he created a food made of whole grains. In 1906, his brother began the Battle Creek Toasted Corn Flake Company. Today, this company has grown to become the world's largest cereal producer. *John Harvey Kellogg, M.D.* by Richard Schwartz (Berrien Springs: Andrews University Press, 1981) is a biography of his life.

John Harvey Kellogg

AUTOBIOGRAPHY

Sometimes, a person will write a book about his or her own life. This kind of book is called an **autobiography** . When reading an autobiography, remember that the person ◀ will usually build up the good things about his or her own life by exaggerating achievements. Also, the writer will usually play down any bad things.

From 1946 to 1978, **Lee Iacocca** worked at the Ford Motor Company, rising to become its president. In 1978, he became president of Chrysler. His efforts saved Chrysler from going out of business. His autobiography is called *Iacocca: An Autobiography* (New York: Bantam Books, 1984).

Most libraries have entire sections devoted to biographies and autobiographies. They are usually not found on the library shelf under the name of the author. Biographies and autobiographies are generally listed in alphabetical order by the **last name of the person the book is about.** For example, a biography of Henry Ford by Carol Gelderman would be under the letter "**F**" and not under the letter "G." You may also try searching the **Internet** for information about the subject of any biography or autobiography.

✔ CHECKING YOUR UNDERSTANDING ✔

Where Would You Find …?

1. In an encyclopedia, under which letter would you look for information about **Walter Chrysler**, the man who began the Chrysler Company in the 1920s?
2. In the library, under which letter would you look to find a biography of **Aretha Franklin** written by Len Hills?
3. In the library, under which letter would you look to find an autobiography by **Thomas Wolfe**, a famous writer of the 1920s?

Walter Chrysler tries his hand at a little golf.

A LIST OF POSSIBLE NOMINEES FOR THE HALL OF FAME

The following list includes people from different ethnic and economic groups who were either born in or lived in Michigan at one time. Each had an impact on the state. The list is offered only as a place to start. You and the members of the group should feel free to select a name not found on this list for your nominee.

GOVERNMENT

❖ **Ralph Bunche** was born in Detroit in 1904. In 1950, he became the first African American to be awarded the Nobel Peace Prize. He received this award for getting Arabs and Israelis to agree to stop fighting in 1948. Bunche was the first black person ever to receive this prestigious award.

❖ **Thomas Dewey** was born in Owosso, Michigan in 1902. In 1942, he was elected Governor of New York. In 1948, he ran as a Republican for President of the United States. He lost to President Harry Truman in a close election.

SPORTS

❖ **Earvin "Magic" Johnson** was born in Lansing in 1959. He played basketball for Michigan State University. Later, Johnson played for the L.A. Lakers. He was on Lakers championship teams in 1980, 1982, 1985, 1987 and 1988.

Thomas Dewey

❖ **Sheila Young** was born in Detroit. In 1976, she won a gold medal at the Olympics for speed-skating. She also won silver and bronze medals in speed-skating, making her the first American to win three medals at the winter Olympic Games.

HISTORY

❖ **Stevens T. Mason** was born in Virginia in 1812. He is sometimes referred to as the "Father" of Michigan because he led the Territory of Michigan into statehood. At age 24, Mason was elected the state's first Governor.

❖ **Malcolm X** was born in Omaha, Nebraska in 1925, but grew up in Lansing. Early in life he adopted the Muslim faith. Afterwards, he became a Black Muslim leader and a defender of African-American rights. In 1965, he was killed by a member of a rival Muslim group.

Malcolm X

LITERATURE

❖ **Edna Ferber** was born in 1887 in Kalamazoo. She wrote novels, plays and short stories. She is best remembered for writing *Show Boat*, published in 1926. The novel was later made into a musical and a movie.

❖ **Ring Lardner** was born in 1885 in Niles. He began his career as a sportswriter for several large Chicago newspapers. Lardner also wrote novels, plays, poetry and an autobiography.

BUSINESS

❖ **Herbert Dow** became interested in medical and other uses of salt water found in Midland, Michigan. In 1890, he started the Midland Chemical Company. Later, it was renamed the Dow Chemical Company. His company grew into one of the world's largest chemical companies.

Ring Lardner

❖ **William Upjohn** was a doctor in Kalamazoo. In the 1880s, he developed better pills that dissolved more easily. Soon he started a company with his brothers. Upjohn Company grew to become one of the nation's largest drug companies.

ENTERTAINMENT

❖ **Berry Gordy, Jr.** grew up in Detroit. In 1959, he started Motown Records. By the mid-1960s, the company was one of the most successful African-American owned businesses in the nation.

❖ **Tim Allen** moved to Michigan at age 11. One day Walt Disney's president saw Allen's comedy act. Soon after, he offered Allen a starring role in his own television show. By the 1990s, Allen had the #1 rated television show and had starred in several movies.

Berry Gordy, Jr.

Research

WHO IS YOUR NOMINEE FOR THE HALL OF FAME?

You and the other members of your group are now ready to go to the library to begin your research. To help you focus your investigation, complete the following "Research Guide" for your nominee.

NAME OF YOUR NOMINEE: _____

❖ **Source used:** Identify **one** source of information—the title of a book, article or section of an encyclopedia you consulted.

❖ **Summary of the person's life.**

❖ **The person's major accomplishments.**

WRITING A DESCRIPTIVE ESSAY

After your group has completed its research, your group has to come to a decision: does this person meet your criteria for greatness? Would you recommend the person to the Michigan Hall of Fame? If so, write a letter to the Michigan Hall of Fame describing this person. Before you start, here are some notes about writing a descriptive essay.

HOW TO WRITE A DESCRIPTIVE ESSAY

▶ | Descriptive writing | paints a mental picture of someone or something. This type of writing is used when you want to describe something. Your description should provide "eyes" for the reader to "see" what you are thinking and writing about.

In descriptive writing, use words that appeal to the five senses. Describe how someone or something looks, smells, feels, tastes and sounds. Avoid vague and overused words such as "nice," "pretty," "good" and "great." Make sure your writing proceeds in a logical order. You might describe someone you know by discussing his or her qualities in the order of their importance. When you are writing such an essay, a very useful writing tool is a thesaurus (thi sôr' əs).

THESAURUS

▶ Peter Mark Roget was an English doctor in the late 1700s. As a hobby, Roget grouped together words that were related to each other. From this hobby, Roget developed the thesaurus. A | thesaurus | is a special reference book used by writers to help them find just the right word to express their ideas. It is usually organized in alphabetical order. Use it by looking up any word that comes to mind that is similar to the word you are looking for. For example, assume you want to find different words to use instead of the word "describe." Here is what a typical entry for "description" might look like:

❖ CONTINUED

DESCRIPTION

Nouns—**1.** description, account, statement, report, expose, disclosure, specification, particulars, summary, brief, abstract.

2. history, biography, autobiography, narrative, memoir, annals, chronicle, tradition, legend, story, tale, personal narrative, journal, novel, experiences, fairy tale.

3. narrator, relator, historian, recorder, biographer, novelist, story-teller.

Verbs—describe, narrate, relate, recite, recount, set forth, draw a picture, portray, represent, characterize, particularize, sum up, run over, rehearse, unfold, tell, enter into details or particulars.

Adjectives—descriptive, graphic, narrative, well-drawn, historical, epic, suggestive, traditional, legendary, anecdotal, expository, storied, biographical, autobiographical

Question: Which of the verbs would you choose to use instead of "describe"?

EXPANDING YOUR UNDERSTANDING

Creating Vocabulary Cards

Biography	Autobiography
What is a "biography"?	What is an "autobiography"?
What information will you find in a biography?	How does an autobiography differ from a biography?

Describing a Candidate for a Community Hall of Fame

A community might also have its own Hall of Fame. If your community had a Hall of Fame, would someone you know be a good candidate? A candidate might include a family member, community leader, teacher, doctor or student. Whom would you select for such a Hall of Fame? Write an essay describing this person.

Locating Information Using a Table of Contents

Imagine you went to the library to find a book about Henry Ford. From the books about him on the library shelf, you select the biography, *The Secret Life of Henry Ford* by John C. Dahlinger.

Suppose you wanted to find information about his marriage. You could search each page of the book, but this would be very time consuming.

Information in a book can sometimes be ▶ found by scanning the **table of contents**. This is usually located in the first few pages of the book. The table of contents contains a list of headings, broken down into chapters, and the pages on which they can be found. In a book about Henry Ford, you might find the following part of a table of contents:

In which chapter would you look for information about Henry Ford's:

1. parents?

2. early years growing up?

3. business partners?

4. home, "Fair Lane"?

5. first automobile?

6. wife?

HOW WOULD YOU CLASSIFY THE LANDMARKS OF MICHIGAN?

4D In this activity, you will learn about some of the landmarks that reflect the rich cultural heritage of Michigan. Look for the following important words:

▶ Museum ▶ Classify

You are about to leave for school when the phone rings. Your older sister is calling from school. She says she forgot her report on famous landmarks in Michigan. She needs the report in school. "Can you get the report from my room and the notecards I left on top of the report?" she asks. "I need these notecards to finish writing my report.

Meet me at the school library at 8:30." You agree to meet her.

Unfortunately, you fall while getting off the school bus. You are not hurt, but the report and the notecards have scattered all over the ground. Your sister will be furious. After picking up the papers, you realize that her notecards were not numbered. What are you going to do? You do not want to disappoint your sister. Quickly, you start reading her report to find out how to arrange the notecards. Here is what you find on the first page:

MICHIGAN: A FASCINATING STATE TO VISIT

Michigan is a wonderful place to live in and a fascinating place to visit. Every year, millions of people make Michigan their vacation spot. It is a state that has just about every recreation a visitor could want—surfing and swimming in the Great Lakes, skiing in mountain resorts and hiking along nature trails.

In addition to these natural wonders, Michigan has many important historic landmarks and buildings. My report focuses on some of these landmarks. There are so many interesting places to visit in Michigan that I have classified the landmarks into four major categories.

❖ CONTINUED

PLACES TO VISIT IN MICHIGAN

In this first part of my report, I will identify each of the four categories of landmarks. They are the following:

- Museums. A **museum** is a place where works of art and other valuable objects are displayed. Michigan has many interesting museums. For example, the **Henry Ford Museum** in Dearborn houses Ford's collection of Americana. The museum contains many interesting artifacts, including

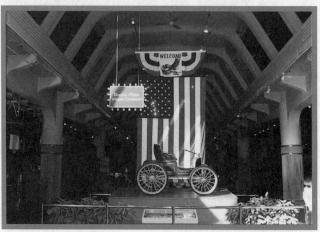

Ford's first car on display inside the Henry Ford Museum.

examples of architecture. Visitors experience history through real objects from the lives of famous Americans. The collection is housed in a building that resembles Independence Hall.

- Historic Sites. Historic sites are places tied to the history of Michigan. They include places that show what life was like in the past. One such historic place is **Fort Mackinac**. The fort protected the Straits of Mackinac for 115 years. It was originally built by the British during the American Revolution to

Soldiers marching during a re-enactment at Fort Mackinac.

protect their fur trade. After the Revolution, it was taken over by the United States. Today, the fort is a national historic landmark.

- Homes of Famous People. This group includes the homes of famous Michiganders. For example, in Dearborn you can visit **Fair Lane**, the home of Henry Ford and his wife Clara. The home was com-

❖ CONTINUED

pleted along the banks of the Rouge River in 1914. The grounds contain servants' cottages, a pony barn and the powerhouse that Ford had connected to the house by a 300-foot-long tunnel. Ford teamed up with his friend Thomas Edison to build an electric power plant to supply electricity to his estate. Today, the

Henry Ford's mansion, Fair Lane.

house is used by the University of Michigan as a conference center.

- Unique Places. This group includes unusual places known for their natural beauty, historical importance or entertainment value. In the Upper Peninsula, there are over 100 waterfalls. The largest in Michigan is the **Tahquamenon Falls**, part of the Tahquamenon Falls State Park. Often called "Little Niagara," the falls are nearly 200 feet across. Almost 50,000 gallons of water a second pour down their 48-foot drop into the canyon below. A special platform allows visitors to stand at the very edge of the falls.

Now you know what you must do. Your sister's notecards describe different landmarks in Michigan. You must categorize her notecards into the types of landmarks she has listed. Before you start, let's look at what it means to classify.

Skill Builder

HOW TO CLASSIFY INFORMATION

To classify is to arrange, organize and sort information. When we classify, we group pieces of information together with other similar information. Classifying is helpful when we want to make sense out of many items that seem disorganized. Could you imagine shopping in a department store if no one in the store knew in which department sneakers were sold? You would have to look through the entire store. To prevent this problem, stores are organized into different departments Grouping similar items together by department makes shopping easier.

THINK ABOUT IT

What other situations can you think of where classifying is used?

CATEGORIZING INFORMATION

Luckily for you, your sister has already set up a classification system for different types of landmarks—historic sites, museums, homes of famous people and unique places. Your task is simply to place each card into its correct category. How can you do this? Here is the procedure you should follow:

1. Look through each card.

2. Think about the landmark's *basic* feature.

3. Categorize each card into the group where it belongs. For example, if a card is about the birthplace of a famous person, you should put that card in the group, "Homes of Famous People."

4. When you have finished, all the cards in the same category should have similar features.

Let's do the first card together:

A

Landmark: Michigan Historical Museum (Lansing)

The state's history museum opened in 1989 in a new home. The museum is built around a center court of 70-foot high white pine trees. It houses many interesting displays. For example, a Native American canoe rests on a stretch of shore in front of a real-looking lake. The museum also has exhibits on the state's many industries. There is a model of a copper mine and a two-story replica of the front of the home of one of Muskegon's lumber pioneers. The third floor of the museum covers the 20th century—the auto industry, the two World Wars and the 1950s.

Notice how the information on this card describes the exhibits of a museum. Since the card is about a museum, it should be categorized under "museums." Copy the following chart to help you keep track as you categorize each card. Place a check mark (✔) in the appropriate column in which the card should be grouped. The first card has already been done for you.

Note: Some of the cards may fit into more than one category.

	Historic Sites	Museums	Homes of Famous People	Unique Places
Card A		✔		
Card B				
Card C				
Card D				
Card E				
Card F				
Card G				
Card H				
Card I				
Card J				
Card K				
Card L				
Card M				

B Detroit Institute of Arts (Detroit)

This museum houses one of the nation's world-famous collections of great art. In addition to dozens of masterpieces, the museum has examples of every major type of art.

C Interlochen Center for the Arts (Interlochen).

This is a music camp and creative arts academy. The idea for the center came from a music teacher at the University of Michigan in 1928.

D Porcupine Mountain Wilderness State Park (Newberry).

Located in the Upper Peninsula, this is one of the state's largest wilderness areas. It has ancient forests and hiking trails that overlook Lake Superior.

E Meadowbrook Hall (Rochester).

This 103-room country estate was built by the widow of John Dodge, an auto pioneer. The home cost $4 million to build in 1926. The estate provides visitors with a close-up view of the life-style of a leading American industrialist.

F Frederik Meijer Gardens (Grand Rapids).

This is a "living" museum. The gardens and five-story conservatory have tropical plants from five continents. There is a 14-foot waterfall and 40 bronze sculptures from around the world.

G Fort Wilkins Historic Complex and Park (Cooper Harbor).

A fort was built here to keep peace between Native Americans and newcomers to the area. Fort Wilkins was the nation's northernmost frontier fort. It was abandoned by the army in 1870 and became a state park in 1923.

H Kellogg Bird Sanctuary (Augusta).

This bird sanctuary was built in 1928 by W.K. Kellogg. He wanted to protect Canadian geese, whose survival was being threatened by the spread of cities. Today, the sanctuary is part of Michigan State University.

I Fayette Historic Townsite (Fayette).

At one time Fayette was owned and operated by the Jackson Iron Company. It was a noisy, grimy iron-smelting town. Today, its fifteen surviving buildings serve as a reminder of the Upper Peninsula's iron-mining era.

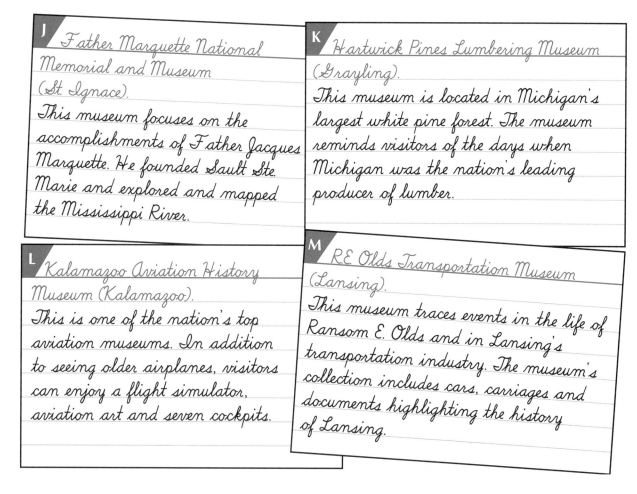

J Father Marquette National Memorial and Museum (St. Ignace).

This museum focuses on the accomplishments of Father Jacques Marquette. He founded Sault Ste. Marie and explored and mapped the Mississippi River.

K Hartwick Pines Lumbering Museum (Grayling).

This museum is located in Michigan's largest white pine forest. The museum reminds visitors of the days when Michigan was the nation's leading producer of lumber.

L Kalamazoo Aviation History Museum (Kalamazoo).

This is one of the nation's top aviation museums. In addition to seeing older airplanes, visitors can enjoy a flight simulator, aviation art and seven cockpits.

M R.E. Olds Transportation Museum (Lansing).

This museum traces events in the life of Ransom E. Olds and in Lansing's transportation industry. The museum's collection includes cars, carriages and documents highlighting the history of Lansing.

Once you have finished categorizing the cards, you have only one task left—to get to the library to meet your sister!

Closing

COMPARING ANSWERS

How does your method of categorizing the landmarks compare with those of other members of your class? Compare how you categorized the different landmarks with what your classmates did.

1. Did you put your cards in the same categories as your classmates?
2. Did any of the landmarks fit into more than one category? If so, which ones?
3. Have you and your family ever visited any of these landmarks?

   ❖ If so, describe your visit.
   ❖ If not, which landmark would you most like to visit? Why?

EXPANDING YOUR UNDERSTANDING

Creating Vocabulary Cards

Museum
What is a "museum"?
Name two museums in Michigan.

Classify
What does it mean to "classify"?
Give an example of a group of
items that can be classified.

Identifying Symbols Associated with Michigan

Michigan is home to some of the nation's top universities. Each school has a symbol to identify it. Do you know the symbol used by each school? Do you have a favorite college team in Michigan that is not mentioned in this chart? If so, feel free to add the name of the college to your copy of the chart.

NAME OF SCHOOL (Location)	NAME ITS TEAM	DESCRIBE ITS TEAM SYMBOL
University of Michigan (Ann Arbor)		
Michigan State University (East Lansing)		
Eastern Michigan University (Ypsilanti)		
Wayne State University (Detroit)		
Your Favorite College Team (where is it located?)		

Creating a Community Travel Brochure

How well do you know the major attractions of your community? Do you know what might interest someone visiting the area where you live? Let's put your knowledge to work. Create a travel brochure or pamphlet for your community's "Visitor Information Center." Your brochure should have the following format:

Name and Outline Map of Your Community

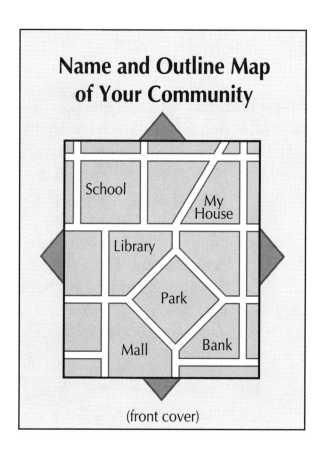

School

My House

Library

Park

Mall

Bank

(front cover)

Facts about Your Area

★ Population
★ Area (size)
★ Names of its
   Elected Officials

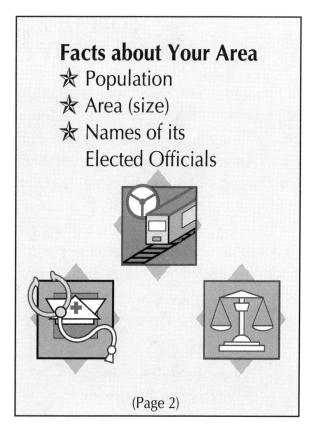

(Page 2)

Special Attractions in the Community

★ Museums
★ State and Local Parks
★ Festivals
★ Historic Sites
★ Cultural Events
★ County Fairs

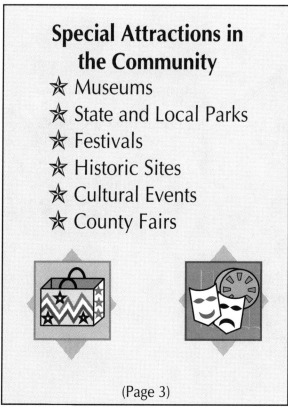

(Page 3)

Presented by

Your Name

(back cover)

CORE DEMOCRATIC VALUES: THE STORY OF OUR FREEDOM

In this unit, you learned how Americans have come from many different backgrounds and learned to live together. Our tradition of individual freedom has helped make this cooperation possible. The story begins in the 1600s when British settlers first came to North America. Many fled their homeland in search of a place to practice their religion freely. People of many different religious beliefs mingled together in the colonies. Eventually, the colonists decided everyone should be free to practice his or her religion.

The colonists also established their own local governments. Power was shared between a colonial governor, appointed by the British government, and a colonial assembly elected by the colonists. Colonists recognized that the right to vote is a basic principle of democracy, a system in which the government represents the people.

To ensure that the government spoke for the people, the colonists also recognized other rights that Americans still respect today:

Freedom of Assembly
People have the right to hold public meetings even if their purpose is to protest against government actions.

Freedom of the Press
People have the right to print their ideas and beliefs even if they criticize the government.

INDIVIDUAL FREEDOMS

Freedom of Speech
People have the right to express their ideas and beliefs when talking with others.

Open and Free Inquiry
People have a right to openly question what is happening in society.

Freedom to Petition Government
People have the right to write to government leaders asking them to make changes.

In the 1770s, the colonists and the British government disagreed over the issue of taxing the colonists. This dispute eventually led to the American Revolution. After the revolution, the people of the United States adopted the U.S. Constitution and the Bill of Rights. These documents further protected the individual freedoms of Americans.

The **U.S. Constitution** stated the basic goals of the new American government. The government was not meant to serve or glorify the rulers of the country. Instead, the purpose of government was to protect and help the people.

According to the U.S. Constitution, our government has three main purposes:

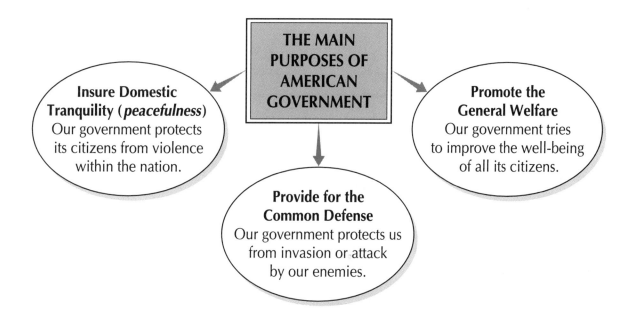

Shortly after the U.S. Constitution was adopted, a **Bill of Rights** was added. The Bill of Rights consists of the first ten amendments (*additions*) to the U.S. Constitution. The Bill of Rights further guaranteed individual rights. The first amendment was especially important. It guaranteed freedom of religion, free speech, a free press, freedom of assembly and the right to petition the government.

Although the Constitution and the Bill of Rights promised to protect individual rights many years passed before all Americans achieved these rights. For example, Native Americans, women, African Americans and other groups had very few rights in the early years of our nation's history.

It took almost two hundred years for the benefits of individual freedom to be enjoyed by all Americans. Today, we recognize that the protection of rights for all groups, especially minorities, is an essential part of individual freedom in a democracy.

SUMMARIZING YOUR UNDERSTANDING

Directions: Use your knowledge to complete the following graphic organizers.

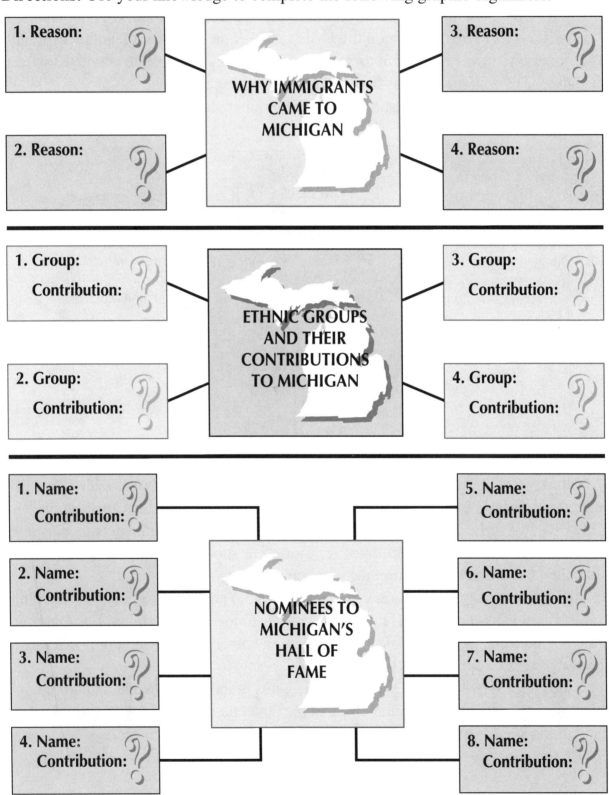

ECONOMICS

Logging was once Michigan's most important industry.

Workers at a winery plant near Traverse City.

Workers lower an engine onto a chassis in a Michigan auto plant.

Economics explains how people earn and spend money. It is also about banks, factories, stores and farms, and how they work. In this unit, you will learn about the things that are needed to produce goods and to provide services—natural resources, human capital, capital equipment and entrepreneurship. You will also learn about starting a new business, conserving natural resources and trading with other countries.

PROFESSOR SMITH VISITS A PIN FACTORY

The year is 1765. Adam Smith, a professor from Scotland, is wearing a handsome light coat, silk stockings, trousers that end at his knees and wide-buckle shoes. He has large eyes and his head shakes slightly when he speaks. He is visiting a factory to find the answers to several questions that confuse him.

"Step right this way, Professor Smith," says a tall, thin man who leads the professor through the doorway. "Thank you kindly, sir," Smith replies. The sound inside the factory is almost deafening. At one end of the room, men are pulling hot iron into long, thin wire. In another corner, a man hammers the wire to straighten it as it cools.

Smith's eyes dance around the workshop. He watches a number of men busily cutting and hammering the red hot iron, making small circles. Each circle is no larger than the head of a pin. "Professor Smith, would you believe that there are 18 separate operations in this workshop for making pins?" says his guide.

Adam Smith

"But wouldn't it be much simpler to have each man make the pins from start to finish?" Smith asks, with some excitement in his voice.

"In my grandfather's day they would have done that," the tall man answers. "But we've discovered that it is more efficient to divide the work up among all the men. This division of labor allows each man to become more skilled at his own individual task. No time is lost by having the men switch from one job to another."

Smith was greatly impressed by what he saw at the pin factory. The division of labor seemed to him to be the secret that made people more productive.

People were growing more food, making more cloth and producing more glass and ironware than ever before in history. And all this came from the simple idea of dividing up the work into separate tasks.

Indeed, it seemed to Professor Smith that division of labor had spread through almost all of British society. Some people were doctors, others were carpenters, farmers or soldiers. Dividing up society's work among separate workers seemed to make society more productive.

However, one thing continued to bother him. In the pin factory, each man had a specialty. One drew iron, while another straightened the iron into pins. The factory owner hired the workmen and told them exactly what to do. The factory owner alone decided everything that went on in the factory.

But what about the society that existed beyond the pin factory? What was the guiding force that told each person in society what to do? Who made sure that there were enough farmers to grow wheat for the bakers? Who told the bakers to make enough bread for everyone who needed bread to eat? Society was like a huge pin factory, but it miraculously ran without a factory owner telling everyone what to do. How did everyone know what job to fill and what to do?

In olden times, people either did the same kind of work as their parents or obeyed the orders of their king or ruler. It was easy to see how those societies worked—everyone was told what to do. But society in Great Britain and America was quite different now. Individuals did what they thought was best for themselves, without a second thought about what was best for society. And yet, society was not falling apart. In fact, things were better than ever.

Smith wondered, could there be some "invisible hand" guiding everyone? Adam Smith spent many years wondering about the answer to this and other economic questions. In this unit you will learn the answers to some of the questions that once puzzled the old professor.

HOW WOULD YOU SPEND YOUR MONEY?

5A   In this activity, you will make decisions about how to spend money. These decisions will introduce you to two ideas in economics— scarcity and opportunity cost. Look for the following important words and phrases:

▶ Economics   ▶ Problem of Scarcity   ▶ Opportunity Cost

A ▶ symbol appears in the margin where the **word** or **phrase** is first explained.

Today must be your lucky day! You just opened the mail and found a birthday card from your favorite aunt and uncle. Inside the card is a gift of twenty dollars. Excitedly, you ask your mother, "What should I do with this money?" She says, "There are many things you could do." She suggests that you make a list of different ways of using or saving the money.

WHAT SHOULD YOU DO WITH THE MONEY?

On a separate sheet of paper, list five things you would do if you had an extra $20:

I Would Want:	It Would Cost:
1.	$
2.	$
3.	$
4.	$
5.	$

What you want to buy will be influenced by your personal tastes and values as well as by the prices that different things cost. If you are like most people, all of the things you want probably cost more than $20. You cannot have everything you want. You have to choose. Whenever you make choices about how to save or spend money, you are
▶ involved with the subject of **economics** (ē kə nom' ekz).

Definition

THE PROBLEM OF SCARCITY

People who study economics are known as **economists**. Economists believe that a central concern of economics is the "problem of scarcity." The **problem of scarcity** (skâr' ◄ si tē) involves two basic ideas:

❖ **People usually have unlimited wants.** There are many things you probably want. Once you had them all, you would most likely find new things that you wanted.

❖ **A society can produce only a limited number of things at any one time.** There is only a certain amount of available goods (*video games, clothes, etc.*). There is only a certain amount of available services (*car-washing, banking services, restaurants, etc.*).

The problem of scarcity exists because:

1. most people want an unlimited number of things; **AND**

2. society does not have enough resources to produce an unlimited amount of goods and services.

In other words, even with your birthday gift of $20, you probably want more things than your $20 could buy. Your scarce resources cannot satisfy your unlimited wants.

✔ CHECKING YOUR UNDERSTANDING ✔

Suppose every person in the world were given a million dollars a year. Do you think this would end the problem of scarcity? If yes, explain how. If no, explain why not.

Because of the problem of scarcity, economists say there is an **opportunity cost** ◄ to every economic decision. This "cost" is the opportunity you give up to do other things. For instance, pretend you have enough money to buy either a radio or a book. You decide to buy the radio. The "opportunity cost" of your radio is the book you might have bought instead. You got the radio at the "cost" of giving up the book.

✔ CHECKING YOUR UNDERSTANDING ✔

Have you made a recent economic decision that involved opportunity cost?

1. What were some of the things you were thinking of buying?
2. What did you finally decide to buy?
3. What was the opportunity cost (*what you gave up*) of your decision?

MAKING AN ECONOMIC DECISION

Now that you are familiar with the problem of scarcity, it is time for you to make a decision about what to buy with your $20. It is sometimes easier to make a decision by using a "decision model." This model will help you plan out your decision by breaking it down into steps. Here is how it is done:

STEP 1	STEP 2	STEP 3
Identify the Problem	1. 3. Create Criteria 2. 4. 1. 3. Create Criteria 2. 4. 1. 3. Create Criteria 2. 4.	**Make Your Decision**

STEP 1: Identify the Problem
Start by identifying the problem. In this case, you must decide how to spend your $20.

STEP 2: Create Criteria
Before you can solve the problem, you must establish criteria for making your decision. Criteria are standards for making a judgment about something. We use these standards to decide which solution is best. For example, in this problem you might consider the following criteria:

❖ **Cost.** What will an item cost? Is it more than you are willing to spend?

❖ **Satisfaction.** Will the item give you satisfaction?

❖ **Opportunity Cost.** If you buy this item, what other items have you given up the opportunity to buy?

❖ **Durability.** Will the item stand up to continued use?

STEP 3: Make Your Decision
Now, review some of the choices for your decision. Based on your criteria, how would you spend your $20? Share your answer with your classmates.

CONSUMERS AND PRODUCERS ◆ IN A FREE MARKET ECONOMY

Every society must answer three basic economic questions:

What should be produced?

How should it be produced?

Who should get what is produced?

How a society answers these three questions is known as its **economic system**. In some societies, the government decides the answers to these three basic economic questions. In other societies, the answers are based on tradition and custom.

The United States has a **free market system**. In such an economic system, producers and consumers decide how resources are used. A **producer** (prə d$\overline{oo}$' sr) is a person or business that supplies goods and services. For example, a farmer produces crops and a doctor provides medical services. **Production** (prə' duk shən) is the act of making or providing these goods and services

In the free market system the consumer is very important. **Consumers** (kən s$\overline{oo}$' mərz) are people of businesses that use goods and services to satisfy their needs and wants. For example, a consumer uses foods by eating them and clothes by wearing them. **Consumption** (kən sump' shən) is the act of using these goods and services.

In a free market, both producers and consumers determine what is made and who gets it. Producers make goods or provide services for consumers and decide the selling price. Consumers buy the goods and services they want from various producers.

Consumers influence what is produced by deciding whether or not to buy particular products. If no consumers want a product, after a while producers

A consumer shops for her family.
What makes someone a consumer?

will stop making it. If consumers like a product, manufacturers will make more of it. In this way consumers help influence what is produced in a free market economy.

EXPANDING YOUR UNDERSTANDING

Creating Vocabulary Cards

Economics
What is "economics"?
State the three basic economic
questions.

The Problem of Scarcity
What is the "problem of scarcity"?
Give an example of a time you
experienced the problem of scarcity.

Dealing with the Problem of Scarcity

Let's see how the problem of scarcity might affect your school. Imagine that the following is a list of problems facing your school:

Problems	Amount Needed to Fix the Problem
The school library needs additional books.	$3,000
New ovens are needed for the cafeteria.	$4,000
The school needs to buy new computers.	$6,000
The school needs a new roof.	$4,000

Your school has $10,000 in its budget. How would you spend this money? Identify which problems you would solve by spending the $10,000. Explain your economic decision.

Dealing with Opportunity Costs

Everything you buy means giving up something else you could have bought. Describe a situation in your life in which you dealt with the problem of scarcity and opportunity costs by using the decision-making grid below.

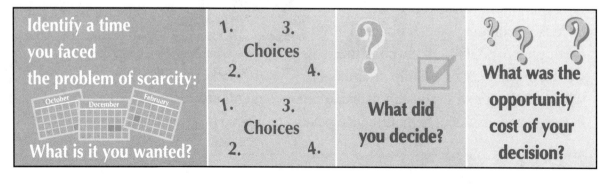

WOULD YOU START YOUR OWN BUSINESS?

5B In this activity, you will learn what it might be like to start your own business. Look for the following important words and phrases:

▶ Business   ▶ Goods and Services   ▶ Demand

▶ Factors of Production   ▶ Profit   ▶ Supply

We live in a society in which people are allowed to start their own businesses. A **business** (biz' nis) is any economic activity in which someone tries to make a profit. ◀ The ability to start a business is possible because America has a free market economy. Under this system anyone has the right to start a business.

If enough consumers buy the products of a business, the business can make a lot of money. No wonder that in 1995 almost nine million new businesses were started in the United States. What would it be like to be a young business owner? In this activity, you will have an opportunity to **imagine** what it's like to start your own business.

STARTING A BUSINESS

Every business begins with an idea. Your class should break up into small groups. Members of your group should think of some kind of work that you all would enjoy and be good at. What follows is a list of suggestions. Do not limit yourselves to the ideas on the list. Your group may have an even better idea for its own business.

❖ **Pet Care:** Caring for household pets: feeding, walking and washing pets.

❖ **T-Shirt Sales:** Selling T-shirts decorated with different designs.

❖ **Laundromat Service:** Helping with laundry loads to be washed and dried.

❖ **Arts and Crafts:** Making quilts, greeting cards or wooden figures.

❖ **Notebook Covers:** Making notebook covers with your own designs.

❖ **Lawn Service:** Mowing and raking lawns.

❖ **Other (Your Group's Idea):** _____?_____

This student earns money by mowing lawns.
What business are you thinking about?

Now it's time for your group to make a decision. Which business would your group members like to try?

> Our business will be _____?_____ because we like _____?_____.

GETTING INFORMATION AND ADVICE

Before starting a business, it is helpful to get some advice from other people. Members of each group should talk with their parents or guardians. You may also wish to invite a businessperson from your community to speak to the class. Explain that you want to know the advantages and disadvantages of starting a business. Make a list of their suggestions.

Advantages	Disadvantages
1.	1.
2.	2.
3.	3.
4.	4.

THE FACTORS OF PRODUCTION

Any person about to start a business must consider the factors of production. The ▶ **factors of production** are all the things needed to produce goods and services. **Goods** ▶ are those items people make, such as toys, foods and cars. **Services** are things that people do or provide for others. For example, electricians, teachers and plumbers are people who provide services.

There are four factors of production: **C**apital equipment, **E**ntrepreneurship, **L**and (*natural resources*), and **L**abor (*human capital*). A useful mnemonic to help you remember the factors of production might be C-E-L-L .

LAND (NATURAL RESOURCES)
Economists use the term "**land**" to mean the resources found in nature. These natural resources include metals, minerals, water, plants and soil.

CAPITAL EQUIPMENT
Capital equipment consists of those things used to make other goods or to perform services. For example, machines and tools are capital equipment.

THE FACTORS OF PRODUCTION

A house under construction.
What factors of production can you identify?

LABOR (HUMAN CAPITAL)
Labor, sometimes called human capital, is the work people do to produce goods or provide services. Labor includes the skills and knowledge of the people who make things and provide services.

ENTREPRENEURSHIP
Land, labor and capital equipment must be combined in an organized manner to make something. People who bring these three factors of production together are called **entrepreneurs** (ön trə prə nûrz').

Your Task

FINDING OUT IF THERE WILL BE A PROFIT

Starting a business takes money to buy raw materials (*land*), tools and equipment (*capital equipment*). Sometimes you may need money to hire other workers (*human capital*). Think about the factors of production and how you will supply each one.

After considering the factors of production, your group should think about how much money it will need to start its new business. Use the chart on the next page to estimate (*approximate*) what the costs might be during your first month of business (*on the left side of the chart*). Then figure out how much money your group might earn from selling your product or service (*on the right side of the chart*). The amount of money left over after you have paid all your bills is your **profit**. ◀

Our First Month of Business

Estimate of Monthly Costs		Estimate of Monthly Income	
A. Cost of materials:	?	Selling price of the good or service:	?
B. Cost of advertising:	?		
C. Other:	?		
(add A, B, C, for monthly costs)		Number of goods or services you think you can sell each month: ?	
		Multiply selling price by number of items sold.	
These are your monthly costs:	?	This is your monthly income:	?

Subtract your monthly costs (*left column*) from your monthly income (*right column*):

Total Monthly Income: $?
− (minus) Monthly Costs: $?
Monthly Profit or Loss: $?

MAKING A DECISION

You and the members of your group now have some idea of what you will need, as well as the risks of starting your own business. If your monthly costs amount to more than your monthly income, then your group will have a loss. Obviously, if your group loses money for too long, you will go out of business. Based on what you have learned in this activity, do you think you would like to start your own business? Explain your answer.

SUPPLY AND DEMAND IN A FREE MARKET ECONOMY

In a free market economy, the basic economic questions are answered by consumers and producers. Producers decide what they will make for sale. Consumers choose what they will buy. The amount of a product that consumers are willing to buy is known as the **demand** for a product.

THINK ABOUT IT

Fewer people will buy a pair of shoes costing $150 than a pair for $30. Why are consumers willing to buy more of a product if it costs less? Explain.

Producers determine the supply of a product. How much of the product is made and is available for consumers to buy is known as the **supply** of a product.

THINK ABOUT IT

Producers are willing to make more pairs of shoes if they can sell them for $150 a pair than for $30 a pair. Can you explain why?

Through their buying decisions, consumers determine which products will sell. This influences what producers are willing to make available. What consumers want to buy and what producers will sell determines what is produced. Here is how these two interact in a free market economy:

❖ If consumers are willing to pay more for a product, then producers will make more of it. This is because producers want to increase the amount of profit they can earn.

❖ If consumers are unwilling to pay as much for a product, then producers have to lower their prices in order to keep selling the product.

❖ If producers raise their prices, not as many consumers will be willing to buy the product.

These women are shopping for pumpkins in the fall.
Why do pumpkins often cost more just before Halloween?

EXPANDING YOUR UNDERSTANDING

Creating Vocabulary Cards

Factors of Production
What is a "factor of production"?
List the four factors of production.

Goods and Services
What is a "good"?
What is a "service"?
Provide an example of each.

Learning about Business Organizations in Your Community

In this activity, you learned about starting a business. There are several ways to organize a business:

- ❖ A **single-ownership** business has only one owner. The owner is responsible for running the business. All final decisions are made by the owner. The owner receives all the profits of the business, but is also personally responsible for all of the **debts** (*money owed*) of the business.

- ❖ A **partnership** is a business owned by two or more people. Each partner is an owner. Responsibilities are shared. Since the partners share the risks, they also share the profits. However, each partner is personally responsible for the debts of the business.

- ❖ A **corporation** is a company formed under the laws of a state. People who invest in a corporation are called **stockholders**. Stockholders give money to the corporation. In return, they receive shares or stock, which represent ownership of a part of the company. Stockholders are not personally responsible for the corporation's debts. The most they can lose is the money they have invested.

How are the businesses in your community organized? Name **two** examples of a single-ownership business, partnership and corporation located in your community.

Interviewing a Local Businessperson

Pretend you and a classmate are hired as reporters. Your first assignment is to interview and write a news article about a businessperson in your community. Family members may suggest someone to interview. **Before** the interview, get your parent's permission to meet with the person. Use what you learned in this activity as the basis for some of your questions. For example, you might want to discuss how that person's business is organized.

Skill Builder

WRITING A NEWS ARTICLE

Next, turn the results of your interview into a news article. Let's begin by looking at some of the steps involved in writing a news article.

❖ A news reporter always writes an article in the "third person." This means using "he" or "she" rather than "I." Do not take sides. Remember, you are reporting the news, not writing your opinion about it.

❖ Your article should have a headline to catch the reader's attention. For example, "New Store to Open in Main Street Mall."

❖ The article's first paragraph is known as the "lead." It gives readers an idea of what the article is about. The rest of the article spells out the details. The first paragraph is written so readers can learn the basic information quickly. Then, if they wish, they can continue reading the article to learn more details. The lead should be interesting, so that your reader will want to find out more. For example:

> To most people, Jones' Pharmacy on Main Street is just another store. Not so to Mark Jones, the man in the white coat behind the counter. As a pharmacist, his job is sometimes filled with excitement. Mr. Jones recalled how one day he saved the life of a young child by …

❖ A newspaper article reports facts to its readers. After reading your article, a person should know the answers to certain basic questions:

- **Who** was involved?
- **What** happened?
- **Where** did it happen?
- **When** did it happen?
- **Why** did it happen?

❖ Like all good writing, preparing a news article requires careful work. First, a reporter uses reference tools to develop knowledge about the topic of the article. Then the reporter visits the place or interviews the people involved.

❖ A good article requires careful editing. You and your partner should divide the work. Each one should write one section of the article. Later, each of you should review your partner's work, make suggestions and correct errors as needed.

When your article has been completed, compare it with those of your classmates. Then put all the articles together in a class newspaper about some of the interesting businesspeople working in your community.

WHAT JOB WOULD YOU LIKE WHEN YOU GROW UP?

5C In this activity, you will learn about some of the major types of jobs available to you when you grow up. Look for the following important words and phrases:

▶ Occupations   ▶ Manufacturing   ▶ Technology
▶ Agriculture   ▶ Service Industries   ▶ Retail Sales

If you are like most Americans, you will spend more than 80,000 hours of your life at work. Selecting your job will therefore be one of the most important decisions you make in your life. Which job do you think you would like to have? Before you answer, let's
▶ look at some of the **occupations** (*jobs*) available to you when you reach adulthood. In general, there are three types of occupations:

Using the land   **Making things**   **Providing services**

USING THE LAND

Farming, fishing and mining are occupations that use the land.

FARMING

Farmers are people involved in
▶ **agriculture** (*growing crops*). To grow crops, farmers use fertilizers that add minerals and other nutrients to the soil. Farming is an important occupation in Michigan. Farmland occupies one-third of the state's land surface. Over fifty thousand families live on farms in Michigan.

A farm in the Lower Peninsula.
What crops are grown on Michigan's farms?

Most of the state's farms are in the Lower Peninsula, where the soil and climate are more favorable for farming.

Most of Michigan is located in our nation's hay-and-dairy belt. Corn, wheat, soybeans, sugar beets, potatoes and hay are the state's leading crops. Along Lake Michigan, in the Lower Peninsula, the land is especially good for growing apples, blueberries, cantaloupes, cherries, grapes, peaches, pears, plums and strawberries.

Many farmers also raise **livestock** (*farm animals*), such as cattle, sheep and hogs. More than forty percent of farm income in Michigan comes from selling animals and animal products. In 1996, cattle and hogs raised in Michigan numbered over a million each. Milk is the state's leading farm product. Dairy farming is especially important throughout the Lower Peninsula.

Turkeys, chickens, ducks and geese are raised in Michigan.

MINING

Miners dig or drill deep holes into the ground to find minerals such as coal or copper. Mining has always played an important part in the state's economy. Petroleum, natural gas, peat and salt mines provide important minerals for Michigan's chemical industries. Michigan also has large deposits of sand and gravel, which are used for construction and road building. At one time, the Upper Peninsula led the nation in the production of copper and iron ore. Today, because these deposits are so deep, it is expensive to mine these minerals in Michigan.

Aerial view of the Empire Iron Mine.
What other items are mined in Michigan besides iron?

FISHING

People catch fish in rivers, lakes and oceans. In Michigan, most fish are caught in the Great Lakes. Other fish in Michigan are raised in hatcheries. Each year, tons of fish are taken from Michigan's rivers and lakes. Whitefish, chubs, lake herring, lake trout, salmon and yellow perch are among the most important varieties of fish caught in Michigan.

✔ CHECKING YOUR UNDERSTANDING ✔

1. What fruits are grown in Michigan?
2. What other crops are grown in Michigan?
3. What types of livestock are raised in Michigan?
4. What minerals are mined in Michigan?
5. How does the geography of Michigan have an impact on the kinds of jobs available?
6. Would any of these jobs interest you?

MAKING THINGS

▶ Many people work at making things. Economists call this **manufacturing** or **industry**. Most people with jobs in industry work in factories. **Factories** are buildings in which goods are made.

Michigan is the nation's sixth leading industrial state. Over 2,200 products bear the label, "Made in Michigan." Automobiles, other transportation equipment, machinery, plastics and office furniture are some of the goods manufactured in Michigan. The state has a central location, large forests, many mineral resources, excellent transportation facilities and a plentiful supply of water

Assembly line in a Ford factory.
What other goods are manufactured in Michigan?

power. The state is also fortunate in that several early leaders in the auto industry, like **Ransom Olds** and **Henry Ford**, were Michiganders. They helped make Michigan the center of our nation's automobile industry.

The state's leading industry today is still the manufacture of automobiles. One out of every four workers in the state is employed in the automobile industry. Many other industries have also developed to meet the needs of automobile manufacturers. For example, metal stamping, tool making, iron and steel production, the manufacture of auto upholstery, and the production of electrical equipment and machinery are important Michigan industries.

Most manufacturing jobs are found in three areas in the southern part of the state:

❖ The **Detroit metropolitan area** is the state's leading industrial center. Automobiles, machinery, metal products, steel, chemicals and medical drugs are made here.

❖ The **Lansing-Grand Rapids-Muskegon area** manufactures automobiles, furniture, household appliances and engines.

❖ The **Kalamazoo-Battle Creek-Jackson area** is known for food processing, paper goods, medical drugs and auto parts.

View of Detroit.
What things are manufactured in Detroit?

In addition to these areas, Saginaw is known for its foundries (*places where metal products are made*) and machine shops. The shipbuilding industry is mainly found in Bay City, Port Huron and Wyandotte. Muskegon is a leading center for sporting goods. One of the nation's largest makers of bowling alley equipment has its plant there.

✔ CHECKING YOUR UNDERSTANDING ✔

1. What types of goods are manufactured in Michigan?
2. What geographic factors helped Michigan become a major manufacturing center?
3. Which cities in Michigan are industrial centers?
4. Would any of these jobs interest you?

PROVIDING SERVICES

Today, many Michiganders work at jobs that do not make goods. Instead, they work in **service industries**. People in these jobs do something for others. Service industries ◀ account for two out of every three dollars earned in Michigan. Service industries are found mostly in Michigan's major metropolitan areas—especially Detroit.

TECHNOLOGY

Many service-directed jobs are related to the development of **technology**. These jobs ◀ deal with the research and development of new products. Engineering and research companies in Michigan receive a large part of their business from the automobile industry.

TRANSPORTATION

People who move goods from one place to another provide the service of **transportation**. Detroit serves as the nation's main entrance for Canadian goods. As a result, Detroit is Michigan's largest and busiest port. Detroit also has one of the nation's most active airports. Ships from Michigan ports carry large cargoes of goods throughout the Great Lakes region. The Soo Locks are among the busiest ship canals in the world.

View of overpasses and underpasses.
Why are modern highways important to Michigan's economy?

Early in the state's history, people mainly traveled by water. The first highway in Michigan was built in the 1820s. In 1908, Michigan became the first state to build a concrete highway. Today, thousands of jobs are tied to the state's 120,000 miles of roads. Michigan's highways are used by cars and trucks transporting goods across the United States and Canada.

FINANCE

Michigan's financial industry employs thousands of people in banks, insurance companies and real estate firms. Many of the nation's leading banks are located in Detroit. Banks play a key role in lending money to businesses. The state's insurance industry is concentrated in Detroit and Lansing. Jackson National Life Insurance, one of the nation's largest insurance companies, has its headquarters in Lansing.

COMMUNICATIONS

Established in 1817, the *Detroit Gazette* was Michigan's first regularly published newspaper. Today, the state's largest newspaper is the Detroit *Free Press*. There are another 40 daily and 325 weekly and semi-weekly newspapers published in Michigan. WWJ, Michigan's first television station, has been in operation since 1947. At present, there are 50 television stations and 370 radio stations around the state.

TOURISM

Tourism is a seventeen-billion dollar industry in Michigan. Over nine million tourists visit Michigan each year. The state is sometimes called a "Water Wonderland" because of its many lakes and rivers. Conventions and business shows attract other visitors to Michigan. With 3,000 hotels, motels, camps and trailer parks, the state's tourism industry employs thousands of people. These people work in souvenir shops, restaurants, hotels and motels.

Summer at the beach in Marquette.   Winter snowmobile races in Mackinaw City.
Summer or winter, millions of tourists flock to Michigan.

RETAIL AND PERSONAL SERVICES

Another type of service industry is **retail sales** . This service is provided by those ◀
who buy goods in large amounts and resell them locally. This is what a department store
or grocery store does. Other people serve us by providing information, teaching us,
cleaning our clothes, cooking and serving our food, and taking care of our health. Doctors, lawyers, grocery store cashiers, teachers, nurses, telephone operators, waiters and
hairdressers all provide us with services.

GOVERNMENT

Government employment is also a service industry. Government jobs include the operation of public schools, public hospitals and military establishments. The public school
system is one of the leading government employers. Federal and state governments have
major branch offices in Detroit and Lansing.

✔ CHECKING YOUR UNDERSTANDING ✔

1. What types of service jobs exist in Michigan?
2. What needs are met by banks and other financial institutions?
3. Why is tourism important to Michigan?
4. Would any of these jobs interest you?

Closing

MAKING A DECISION

Now that you have had a chance to look at the many types of occupations, it's time to
come to a decision. Which job do you think you would most like to have? Why?

EXPANDING YOUR UNDERSTANDING

Creating Vocabulary Cards

Occupations
What is an "occupation"?
What occupations will be open to
you as an adult?

Manufacturing
What does "manufacturing" mean?
What are some Michigan businesses
involved in manufacturing?

Interpreting a Pie Chart about Occupations

MICHIGAN'S NON-FARM OCCUPATIONS, 1994

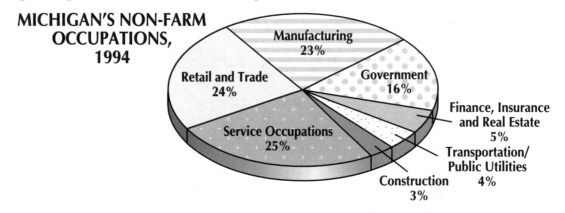

- Manufacturing 23%
- Government 16%
- Finance, Insurance and Real Estate 5%
- Transportation/Public Utilities 4%
- Construction 3%
- Service Occupations 25%
- Retail and Trade 24%

✔ CHECKING YOUR UNDERSTANDING ✔

Use the information in the pie chart to answer the following questions.

1. What is the title of the pie chart?
2. What percentage of Michigan non-farm workers were government workers in 1994?
3. In which type of occupation were the most Michiganders employed?
4. In which type of non-farm occupation were the fewest Michiganders employed?
5. In the years to come, which job sector do you think will grow the fastest?

A police officer is a government employee.
Do you have friends or relatives who are government employees?

HOW WOULD YOU PROMOTE THE ECONOMY OF MICHIGAN?

5D In this activity, you will look at Michigan's many important resources. Then you will design a campaign to persuade foreign businesses to locate in your state. Look for the following important words and phrases:

▶ Investments   ▶ Product Map   ▶ Minerals

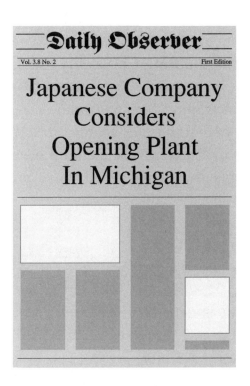

THE IMPORTANCE OF NEW BUSINESSES TO MICHIGAN

You may have noticed headlines such as those above in your local newspaper. Like other states, Michigan tries to attract foreign companies and new businesses to the state. **Investments** (*such as building a factory or relocating a business to Michigan*) can ◀ mean more tax dollars for state government and more jobs for state residents. The growth of new jobs is very important to the future health of the state's economy.

Many factors attract investors to a state. One key factor is the availability of an educated and skilled workforce. Michigan ranks high among states in the number of children enrolled in public schools. Michigan's public school system has more than $1\frac{1}{2}$ million students: they attend over 3,600 elementary, junior and senior high schools.

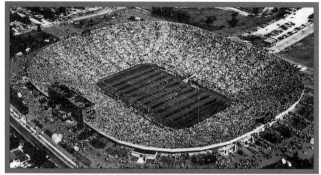

Stadium of the University of Michigan.
In which city is its main campus located?

The state also has an excellent state-supported university system. Michigan has 13 four-year state universities and 29 two-year colleges.

Michigan State University in East Lansing is one of the largest single-campus colleges in the nation. The **University of Michigan** is one of the nation's finest colleges. Its main campus is in Ann Arbor.

Another important factor attracting investments is the abundance of natural resources. These include plentiful water, the land used to grow food, and the minerals and plants used to make many other products.

You already know that maps can be used to provide different kinds of information. The map to the right is called a product map. Look at the map carefully. Then read the following Skill Builder to help you interpret the map.

INTERPRETING A PRODUCT MAP

A **product map** is a type of theme map. This one shows the boundaries of Michigan and identifies where various state products are made. On a product map, picture symbols are used to stand for agricultural and mineral products.

Based on the map, complete the following:

❖ List **three** crops grown in Michigan.

❖ Name **two** animals raised in Michigan.

❖ Locate **two** places where minerals are found in Michigan.

The **legend** explains what each symbol represents. For example, each area in Michigan that grows corn is shown on the map with a small ear of corn 🌽.

Answer the following questions:

❖ What does the 🏭 represent?

❖ What does the 🐄 represent?

❖ Name a city located close to where fruit is grown.

❖ What symbol is used for manufacturing?

CREATING AN ECONOMIC PROFILE OF MICHIGAN

The Governor of Michigan has many responsibilities. One of the most important of these is to promote the state's economy. Imagine that the Governor has called on your class to design a series of advertisements to attract companies to Michigan.

Your teacher decides to divide the class into small groups to develop these advertisements. Each group will be responsible for creating an advertisement. Remember, the focus of your advertisement should be on attracting companies from around the nation and the world to settle in Michigan.

Before your group can begin, you will need to gather information about the economy and resources of Michigan. Members of your group should use an almanac, encyclopedia or the Internet to conduct your research. Use the information on the next page to guide your research. The information you find can then serve as the basis for creating your advertisement.

Information Sheet About Michigan

I. The Geography and People of Michigan

Total Area: _____   Acres of Forest Land: _____

Climate: _____

Major Geographic Features: _____

Population: _____   Rank in Population: _____

Population Density: (*see page 65*) _____

II. The Economy of Michigan

Major Natural Resources: _____

Major Industries: _____

Chief Agricultural Crops: _____

Major Ports: _____

Average Household Income: _____

Unemployment Rate: _____

III. Other Information about Michigan

State Taxes: _____

Major Tourist Attractions: _____

Famous People Born in Michigan: _____

Any Other Information about Michigan: _____

The following section provides an overview of some of the information you will need.

THE NATURAL RESOURCES OF MICHIGAN

In the 1830s, Michigan was given the Upper Peninsula by Congress. Many Michiganders complained that the land was worthless. In fact, this area has proven to be a treasure chest of natural resources.

FORESTS

One of Michigan's most valuable natural resources is its forests. At one time, forests covered almost the entire state. As settlers arrived, forests were cut down to prepare the land for agriculture. In the 1840s, large-scale cutting of the forests for lumber began. Lumbering became Michigan's most important industry. At one time, over 100,000 lumberjacks worked in the state's forests.

By 1900, many of Michigan's forests were gone—either cut down by lumberjacks or destroyed by forest fires. The state legislature then passed new laws to rebuild Michigan's forests. A seedling had to be planted for every tree that was cut down. Look-out stations were constructed to allow forest rangers to watch for forest fires. This program was so successful that today over half of Michigan is again covered by forest land. In

These Plantation Pines were planted as part of a conservation program to replace cut trees.

the north, white pine and birch trees are now found. In the south, oak, maple and hickory are the main types of trees.

Forests continue to play a key role in the economy of the state. They provide valuable recreational areas. The forests also support a key state industry: furniture making. Furniture making developed because of the availability of lumber from trees.

Some trees are used to make **pulpwood**. Trees are cut down and trucked to paper mills where they are washed and chopped into tiny pieces. The resulting pulpwood is used to make products such as writing paper, cardboard and paper bags.

Michigan is also the nation's largest grower of Christmas trees. The state ships more than 4 million of them each holiday season.

Logs being readied at a pulpwood plant.
What is pulpwood used to make?

✔ CHECKING YOUR UNDERSTANDING ✔

1. Why are forests important to Michigan's economy?
2. Why were new state laws needed to rebuild Michigan's forests?
3. List some products in your home that might have come from the state's forests.
4. What kinds of trees can you find growing in Michigan?

MINERALS

▶ A **mineral** is a substance found in the earth. Large deposits of iron ore and copper are found in Michigan's Upper Peninsula. Three ranges contain iron ore: the Gogebic, Menominee and Marquette. In 1969, an oil and natural gas field was discovered in the northern part of the Lower Peninsula. There are now 6,000 active oil and gas wells operating in Michigan. Oil and gas have become the state's most important mineral resource. Most of the state's electric power is coal-produced

The Palisades Nuclear Plant.
What does a nuclear plant produce?

electricity. Five nuclear power plants help supply the state's electric power needs.

Other minerals found in the Lower Peninsula include salt, limestone, gypsum, sand and gravel. Almost one-third of the nation's salt deposits are found in Michigan. Salt is used by the state's chemical industry. Gypsum is used to make plasterboard. Limestone is used for blast furnaces, in chemicals and in the production of cement. Michigan is also a major producer of cement, a major ingredient in concrete.

FAMOUS PLACES: THE TILDEN MINE

At one time Michigan had many iron mines. Today, most of the iron ore is too far below ground to be profitably mined. The Tilden mine, near Marquette, employs 850 workers, metallurgists and engineers. At the mine, small particles of iron are separated from powdered rock and

Some of the equipment used at the Tilden mine.

made into pellets. Groups visiting the mine can see how it operates. The mine is now more than 500 feet deep.

✔ CHECKING YOUR UNDERSTANDING ✔

1. Why are minerals important to Michigan's economy?
2. List some products in your home made from Michigan's minerals.

WATER

Michigan is surrounded by water. It is one of Michigan's most important resources. There are 11,000 lakes throughout the state. They attract many tourists. Michigan's drinking water is considered among the best in the nation. However, water pollution caused by industrialization and a growing population has become a serious problem. For example, Michigan's industries produce 900 pounds of waste per person in Michigan, per year! Unfortunately, some industries dump their waste products into Michigan's rivers.

A ride on board the Meamont Belle on one of Michigan's 11,000 lakes.
Which lake do you live near?

✔ CHECKING YOUR UNDERSTANDING ✔

1. Why is water important to Michigan's economy?
2. Why is water in Michigan facing a threat?

SOIL

Farmland covers about one-third of the state. The southern part of the Lower Peninsula has the state's richest soils. These soils are well-suited to agriculture. Michigan's main agricultural crops are corn, beans, vegetables, potatoes and fruits.

The state also produces some unusual crops. Michigan is one of the few states to grow mint. It is the largest producer of peppermint and spearmint in the nation. The Upper Peninsula has a variety of soils. Some are very fertile, while others are unfit for agriculture.

A farm in the Lower Peninsula.
Can you tell what is being grown here?

✔ CHECKING YOUR UNDERSTANDING ✔

1. Where can the best soil in Michigan be found?
2. List some of the agricultural products in your home that may have been grown in Michigan.

DESIGNING YOUR ADVERTISING CAMPAIGN FOR MICHIGAN

Closing

On a separate sheet of paper, your group should create an advertisement. Think about what information would make Michigan most appealing. Your goal is to attract businesses to your state. Remember:

❖ Artistic talent is **not** important in designing the advertisement.

❖ Creating an interesting advertisement is essential.

❖ Search magazines and newspapers for pictures to use in your advertisement.

❖ Members of your group may want to ask their parents for help. Parents may suggest ideas or help take photographs for use in the advertising campaign.

EXPANDING YOUR UNDERSTANDING

Creating Vocabulary Cards

Investments
What are "investments"?
How do investments help
Michigan?

Minerals
What are "minerals"?
Name three minerals found in
Michigan.

Creating an Economic Map of Community Businesses

Your neighborhood may have an industrial park where factories are located. It may also have a mall where people shop. Create an economic map of your community. If your community has any of the following show where they are located:

❖ shopping malls   ❖ industrial parks

❖ farms   ❖ new businesses

❖ banks   ❖ office buildings

Greektown in Detroit is filled with shops and restaurants.
What items will your economic map include?

HOW INTERDEPENDENT ARE WE WITH FOREIGN COUNTRIES?

5E In this activity, you will learn how people in different countries have become economically interdependent (*dependent on each other*). Look for the following important words:

▶ Interdependent   ▶ Exports   ▶ Imports   ▶ Hypothesis

Technologies like the telephone, fax, television, jet plane and computer are said to be "shrinking" our world. Of course, the world isn't actually getting smaller. It just seems that way. Because of these new technologies, people have more contact with distant places than they did in earlier times.

THE WORLD'S GROWING INTERDEPENDENCE

Increased contact has made people around the world much more interdependent. Nations are **interdependent** (in tər di pen' dənt) when they depend on trade with other nations for goods and services. For example, many American jobs depend on exports.

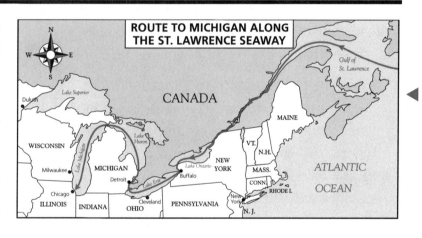

Exports are goods and services made in one country and sold in another country. ◀ Trade with foreign countries is important to Michigan's economic health. Michigan's location in the heart of the Great Lakes region has played a key role in its economic development.

The Detroit River is one of the world's busiest ship thoroughfares. Ships from Michigan carry minerals, grains and manufactured goods through the **Great Lakes-St. Lawrence Seaway** system to other ports and foreign countries. In 1962, an **International Bridge** was completed across the St. Mary's River at Sault Ste. Marie to Canada. The bridge has helped increase trade between Michigan and Canada. Michigan is also linked to Canada by other bridges and a tunnel that runs from Detroit to Windsor.

▶ The United States also depends on imports. **Imports** are products from other countries brought into a country for sale. Other countries equally depend on importing products from America and exporting products to us.

THINK ABOUT IT

1. How has global interdependence affected your life?

2. How many goods in your home do you think came from foreign countries?

❑ less than half   ❑ about half   ❑ more than half

▶ At this point, your answer is only a hypothesis. A **hypothesis** (hi poth' i sis) is an educated guess. It may or may not turn out to be correct. In this activity, you will find out if you guessed correctly by taking an inventory of items in your home.

Your Task | TAKING A HOME INVENTORY

With the help of your parent or guardian, examine the contents of any two rooms of your home.

❖ You will find many things that have the name of their **country of origin** (*country where they came from*) stamped somewhere on them. For example, in the kitchen you might find a can of coffee. Look closely at its label. You will see that it probably says it came from Brazil or Colombia. If you cannot identify where an object came from, move to another item.

❖ If an object is made in the United States, include it on your list. You are not just looking for goods made in foreign countries, but also those made in America. If an item has been partly made in two countries, list the names of both countries (Example: USA / Spain).

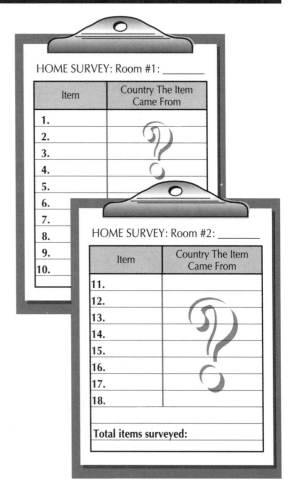

FINDING THE PERCENTAGE OF IMPORTED PRODUCTS

Make a separate list of all the countries on your chart. Next to each country, write the number of items you found from that country in your two rooms. Turn that number into a fraction. Here is how it's done: divide the number of items from each country by the total number of items in your survey. For example, if you found:

$$\frac{3 \text{ items from Brazil}}{20 \text{ is the total number of items}} = \frac{3}{20}$$

In this case, three out of twenty items came from Brazil. You may have studied percentages in your mathematics lessons. A **percentage** is a fraction with a denominator of 100. Here, 15 percent of the items came from Brazil. Percentages make it easier to compare different fractions.

You can turn each fraction into a percent by using your calculator. First, divide the **numerator** (*top number of the fraction*) by the **denominator** (*bottom number of the fraction*). This turns the fraction into a decimal. Now you can change the decimal into a percentage by moving the decimal two places to the right and adding a percentage sign (%). This method will show you the percentage of products in the two rooms that were made in the United States. It will also show you the percentage of products from other countries. Use the following chart to keep track of your calculations.

Country	Number of Products	Fraction	Decimal	Percent
1.				
2.				
3.				
4.				
5.				

THINK ABOUT IT

1. Was the percentage of products from the United States greater than half (*over 50%*)?
2. Which country, other than the United States, supplied the most products in your survey?

MAPPING THE COUNTRIES OF ORIGIN

Find an atlas in your school or public library. Use it to locate each country on your home inventory chart. Make a copy of the map below. Then list the items around the outside margin of the map. Finally, draw a line from each item to the location of its country of origin. For example, if one item in your inventory was coffee, write the word "coffee" in the margin of your map. Then draw a line from that word to its country of origin—probably Brazil or Colombia. To help you locate the countries in your survey, team up with a partner from your class. You and your partner can work together finding the countries on each of your charts.

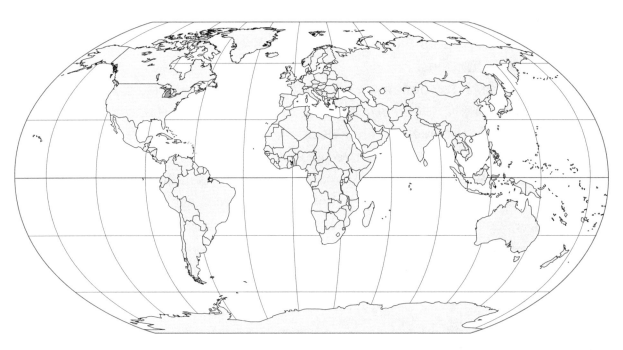

WAS YOUR HYPOTHESIS CORRECT?

Now that you have taken your home inventory, it's time to see if your original hypothesis was correct.

1. How many items in your inventory came from foreign countries?
2. How accurate was the original hypothesis you made when you began this activity?
3. Were you surprised by the results of your inventory? ☐ **Yes** ☐ **No** If so, how? If not, why not?
4. What conclusions about global interdependence can you draw from the results of your inventory and those of your classmates?

EXPANDING YOUR UNDERSTANDING

Exports	Imports
What is an "export"?	*What is an "import"?*
Name a product that is exported from the United States.	*Name a product that is imported into the United States.*

Finding Out About Our Major Trading Partners ———————

In this activity, you learned about economic interdependence. With which foreign nations does the United States trade the most? What goods does our country most often export? What things do Americans most often import? Use an almanac to find the following information:

MAJOR TRADING PARTNERS OF THE UNITED STATES

1. Which nations do we export the most goods to, in terms of dollar value?
2. Which nations do we import the most goods from, in terms of dollar value?
3. What kinds of products do we sell the most to other nations?
4. What kinds of products do we buy the most from other nations?

FAMOUS PLACES: THE SOO LOCKS

St. Mary's River connects Lake Superior to Lake Huron, which in turn connects with lower lakes. However, Lake Superior is 21 feet higher than Lake Huron. As a result, large ships could not pass between the two lakes. This problem was solved in 1855, when the Soo Locks were built at Sault Ste. Marie. The canal's locks raise or lower the water level so that ships can pass between Lake Superior and Lake Huron. Today, the Soo Locks are among the busiest ship canals in the world. Twelve thousand ships a year travel through its four locks.

A ship passes through the Soo Locks.

SUMMARIZING YOUR UNDERSTANDING

Directions: Use your knowledge to complete the following graphic organizers.

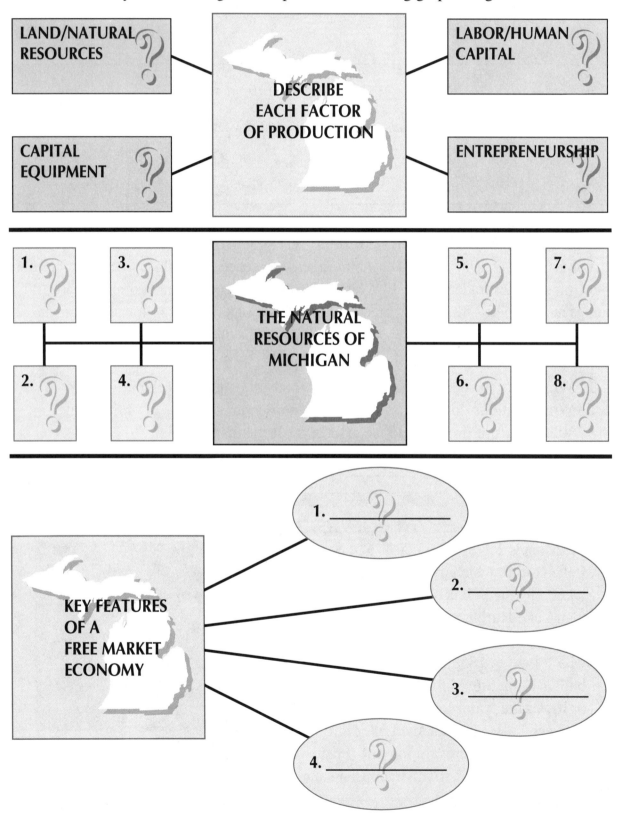

GOVERNMENT

President Bill Clinton.

City Hall in Bay City.

Lansing mounted police.

Every society has some kind of government. A democratic government provides a way for people to cooperate. People work together through the government to make new laws or to change laws they believe are unfair. A government also has a system to punish people who break the laws. In this unit, you will find out how governments are organized. You will also learn some of the main features of your local, state and national governments.

A YOUNG AUTHOR STRUGGLES
THROUGH THE NIGHT

homas Jefferson, a tall, red-haired Virginian, sat alone at his desk. Candles lit up the large, spacious room. It was a hot Philadelphia night in July 1776, and the sweat rolled from his brow.

Thomas thought about the exciting events of the past few years. He remembered the taxes that the English Parliament had forced on the American colonists. The Americans were not allowed to vote on whether these taxes were fair. Then Thomas thought about his own role in leading the young representatives in the colonial assembly of Virginia to protest against these unfair policies. The problems with England had quickly led to war.

Thomas had been one of Virginia's representatives to the Continental Congress in Philadelphia. George Washington, another Virginian, was appointed to lead the Continental Army. But the English had sent thousands of well-trained troops to fight the colonists. Thomas thought it would be hard for the colonists to defeat such a well-trained army. Perhaps he and the other members of the Continental Congress would be hanged as traitors if the colonists lost.

The Continental Congress knew that it needed the support of most colonists in order to win the war. A few key members of the Congress had formed a committee to write a public announcement. The announcement would explain to the colonists and to others around the world why the American colonies should declare independence from England. The other members of the committee were older and more experienced than Thomas. But they thought that he would do the best job in writing the declaration. Now it was all up to him.

Thomas Jefferson

Thomas was only 33 years old. He was an experienced writer and lawyer. However, a very difficult job lay ahead of him. Could he write something so powerful that it would inspire his fellow countrymen to support independence? Could he also convince the French to enter the war on the side of the Americans, against the English?

Thomas paced back and forth between the fireplace and the open windows of his parlor room. Again and again he wondered: What should he say in the declaration? What could he write that would inspire others to risk their lives for independence?

Thomas' thoughts went back to his days at college and to Dr. William Small, his favorite teacher. Dr. Small had often talked about the different types of governments. He had also discussed other people's views about which type of government was the best.

In recalling these ideas, many new questions entered Thomas' mind. What did the future hold for the American colonists? Would each colony break away and become a separate and independent country? Or would each of the colonies be willing to give up some power and unite together into a single country? What kind of government should they set up? Should they become a *democracy*—a government in which people choose their own government officials? Could such a system of government work in a new and inexperienced nation?

Thomas put down his feather pen on the desk and stared blankly out the window. A cool breeze entered the room. He was filled with conflicting emotions. He felt both fear and hope as he thought about the future.

What should he write in this declaration? What could he say to make things easier for his countrymen in the difficult years ahead? As you read through this unit, you will learn the answers to many of the questions about the American system of government that raced through the mind of Thomas Jefferson over two hundred years ago.

WHAT RULES WOULD YOU MAKE FOR YOUR CLASS?

6A In this activity, you will learn how governments work by writing a set of rules for your class. Look for the following important words:

▶ Rule   ▶ Government   ▶ Law

A ▶ symbol appears in the margin where the **word** is first explained.

People are social beings. They need to live with other people in groups or communities.
▶ A community protects its members by developing rules of behavior. A **rule** tells people what they can and cannot do. With rules, we know how to behave and how we can expect others to behave. Can you imagine what life would be like if there were no rules?

LAWS AND PENALTIES

▶ A **government** (guv' ərn mənt) is the organization that makes a community's rules,
▶ settles its disputes and protects its members from others who may be hostile. A **law** is a rule made by the government. Laws help guide our lives and help citizens avoid disagreements and conflicts. Once a law is made, there is a **penalty** (*punishment or consequence*) for breaking it. For example, a law may state that cars must stop if a traffic light is red. If a car does not stop at a red light, the driver has broken the law. The penalty for breaking this law is usually that the driver pays a fine.

✔ CHECKING YOUR UNDERSTANDING ✔

Can you identify a law that tells us something we **cannot** do? What is the penalty for breaking that law?

MAKING RULES FOR YOUR CLASS

Imagine it is the first day of school. Your teacher begins by talking about the rules of behavior for the class. Your teacher announces that the class will make up these rules. The class must keep in mind that the rules should protect the rights of all class members. The rules should allow class members to do their work without being distracted.

As an example, your teacher suggests the following rule about class discussions: *only one student may speak at a time*. The teacher recommends that a student who breaks this rule will have to write a note of apology to the student who was interrupted.

Now it's your turn. Let's see how good you are at making rules and setting consequences for breaking them. What rules and penalties do you suggest? Some topics for rules are listed below:

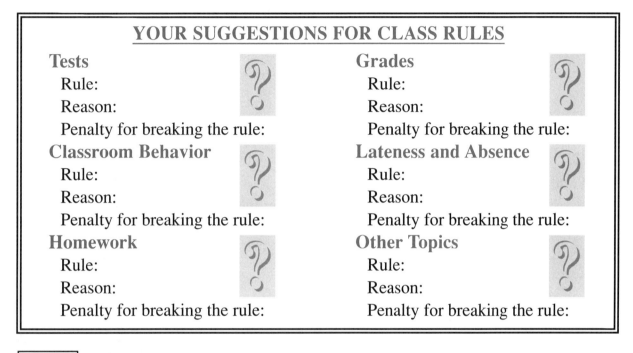

YOUR SUGGESTIONS FOR CLASS RULES

Tests
  Rule:
  Reason:
  Penalty for breaking the rule:

Grades
  Rule:
  Reason:
  Penalty for breaking the rule:

Classroom Behavior
  Rule:
  Reason:
  Penalty for breaking the rule:

Lateness and Absence
  Rule:
  Reason:
  Penalty for breaking the rule:

Homework
  Rule:
  Reason:
  Penalty for breaking the rule:

Other Topics
  Rule:
  Reason:
  Penalty for breaking the rule:

Closing

REACHING AN AGREEMENT ON YOUR CLASS RULES

Are your rules and penalties similar to those of your classmates? Compare your list with those of your classmates and your teacher. Try to reach a **consensus** (kən sən'səs) (*agreement*) on a set of class rules. Be sure to include the penalty as part of the rule. List the rules on a separate sheet of paper. Then submit them to your teacher for approval.

Rules for the Class

Rule #1:
Rule #2:
Rule #3:
Rule #4:
Rule #5:

EXPANDING YOUR UNDERSTANDING

Creating Vocabulary Cards

Rule
What is a "rule"?
Give an example of a rule.

Government
Define "government."
Why does a government make laws?

Finding Examples of Rules and Laws in Your Community

Rules and laws affect how we live. For example, look at the photograph on the right. What does it tell you about what drivers should and should not do? These street signs are probably similar to some in your own area. Find **two** signs with rules or laws in your community. For each sign:

❖ write or draw what is written on the sign

❖ explain the meaning of the rule or law

These signs state rules affecting motorists who park on the street.
How many of these rules can you explain?

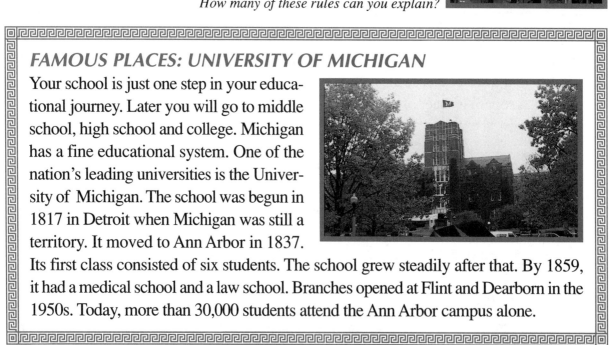

FAMOUS PLACES: UNIVERSITY OF MICHIGAN

Your school is just one step in your educational journey. Later you will go to middle school, high school and college. Michigan has a fine educational system. One of the nation's leading universities is the University of Michigan. The school was begun in 1817 in Detroit when Michigan was still a territory. It moved to Ann Arbor in 1837.

Its first class consisted of six students. The school grew steadily after that. By 1859, it had a medical school and a law school. Branches opened at Flint and Dearborn in the 1950s. Today, more than 30,000 students attend the Ann Arbor campus alone.

WHAT CHARACTERISTICS
MAKE A PERSON A GOOD LEADER?

6B Democratic societies depend upon good citizens stepping forward to fill positions of leadership. In this activity, you will identify the characteristics that make a person a good leader. Look for the following important words and phrases:

▶ Social Scientist　　　▶ Leader　　　▶ Gettysburg Address

▶ Hypothesis　　　▶ Dictionary　　　▶ "I Have A Dream" Speech

A **social scientist** is someone who applies the methods and procedures of science to ◀ study how people behave. Social scientists look for patterns of behavior that help explain why people act as they do. Here are some examples of social scientists:

❖ **Political Scientists** study how people govern themselves, choose their leaders and what kind of government they have.

❖ **Economists** study the ways in which people make goods and perform services, and distribute and consume these goods and services.

❖ **Sociologists** study social relationships in society, such as social groups and the movement of people between these groups.

HOW A SOCIAL SCIENTIST
CONDUCTS AN INVESTIGATION

Like other scientists, a social scientist will often investigate a specific question. The social scientist will try to think of some kind of explanation, or **hypothesis** ◀ (*educated guess*), to answer the question. As in other sciences, the social scientist then examines evidence to see if the hypothesis is correct. The social scientist often looks at **statistics** (*numbers that show how people have reacted in certain conditions*) and other data.

In this activity you will act as an "amateur social scientist." You will be asked to investigate an important question: what personal qualities make someone a good leader?

—— **THINK ABOUT IT**

Identify a person who you think is a leader. What qualities make him or her a leader?

CHARACTERISTICS OF A LEADER

▶ Most political scientists say that a **leader** must meet three requirements. A leader has to:

have a vision for the future	be able to communicate that vision to others	have the ability to get others to act

What personal characteristics do you think leaders need to meet these requirements? A **characteristic** (kar ik tə ris' tik) is a special trait or quality. Which of these qualities do you think most help someone to become a leader? Consider the following:

- fair
- unselfish
- compassionate
- courageous
- generous
- expressive
- honest
- dishonest
- skillful
- intelligent
- arrogant
- ruthless

You may not know the meaning of some words on this list. Use a dictionary to look up words you do not understand.

LEARNING TO USE A DICTIONARY

▶ A **dictionary** (dik' shə ner ē) is a reference book with many thousands of words arranged in alphabetical order. Dictionaries explain how to say each word correctly. The word is divided into syllables (*parts*), showing which syllables are accented. Some dictionaries tell you the origin of the word (*where it comes from*). Dictionaries also list the different parts of speech (*noun, verb, etc.*) that the word might have. Finally, a dictionary lists the meaning of the word for each part of speech. Sometimes a dictionary gives a sample sentence to make the meaning of the word clearer. Often a word has several meanings. You have to pick the one that makes the most sense in the sentence you are reading. Here's a typical dictionary entry for the first word on the list above:

fair (fër). [Old English "foeger"] *Noun.* Gathering for sale of goods or display of goods or farm products, as in "state fair."
Adjective. **1.** Beautiful, pleasing. **2.** Clear and sunny, as in "fair weather." **3.** With blond hair and light complexion. **4.** Just, unbiased, impartial, with equal treatment for all, as in "he received a fair trial."

Now that you understand some of the words used to identify the characteristics of a leader, are there any words you would add to the list? If so, what are they?

Let's return to our original question: *what personal characteristics do you think a person needs to be a leader?* Your answer to this question forms your hypothesis about the qualities of a leader. Is your hypothesis correct?

LOOKING AT TWO IMPORTANT LEADERS

To see if your hypothesis is accurate, you must investigate the evidence. Begin by looking at case studies of two people considered by many to have been good leaders.

❖ **Abraham Lincoln** was President of the United States from 1861 to 1865.

❖ **Dr. Martin Luther King, Jr.,** was a Civil Rights leader in the 1950s and the 1960s.

ABRAHAM LINCOLN (1809–1865)

Some people consider **Abraham Lincoln** to have been the greatest American President. Lincoln was born in a log cabin. He struggled hard to become a lawyer. People liked his intelligence and plain style of speaking. He was known for his honesty. Lincoln soon went into politics. At that time, the most important issue facing the nation was the existence of slavery. Lincoln helped form a new political party that opposed the spread of slavery to new states joining the United States.

Abraham Lincoln

Lincoln was elected President in 1860. People from the Southern states did not know of Lincoln's patience and understanding. In spite of his personal feelings, Lincoln promised that he would not abolish slavery in the South where it already existed. Many Southerners did not believe him. Soon several Southern states declared they would leave the United States and form their own country—the **Confederate States of America**.

Lincoln believed it was important to keep all the states together in one nation. He told the Southern states that he would not permit them to leave the United States. Despite Lincoln's warnings, they did so anyway. Soon afterwards, the North and South went to war. Gradually, Lincoln came to believe that the United States could not survive "half free" and "half slave." At the end of 1862, Lincoln issued the **Emancipation Proclamation**. This freed all persons who were slaves in the rebelling Southern states.

❖ CONTINUED

The Civil War lasted for four years and was the bloodiest war in American history. Many people doubted the wisdom of Lincoln's decision to go to war. But Lincoln thought the war was necessary. He had the personal courage to see the war through. Eventually, the North won and the country was reunited. The **Thirteenth Amendment** to the U.S. Constitution was passed in 1865, ending slavery throughout America.

Near the end of the war, President Lincoln went to Gettysburg to dedicate a cemetery where thousands of soldiers would be buried. At the time, his Gettysburg Address attracted little attention. It is now recognized as one of the greatest expressions of the ideals of American democracy. The Address demonstrated Lincoln's excellence as a public speaker.

Lincoln came to Pennsylvania to dedicate a cemetery to soldiers killed at Gettysburg.

Four score and seven [87] years ago our fathers brought forth on this continent a new nation conceived [begun] in liberty, and dedicated [devoted] to the proposition [idea] that all men are created equal ...

Thinking about those who had lost their lives in the battle, Lincoln noted that nothing he could say could be more important than what those soldiers had already done. They had given their lives for their country. He then ended his speech with these words:

We here highly resolve [determine] ... that this nation, under God, shall have a new birth of freedom; and that government of the people, by the people, and for the people shall not perish [be destroyed] from the earth.

With the war over, Lincoln drew up plans to rebuild the South. He was generous enough to welcome Southerners back into the Union as equals. However, Lincoln was **assassinated** (*murdered for his political beliefs*) just as the Civil War was ending. It was left to others to reunite the country.

QUESTIONS ABOUT ABRAHAM LINCOLN

1. Go back to your list of personal characteristics. Did Lincoln possess any of the characteristics you thought were important? Explain.

2. It has been said that Lincoln helped to strengthen democracy in the United States. Would you agree? Explain.

DR. MARTIN LUTHER KING, JR. (1929–1968)

Nearly a century after the Civil War, the rights of African Americans were still being violated by the laws and practices of many states. For example, African Americans in many Southern states were legally **segregated** (*separated by race*) in schools and forced to use separate public places such as restaurants, drinking fountains and seats on buses. In addition, groups like the **Ku Klux Klan** committed violent acts against African Americans.

A segregated drinking fountain. Dr. King sought to eliminate such segregation in the nation.

Dr. Martin Luther King, Jr. was born in Atlanta in 1929. After graduating from college he became the pastor of a church in Montgomery, Alabama. In the 1950s and 1960s, the Civil Rights Movement struggled to end racial segregation. Dr. King became one of its leaders. King and others felt the time had come to end segregation. But King was a patient man who believed in non-violence. Unlike some leaders, he opposed the use of violence to end segregation. If the government passed an unfair law, King felt people should oppose it with non-violent marches and strikes. He felt that peaceful resistance would eventually change people's attitudes. King was very effective in using non-violent demonstrations and **boycotts** (*refusal to buy certain products*) to fight against segregation.

Martin Luther King, Jr.

❖ CONTINUED

King helped bring hundreds of thousands of people together for a **March On Washington** in 1963. King was a gifted speaker. During this rally he delivered his **"I Have A Dream" Speech**. Dr. King told Americans of his dream that someday our country would be free of prejudice and hatred.

I have a dream. It is a dream deeply rooted in the American dream. I have a dream that one day this nation will rise up and live out the true meaning of its creed [beliefs]. We hold these truths to be self-evident [clear], that all men are created equal. I have a dream that one day in the Red Hills of Georgia the sons of former slaves and the sons of former slave owners will be able to sit down together at the table of brotherhood.

Dr. King and his followers helped end public segregation. New laws made segregation illegal in public transportation, hotels and restaurants. King also helped end requirements that had kept African Americans from voting.

In organizing demonstrations, King showed great personal courage. He sometimes risked imprisonment, violence and death. Enemies threatened King

Dr. King led the March on Washington in 1963.

and his family. They tried to blow up his house. They threw him in jail. Still, he refused to give up. In 1968, King was assassinated by an opponent of Civil Rights.

Dr. King was able to inspire people to act non-violently. He organized supporters of Civil Rights from all races. King and his followers achieved major changes in America and served as an example to other groups around the world. Even after his death, King remained a symbol of the Civil Rights Movement. In 1986 King's accomplishments were once again recognized by the nation. His birthday, January 15, became a federal holiday.

QUESTIONS ABOUT MARTIN LUTHER KING, JR.

1. Go back to your list of personal characteristics. Did King possess any of the characteristics you thought were important? Explain.

2. Do you think King helped strengthen the rights of all Americans? Explain.

WHAT MAKES SOMEONE A GOOD LEADER?

Closing

Now that you have looked at two case studies, you should test your hypothesis against the evidence. What personal qualities did these leaders have? Let's use a Venn diagram to compare and contrast the personal characteristics of Abraham Lincoln and Martin Luther King, Jr.

A **Venn diagram** is used to compare two or more items to show what they have in common and what is different between them. Each item is represented by a circle. The area where the circles overlap shows what the items share, while the outer part of each circle shows how each item is different.

The Venn diagram below has been started for you. Make a copy of the diagram. Then complete the blanks in the circles by listing the qualities both men shared, and those qualities unique to each leader.

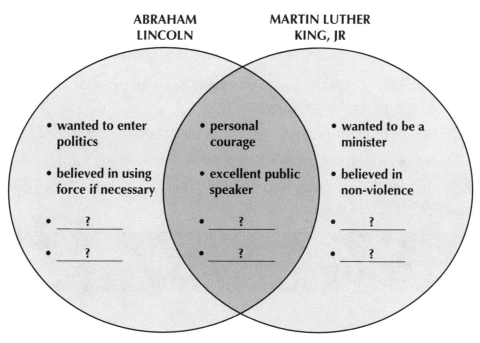

ABRAHAM LINCOLN — MARTIN LUTHER KING, JR

- wanted to enter politics
- believed in using force if necessary
- ___?___
- ___?___

- personal courage
- excellent public speaker
- ___?___
- ___?___

- wanted to be a minister
- believed in non-violence
- ___?___
- ___?___

---

1. Did Lincoln and King have the personal qualities that you thought good leaders should have?
2. Would you now change your original hypothesis? Why or why not?
3. How might you continue your investigation of the personal qualities of leaders?

EXPANDING YOUR UNDERSTANDING

Creating Vocabulary Cards

> *Social Scientist*
>
> *What is a "social scientist"?*
>
> *Identify three types of*
>
> *social scientists.*

> *Leader*
>
> *What are three requirements*
>
> *of good leadership?*
>
> *What are some of the personal*
>
> *qualities of good leaders?*

Identifying People with Leadership Qualities

In this activity, you learned about leadership qualities. One way to continue your investigation of leadership qualities might be to discuss this question with others.

❖ Ask **two** adults if they would help you with a school project. One of them should be your parent or guardian.

❖ Ask each adult to identify a person whom they think has leadership qualities.

❖ Finally, ask for a description of that person's characteristics.

❖ Make a copy of the following chart to help you keep track of the information you gather.

PERSON INTERVIEWED	PERSON IDENTIFIED AS LEADER	LEADERSHIP QUALITIES

WHO REPRESENTS YOU IN THE NATIONAL GOVERNMENT?

6C In this activity, you will learn who represents you in the national government. Look for the following important words and phrases:

▶ Democracy ▶ Federalism ▶ Executive power

▶ Representative ▶ Legislative power ▶ Judicial power

In Activity 6A, you learned that a **government** is the organization that people set up to protect their community and to make rules for themselves. By making and enforcing rules, the government keeps order, protects people's lives and safeguards property. Democratic governments act with the permission of the community. The **authority** (*power*) of a democratic government is limited to what the community decides its government leaders can do. Although our country is a democracy, other forms of government are also possible.

TYPES OF GOVERNMENT

Throughout history, there have been three main types of government: monarchy, dictatorship and democracy.

MONARCHY

A **monarchy** (mon' ər kē) is a government in which a king or queen has political power. A monarch inherits power. When the king or queen dies, power passes to one of the monarch's children or a relative. Years ago, monarchs claimed they were chosen to rule by God. These absolute monarchs had power without any limits. In other types of monarchy, the monarch shares power with an elected law-making body. This form of government is called a **constitutional monarchy**.

King Louis XIV claimed God chose him to rule France.

DICTATORSHIP

A **dictatorship** (dik tā' tər ship) is a system in which all government power is in the hands of one person or a small group. This person or group is in charge of the government, and claims to know what is best for the society. Often, the person or group uses force and violence to maintain its rule. A dictator usually has absolute power. The ruler or ruling group decides what to do, and is not concerned with what other people want. With all power in the hands of a single person or group, most people have no rights.

DEMOCRACY

▶ In a **democracy** (di mok' rə sē), the government's power comes from the permission of the people it governs.

▶ **Representatives** (rep ri zen' tə tivz), officials elected by the people, usually decide key issues. This type of government, known as a **representative democracy**, exists in the United States and most other democracies. In a democracy, the powers of officials are limited by the rule of law. They can only exercise the authority that the citizens have given to them.

Joseph Stalin was a dictator of the Soviet Union.

> We live in a democracy where people elect their officials.
> **Do you know the names of the people who represent you?**

Like many Americans, you may not know the names of all the people who represent you. In this activity you will learn about some of these people. Let's begin by looking at how the government of the United States is organized.

THE DIVISION OF POWERS

In our system of government, power is shared among several levels of government. This
▶ division of governmental power is called **federalism** (fed' ər ə liz əm).

❖ One level is the **national** or **federal** government. It deals with matters affecting the whole country, such as defense.

❖ At another level are **state governments**. Each state government handles matters occurring within that state. For example, states make laws about who may drive a car.

❖ At a third level are **local governments**. They deal with county, city, town and village matters. For example, local governments clean and repair neighborhood streets.

With this division of powers, the national government can decide issues of national importance, while state and local governments can handle matters closer to home.

THE SEPARATION OF POWERS

All governments—national, state and local—are given three powers to carry out their authority. These powers are:

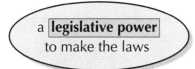

a **legislative power**
to make the laws

an **executive power**
to enforce the laws

a **judicial power**
to interpret the laws

On the state level, the **legislature** decides what laws to create. For example, it may pass a law saying that all students must learn music in school. The **executive** enforces the law. Executive officials make sure that all schools teach music. Finally, the **judicial** power interprets the laws. If a school district cancels music classes, a parent could take it to court. A state judge would then order the school district to obey the law by providing music classes.

Each level of government—national, state and local—has special institutions or **branches** to help carry out these powers. The following chart lists these different levels of government and their branches.

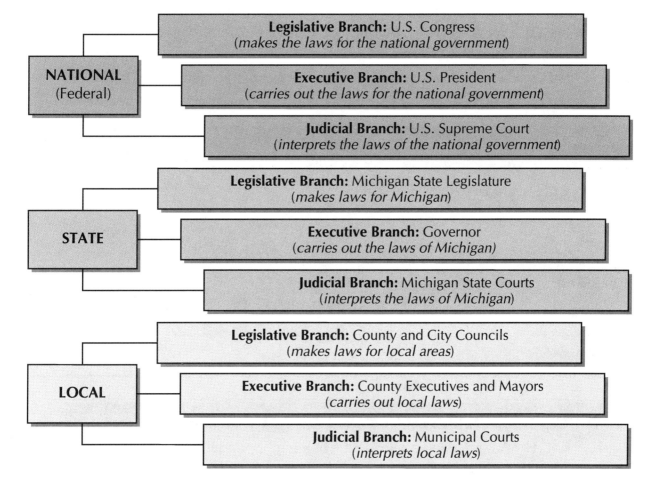

NATIONAL
(Federal)

Legislative Branch: U.S. Congress
(*makes the laws for the national government*)

Executive Branch: U.S. President
(*carries out the laws for the national government*)

Judicial Branch: U.S. Supreme Court
(*interprets the laws of the national government*)

STATE

Legislative Branch: Michigan State Legislature
(*makes laws for Michigan*)

Executive Branch: Governor
(*carries out the laws of Michigan*)

Judicial Branch: Michigan State Courts
(*interprets the laws of Michigan*)

LOCAL

Legislative Branch: County and City Councils
(*makes laws for local areas*)

Executive Branch: County Executives and Mayors
(*carries out local laws*)

Judicial Branch: Municipal Courts
(*interprets local laws*)

OUR NATIONAL GOVERNMENT

Now let's take a closer look at the national level of government.

LEGISLATIVE BRANCH

Our national government is located in **Washington, D.C.** The legislative or law-making branch is called **Congress**. The main job of Congress is to make laws for the nation. Congress has two parts, known as **houses**, which meet and vote separately. The two houses of Congress are the **Senate** and the **House of Representatives.**

Members of the U.S. House of Representatives.

The U.S. House of Representatives has 435 members. Each state sends at least one representative, but may send more depending on the size of its population. Every 10 years, the U.S. government takes a **census** (*count*) to decide how many representatives will come from each state. Since the last census, Michigan has sent 16 representatives to the U.S. House of Representatives, based on its population.

	House of Representatives	**Senate**
Number of members:	435	100
Length of term:	2 years	6 years
Representation is based on:	The size of the state's population	Two from each state
Elected by:	Voters from a particular Congressional district	Voters from the entire state
Michigan has:	16 Representatives	2 Senators

✔ CHECKING YOUR UNDERSTANDING ✔

How many people represent Michigan in the U.S. Congress?

EXECUTIVE BRANCH

The main job of the **executive branch** is to carry out or enforce laws. Our nation's chief executive is the **President of the United States**. The President is responsible for the agencies of the executive branch. For example, the President is the final authority over the Federal Bureau of Investigation (F.B.I.). The President also represents our country to other nations and serves as Commander-in-Chief of our armed forces. The President lives in the **White House** in Washington, D.C.

Bill Clinton being sworn in as President of the United States.
What is the main job of the President?

While many government officials are elected by voters, other officials are **appointed**. An appointed official is chosen by some other official, rather than by voters. The President appoints many officials to assist in running the executive branch. Most appointments must be approved by the Senate. This practice began two hundred years ago. President George Washington appointed a Secretary of State, a Secretary of the Treasury, a Secretary of War and an Attorney General to help him run the executive branch of government. These officials became known as the **Cabinet**.

The President	
Length of term:	4 years
Number of terms:	A maximum of two full terms.
Qualifications:	35 years old, a resident of the United States for 14 years, and born in the United States.

FAMOUS MICHIGANDERS: GERALD R. FORD

Gerald Ford was born in Grand Rapids. In 1948, he was elected to the U.S. House of Representatives. When the Vice President resigned in 1973, Ford was appointed as the new Vice President. In August 1974 President Nixon resigned. As a result, Ford became the 38th President of the United States. Gerald Ford is the only person who became President without being elected. He is also the only Michigander to have held that office. In 1976, Ford failed in his election attempt for another term as President.

JUDICIAL BRANCH

The role of the **judicial branch** is to interpret the laws by applying them to individual cases. The **U.S. Supreme Court** is the highest court in the nation. It meets in Washington, D.C. The Justices of the U.S. Supreme Court often base their decisions on whether or not a law agrees with the U.S. Constitution. Other federal courts, such as the Federal District Courts, also interpret our national laws.

The courtroom of the U.S. Supreme Court.

The U.S. Supreme Court	
Length of term:	Justices serve for life
How Justices are selected:	Nominated by the President, but must be approved by the U.S. Senate
Number of Justices:	Nine
Qualifications:	No qualifications for Supreme Court Justice are mentioned in the U.S. Constitution.

Closing

WHO ARE YOUR REPRESENTATIVES IN THE NATIONAL GOVERNMENT?

Now that you know how the national government is organized, let's find out who represents you. List the names of the officials who represent you in the national government. Also, try to provide a photograph of each. Use the following sources to help you:

❖ Visit or call your local office of the **League of Women Voters**.

❖ Look in a current almanac.

❖ Look in the pages of your phone book under "Government."

❖ Search local newspapers for pictures of your elected officials.

❖ Search electronic media, such as the **Internet**.

❖ Use the *Michigan Manual* (published by the Legislative Service Bureau).

YOUR REPRESENTATIVES AT THE NATIONAL LEVEL OF GOVERNMENT

A. President of the United States:
(name) _____   (photo)

B. Vice President of the United States:
(name) _____   (photo)

C. U.S. Senators from Michigan:
1. (name) _____   (photo)
2. (name) _____   (photo)

D. Your Representative in the U.S. House of Representatives:
(name) _____   (photo)

EXPANDING YOUR UNDERSTANDING

Creating Vocabulary Cards

Federalism
Define "federalism."
Which level of government is
responsible for raising an army?

Legislative Power
Define "legislative power."
What institution has legislative
power in the national government?

Identifying Whom a Place Is Named After

Have you ever visited John Ball Zoo, the Henry Ford Museum or John Kellogg Park? If you have, maybe you wondered about the person the place was named after. Often schools, zoos, parks, hospitals, bridges, tunnels or streets are named after famous individuals.

Are any buildings or streets in your community named after a famous person? Let's find out! To keep track of information you find, make a copy of the chart on the next page. For each place in the chart, list **one** example. Then write a short description of the person that the site was named after. A sample is provided on the first line.

The Henry Ford Museum

Place	Named After	Brief Descrpition
John Ball Zoo	John Ball	John Ball was a legislator and lawyer. He gave the city of Grand Rapids a gift of 40 acres to build a zoo.
School		
Hospital		
Government Building		
Museum		
Other		

FAMOUS PLACES: THE VAN ANDEL MUSEUM CENTER

Museums are often named after people. The Van Andel Museum in Grand Rapids was named after Jay Van Andel. He is the co-founder of a company called Amway. He gave the museum a large gift of money to construct a new building. The museum has a 76-foot whale skeleton hanging above its three-story main galleria. In addition, there are exhibits about Michigan's Native American population, natural environment and early history. One exhibit features a 1910 furniture factory. This is a tribute to the furniture craftspeople of Michigan. Videos recreate the lives of people who once worked at the factory.

A whale skeleton hangs in the museum's main gallery.

WHO REPRESENTS YOU
AT THE STATE AND LOCAL LEVEL?

6D In this activity, you will learn about state and local governments. Look for the following important words and phrases:

▶ House of Representatives   ▶ Governor   ▶ Special District

▶ Senate   ▶ County Government   ▶ Taxes

The United States is divided into 50 states. Each state has its own government.

STATE GOVERNMENT

Michigan's **state government** handles matters that affect people throughout the state. The state government provides money for schools, builds and maintains state roads and provides a system of justice. It also protects the safety and health of its citizens. Just like the national government, the state government is divided into legislative, executive and judicial branches. The state capital is located in **Lansing**.

COMPARING PHOTOGRAPHS

State Capitol Building (1880).

State Capitol Building (1997).

What differences do you notice between these pictures?

Let's begin our study of state government with a question:

**Do you know the names of any of the people
who represent you in state government?**

In this activity you will learn about the people who represent you in state government. First let's look at how Michigan's state government is organized.

LEGISLATIVE BRANCH

The state legislature of Michigan makes the laws for Michigan. It meets in Lansing. The state legislature consists of two **houses** that meet and vote separately: the **House of Representatives** and the Senate. The Michigan House of Representatives has 110 members. Members are elected in even-numbered years—such as 1996 and 1998. Members serve for a term of two years.

Members of the House of Representatives meet in this room in the State Capitol.

✔ WHICH MICHIGAN HOUSE DISTRICT DO YOU LIVE IN? ✔

The map below is a district map of Michigan. Its 110 representatives serve in the state's House of Representatives.

On a separate sheet of paper, answer the following questions:

1. In which district do you live?
2. Name the districts that border your district.

The other part of the state legislature is called the **Senate**. There are 38 senators in the Michigan Senate. Members of the Senate are elected at the same time as the Governor. Senators are elected for a four-year term.

The Senate Chamber of the State Legislature.

✔ WHICH MICHIGAN SENATE DISTRICT DO YOU LIVE IN? ✔

The map below is a Senatorial map of Michigan. Voters in each of the 38 districts elect one State Senator. The 38 Senators serve in the State Senate.

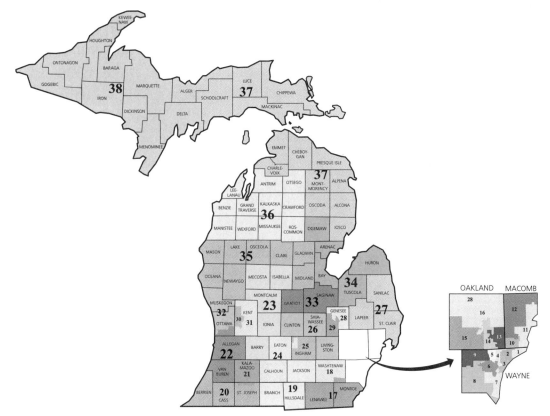

On a separate sheet of paper, answer the following questions:

1. In which district do you live?

2. List the numbers of the districts that border your district.

FAMOUS PLACES: THE MICHIGAN STATE CAPITOL

When Michigan was a territory, Detroit served as its capital. Many Michiganders felt the capital should be located in the geographic center of the state. A new town was built to be the capital. It was called Michigan, Michigan. The name was soon changed to Lansing. Construction began on a permanent State Capitol Building in 1871. It took six years to build. In 1988, the Capitol Building underwent a restoration project, which lasted four years.

The spectacular dome of the State Capitol.

EXECUTIVE BRANCH

▶ The chief executive of Michigan's state government is called the **Governor**. Like the President, the Governor is in charge of the executive branch of government. The Governor's job is to enforce laws passed by the state legislature and to maintain order in the state. The Governor is in charge of several departments, bureaus and agencies that help run the state government. The Governor is also the Commander-in-Chief of the state's National Guard.

The Governor has a great deal of power. After the state legislature approves a bill, it is sent to the Governor. If the Governor signs the bill, it becomes a law. The Governor may also choose to **veto** (*reject*) a bill. If the Governor vetoes a bill, it is sent back to the state legislature.

The Governor is elected by the voters for a term of four years. The Governor can serve for any number of four-year terms. Assisting the Governor is the **Lieutenant Governor**. The Lieutenant Governor carries out the duties of the executive branch when the Governor is out of the state. The Lieutenant Governor is also elected by the voters of the state for a four-year term.

In addition to the Governor and Lieutenant Governor, several other state officials are elected. For example, the voters of Michigan elect the Attorney General and Secretary of State. Other state officials are appointed by the Governor, rather than elected by the voters. The Governor appoints the heads of many executive departments. For example, the heads of the Departments of Correction, Commerce, Labor and Transportation are all appointed by the Governor.

FAMOUS MICHIGANDERS: GOVERNOR JOHN ENGLER

John Engler was born on his parents' farm near Mt. Pleasant, Michigan in 1948. After high school, he attended Michigan State University. By the time he graduated from college, he knew he wanted to follow a career in government service. At age 22, he was elected a State Representative. He then went on to become a Michigan Senator. While serving as a Senator, he graduated from law school. Engler ran as a Republican for Governor. In 1991, he was elected Governor of Michigan. Who knows, maybe one day your picture will be here as Governor!

JUDICIAL BRANCH

The highest court in the state is the **Michigan Supreme Court**. This is Michigan's equivalent to the U.S. Supreme Court. It is called the state's "highest court" since there is no further appeal from its decisions except to the U.S. Supreme Court. The Michigan Supreme Court meets in Lansing. It has seven members: one Chief Justice (*judge*) and six Associate Justices. These Justices are elected by popular vote for a term of

The room in the State Capitol where the Michigan Supreme Court met until 1970.

eight years. The Justices elect one of their members to serve as the Chief Justice. Below the Michigan Supreme Court are lower courts. All other judges are elected for a term of six years.

MICHIGAN'S CONSTITUTIONS

A **constitution** is a written plan of government. Michigan, like our national government, has a constitution. Since Michigan became a state, its citizens have lived under four state constitutions: 1835, 1850, 1908 and 1964. Each document was the product of a convention of delegates elected to draft a new constitution. Each constitution has also been changed by *amendments* (revisions).

Focus on Documents: *Michigan's Constitutions*

Constitution of 1835. Delegates met at the territorial capital of Detroit to draft a new constitution. This was a key step in the process of achieving statehood. Michigan's first state constitution called for a division of power among the legislative, executive and judicial branches. The constitution also provided that children attend school for at least three months a year. Money to educate these children was to come from selling a section of land in each township.

The first constitution approved by the voters of Michigan in 1835.

Constitution of 1850. Financial troubles associated with the state's new road building program brought calls for electing rather than appointing officials to certain offices. In 1850, Michiganders wrote a new constitution. It gave the right to vote to whites born in other countries. It also granted the right to vote to Native Americans who gave up loyalty to their tribe. However, it denied the right to vote to African Americans and to all women. This constitution also provided that the question of further revising the constitution should be decided by voters every sixteenth year.

Constitution of 1908. The start of the twentieth century created many problems for Michiganders. Corruption in government and abuses by large corporations became widespread. Demands for reform created a need for a new constitution. There was strong pressure to give voters greater control over their government. Although it was discussed, the right to vote in state elections was still denied to women. However, special provisions were created to protect women and children from abuses in the workplace.

Constitution of 1964. The state's present constitution went into effect on January 1, 1964. The new constitution banned discrimination on the basis of religion, color, race or national origin. It created a Civil Rights Commission to investigate discrimination. The Governor's term was changed from two to four years. The Governor and Lieutenant Governor began to be elected jointly. In addition, over a hundred government agencies were reduced to 20 departments. Since going into effect, this document has been amended at least twenty times. The voters of Michigan continue to decide every 16 years whether or not they want to revise their constitution.

LOCAL GOVERNMENT

Local governments—counties and towns—provide the most direct contact that citizens have with their government. Each government you live under has a special purpose and specific jobs it performs. Do you know who represents you in local government? Let's first look at how local government in Michigan is organized.

The Genesee County Courthouse, a part of local government in Michigan.

COUNTY GOVERNMENT

Just as the United States is divided into 50 states, Michigan is divided into 83 counties. A **county government's** powers come from the state constitution and the laws passed by the state legislature.

County governments conduct elections, register voters and provide health care services to their citizens. They also operate courts, run county prisons and build and maintain county roads.

In most of the 83 counties, a governing board represents the towns and cities. Voters in the county elect these **boards of commissioners**. The commissioners handle such business as spending county tax funds. Usually the commissioners meet once a month at the county seat.

✔ WHICH COUNTY DO YOU LIVE IN? ✔

The map below shows the 83 counties that make up Michigan.

Answer the following questions:

1. Which county do you live in?
2. Name the counties that border your county.

The **county seat** is the place where county offices are located. Many counties have a county executive, called a chairperson. The chairperson's job is to be in charge of meetings of the board of commissioners.

In addition to commissioners, each county has several other officials. These officials include the county clerk, county treasurer, county attorney, sheriff and register of deeds. The register of deeds keeps records on the buying and selling of property.

TOWNSHIP GOVERNMENTS

There are 1,242 townships in Michigan. Townships differ greatly in size. For example, in 1990 only 21 people lived in Grand Island Township in Alger County. The population of Clinton Township in Macomb County is more than 85,000. Townships pass zoning ordinances, collect taxes, maintain street lights, provide police and fire protection and handle other local matters.

CITY GOVERNMENTS

Counties are also divided into cities and villages. The powers of these local governments extend to regulating (*controlling*) property and managing local affairs. There are over 500 cities in Michigan. Most of these cities are governed by a **mayor** and city council. However, some cities are governed by a city manager.

Dearborn City Hall.
Which officials run most city governments?

FAMOUS MICHIGANDERS: COLEMAN YOUNG

Coleman Young was born in Alabama in 1918. His family moved to Detroit when he was only five years old. In 1973, Young was elected Mayor of Detroit. He was the city's first African-American mayor. As mayor, Young worked to improve Detroit's economy, end racial prejudice and improve conditions for the poor. Partly through his efforts, the Renaissance Center in downtown Detroit was built.

SPECIAL DISTRICTS

Sometimes a need arises for a service that is not provided by a county or city government. In such cases, a **special district** is created to provide that service. ◄ The service is paid for by taxing the people living in the district receiving the service. Michigan has about 280 special districts. They handle such matters as recreation, water, airports, natural resources, fire protection, housing and community development.

Airports such as this one are often run by a district government.
What other matters are handled by special districts?

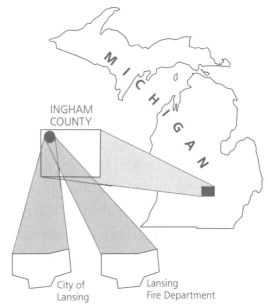

INGHAM
COUNTY

City of
Lansing

Lansing
Fire Department

HOW STATE GOVERNMENT IS FINANCED

State government performs many important services for the people of Michigan. To pay for these services, the government collects taxes. **Taxes** are money that people pay to the government. Without taxes, government would not have enough money to provide needed services.

Parks like this one in Kalamazoo are built and maintained by money collected from taxes.

One form of tax that the state government collects is income tax. People who earn money pay a part of their earnings, or income, to the government. Businesses are also required to pay income taxes.

Another form of state tax is the sales tax. This is collected each time someone buys an item. The amount of sales tax is added to the price of the item purchased.

State government also collects a variety of fees for licenses and other services. For example, drivers pay a fee to renew their drivers' licenses and license plates. This money helps to pay for roads and road safety. The government also uses the money it collects to pay for such things as government workers' salaries, building new highways, assisting schools and maintaining prisons.

Sometimes the government does not collect enough tax money to pay for all its bills and programs. When that happens, the government borrows money by selling bonds. People buy the bonds and the state government repays them at a later date.

Each year the Governor proposes a budget (buj' it) to the state legislature. The budget indicates how much money the state government will spend. The legislature discusses the proposed budget and often makes changes to it.

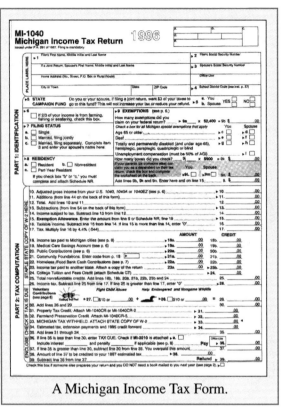

A Michigan Income Tax Form.

✔ CHECKING YOUR UNDERSTANDING ✔

The pie charts below show where Michigan gets its money and how it spends it.

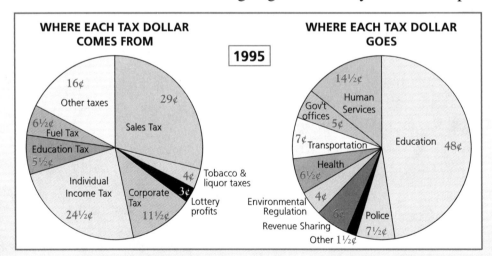

1. Where does the state government get most of its money from?
2. What is the largest item in the state budget?
3. How much does the state spend out of each dollar on human services?
4. Ask your parents how they would like to see state tax money spent.

WHO REPRESENTS YOU IN STATE AND LOCAL GOVERNMENT?

Closing

Now you know how your local and state governments are organized. Can you identify the names of the officials who represent you in state and local government? Let's find out. Use the same sources of information that you did in the previous activity.

YOUR REPRESENTATIVES AT THE STATE LEVEL OF GOVERNMENT

A. Governor of Michigan:
(name) _____   (photo)

B. Senator from your State Senate District:
(name) _____   (photo)

C. Representative from your State House of Representatives District:
(name) _____   (photo)

YOUR REPRESENTATIVES AT THE LOCAL LEVEL OF GOVERNMENT

A. County Legislator:
(name) _____   (photo)

B. County or City Judge:
(name) _____   (photo)

C. Mayor, City Manager or other local executive:
(name) _____   (photo)

EXPANDING YOUR UNDERSTANDING

Creating Vocabulary Cards

Michigan State Legislature	County Government
What is the job of the Michigan State Legislature?	Define "county government."
Which two houses make up the state legislature?	What responsibilities do county governments have?

Writing to an Elected Official

Elected officials usually like to hear from their constituents. **Constituents** (kən stich' o͞o əntz) are the people who live in an official's district. An elected official represents his or her constituents in government. Write a letter to one of your elected officials—your mayor, county commissioner or local judge. In your letter, you may want to:

❖ Ask why he or she wanted to become an elected official.

❖ Ask what he or she finds most interesting and important about the job.

❖ Discuss your view of an issue you think is important.

Skill Builder

WRITING A BUSINESS LETTER

Let's look at the proper form for writing a business letter about an issue that concerns you:

Heading: Start your letter with your address and today's date.

12 Main Street
Marquette, Michigan 49855
November 14, 1998

Inside Address: List the name, title, organization and address of the person to whom you are writing.

Body: The body starts with a greeting. It is proper to address the person as: "Dear Mr." or "Dear Ms.," followed by the name. When writing to government officials, use their title. If you are writing to an agency and you do not know the name of the person who will receive the letter, start with "Dear Sir or Dear Madam."

Honorable John Engler
Governor of Michigan
Executive Office Chambers
Lansing, Michigan 48901

Dear Governor:

I am a fourth grade student at an elementary school in Marquette, Michigan. I am writing to give you my view about helping children who do not have health insurance.

Our class has been studying some of the problems faced by these children. One very important problem is that parents take them to the emergency rooms of hospitals. This costs a lot of money and leads to long waiting periods in hospitals. To prevent this problem I think our state should set up a special health insurance program for children.

Thank you for your attention. I look forward to hearing from you shortly on this matter.

An introductory paragraph tells who you are and what the letter is about.

The main part of your letter is where you discuss your message. The tone of your letter should be respectful. You should not be as casual as you would be if you were writing to a friend.

Signature: Sign the letter between the closing and your printed name.

Yours truly,
Sally Jones
Sally Jones

Closing: It is proper to end with "Yours truly," or "Sincerely yours."

YOU BE THE JUDGE

6E In this activity, you will learn about some of the rights that citizens have in a democracy. Look for the following important words:

▶ Due Process

▶ Equal Protection

▶ Jury

▶ U.S. Supreme Court

In the United States, our government tries to protect the rights of citizens. In fact, the **Declaration of Independence** states that the main goal of government should be to protect the rights of citizens to "life, liberty and the pursuit of happiness." However, this document did not spell out what *specific* rights Americans should have. The **U.S. Constitution** originally listed a few of these rights. After the Constitution was written, it was sent to the states for approval. Many Americans believed the new constitution should be rejected because it failed to list most of the basic rights of citizens. They feared that without a guarantee of those rights, a strong national government might mistreat its citizens.

The Declaration of Independence being read to citizens.

Definition

THE BILL OF RIGHTS
AND OTHER PROTECTIONS

The U.S. Constitution was approved only after its supporters promised that a "Bill of Rights" would be added soon. The first ten amendments were adopted in 1791, and became known as the **Bill of Rights**. Since then, 17 additional amendments have been approved. Many of these later amendments also focus on protecting the rights of citizens.

The Bill of Rights guarantees each of us special rights that cannot be taken away by the government. These special rights generally fall into two categories:

❖ **Rights that protect our freedom of expression.** Example: the First Amendment guarantees each of us freedom of speech.

❖ **Rights when we are accused of a crime.** Example: the Sixth Amendment guarantees each of us a fair trial with a jury that is impartial—fair and not prejudiced against us.

▶ Some rights are called **"due process"** rights. This means the government court must follow certain procedures when it takes away someone's property or accuses someone of a crime. The government cannot use unfair methods in carrying out its responsibilities.

Many of the amendments that came after the Bill of Rights went even further in protecting our rights. Some amendments guaranteed special groups the right to vote. Another amendment guaranteed the

▶ **"equal protection"** of the law to all citizens. The equal-protection clause guarantees that all citizens will be treated equally by any law that the government makes.

Under our system of government, a person cannot be put in prison without "due process of law."

Disagreements sometimes arise over how a particular constitutional right is to be interpreted. No general rule can ever be so exact that it can tell in advance all of the situations that might arise. For this reason, courts apply our laws to specific situations. The courts determine if a specific situation falls within a particular rule. For example, a sign might read:

NO VEHICLES
IN THE PARK

THINK ABOUT IT

We are fairly sure the sign means no cars or trucks are allowed in the park. But what about bicycles, baby strollers and wheelchairs? Are they "vehicles" in the sense intended by the sign? Explain your answer.

A court must examine the words of a law to decide just what they mean. A court might say that the purpose of the rule prohibiting vehicles in the park is to avoid danger to pedestrians (*walkers*). Since wheelchairs and baby strollers pose no danger to pedestrians, they are not "vehicles" in the sense intended by the rule.

Because we live under the "rule of law," we want each person to be treated fairly. In any court, each party has certain rights. These rights include the right to have a lawyer, to hear opposing evidence and to present one's case. In criminal cases, the defendant also has the right to have the case tried by a panel

▶ of unbiased citizens known as a **jury** .

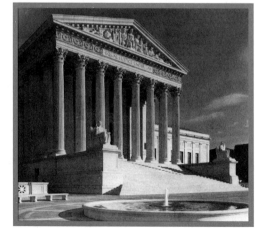

The U.S. Supreme Court meets here to review cases.

The losing side in a trial will often ask a special court, known as a court of appeals, to re-consider the decision. The court of appeals will only change the decision if there was an error in interpreting or applying the law. This would include any action by the trial court that violated a party's constitutional rights.

The **U.S. Supreme Court** is the nation's highest court of appeals. The Supreme ◄ Court often hears appeals requiring it to interpret what is in the Constitution.

THE EXERCISE OF JUSTICE

What would it be like to be a U.S. Supreme Court Justice? In this activity, you will have a chance to play this role. You will review a case that once appeared before the U.S. Supreme Court. Like a real Justice, you will weigh the evidence presented by both sides. Then you will make a decision based on your understanding of the law. Good luck on your first case—your Honor!

SCHENCK V. UNITED STATES (1919)

THE FACTS OF THE CASE

Mr. Schenck was a member of a political party that was against U.S. participation in World War I. When the government called up men to serve in the military, Schenck mailed leaflets telling these men that the war was immoral and against the law. The pamphlet never directly stated that the men should refuse to serve, since such advice would have been against the law. Schenck was accused of preventing the government from calling up men for the army. He was also accused of encouraging soldiers to disobey their officers. At his trial, he was found guilty. He appealed his decision to the U.S. Supreme Court. Schenck claimed that the guilty verdict violated his right to free speech.

ARGUMENTS USED BY SCHENCK

Schenck's lawyer argued that Schenck's right to free speech had been violated. The purpose of free speech is to allow people to criticize their government. His lawyer admitted that it would be wrong to use free speech to call for an armed uprising against the government. But the lawyer said Schenck had done nothing of the kind. He merely gave his readers a different view about the war, and asked that they act for themselves. The lawyer argued the government should not be allowed to imprison Schenck for questioning its decision to go to war. What other things might the government do if its citizens were not allowed to engage in free debate? The lawyer concluded that Schenck was not guilty and should be set free.

❖ CONTINUED

ARGUMENTS USED BY THE U.S. GOVERNMENT

The lawyers for the United States argued that Schenck's pamphlet encouraged men to disobey the law. Any person who believed what Schenck wrote would probably refuse to serve in the armed forces. People have a right to discuss whether or not the country should go to war. However, they do not have a right to refuse to serve if called. Telling people not to serve is disobeying the law.

The government's lawyers recognized the right to free speech. But they said there are some limits to free speech. They argued that a person cannot shout "fire" in a crowded theater as a joke, and then claim to be exercising free speech. No one has a right to use words that would create an *obvious* and *immediate* danger. Schenck's pamphlet clearly created an immediate danger. If people listened to Schenck, they would refuse to serve in the armed forces. They might even disobey their officers by refusing to fight. The government's lawyers concluded that Schenck therefore deserved to be kept in prison.

Closing

HOW WOULD YOU DECIDE THIS CASE?

You have now heard the evidence. The time has come for you to decide the case. Before doing so, let's review what you have heard in this case:

1. Summarize **two** arguments used by Schenck's lawyer.
2. Summarize **two** arguments used by the lawyers for the U. S. Government.
3. Based on the facts of the case and your understanding of the law, how would **you** decide the case? Explain your decision.

EXPANDING YOUR UNDERSTANDING

Creating Vocabulary Cards

Bill of Rights
What is the "Bill of Rights"?
List two rights protected by
the Bill of Rights.

U.S. Supreme Court
What is the "U.S. Supreme Court"?
What is the role of the U.S.
Supreme Court in interpreting
our laws?

Listing Constitutional Rights

The rights of Americans can be classified, based on whether they protect political, social, economic or religious rights. Here is what each of these categories of rights means:

- ❖ **Political rights** allow citizens to participate in government.
- ❖ **Social rights** deal with our ability to live in a community.
- ❖ **Economic rights** concern our ability to function in the economy.
- ❖ **Religious rights** protect our freedom of worship.

Make a copy of the following chart. The class should be divided into groups. Each group should list **five** other rights enjoyed by all Americans. Then place a check mark (✔) in the appropriate column indicating the main category of that right. The first one has already been done for you.

Note: Some rights may fit into more than one category. Check each category that applies.

A political demonstration in front of the U.S. Supreme Court illustrates the right of Americans to peacefully assemble.

Description of the Right	Political Right	Social Right	Economic Right	Religious Right
Government cannot set up an official religion or limit people's freedom of religion				✔

CORE DEMOCRATIC VALUES: PRINCIPLES OF AMERICAN GOVERNMENT

In drawing up the U.S. Constitution, our national leaders wanted to design a system that was effective. They also wanted a government that would protect individual rights. They were especially influenced by their experiences with the British government before the American Revolution.

The British government had taxed the colonists without their permission. The British had also sent troops to live in the houses of some colonists. It seemed the colonists had few rights they could really count on.

In creating a new form of government in 1787, American leaders were careful to make sure that these kinds of abuse could not be repeated. Their new system was based on the idea that government should protect individual rights, secure the safety of the community and promote the public good. To guarantee these rights, they wrote certain key principles into the new Constitution:

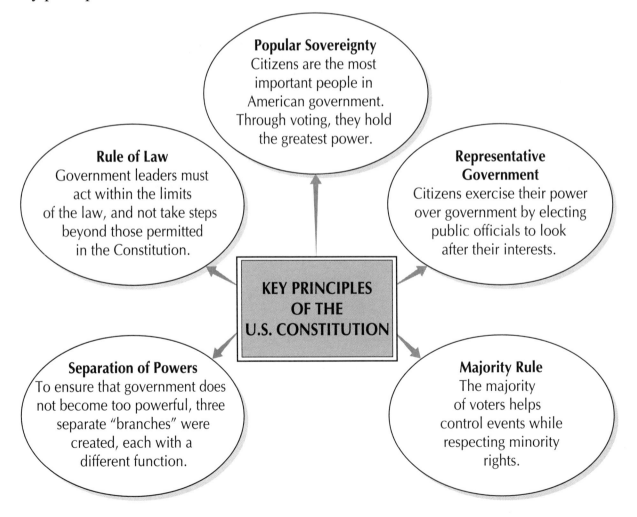

Popular Sovereignty
Citizens are the most important people in American government. Through voting, they hold the greatest power.

Rule of Law
Government leaders must act within the limits of the law, and not take steps beyond those permitted in the Constitution.

Representative Government
Citizens exercise their power over government by electing public officials to look after their interests.

KEY PRINCIPLES OF THE U.S. CONSTITUTION

Separation of Powers
To ensure that government does not become too powerful, three separate "branches" were created, each with a different function.

Majority Rule
The majority of voters helps control events while respecting minority rights.

The U.S. Constitution divided power between our national government and the government of each state. The powers of our national government are strictly spelled out in the Constitution. All powers not listed in the Constitution were left to the state governments or to the people. By doing this, the authors of the Constitution once again wanted to prevent our national government from becoming too powerful.

There are also several other core values that are important to the success of our constitutional system:

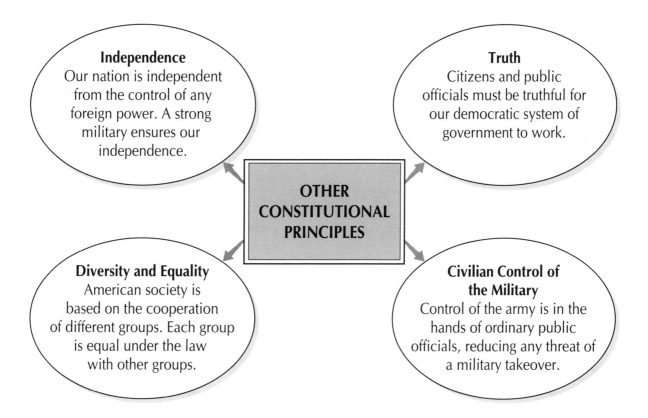

Independence
Our nation is independent from the control of any foreign power. A strong military ensures our independence.

Truth
Citizens and public officials must be truthful for our democratic system of government to work.

OTHER CONSTITUTIONAL PRINCIPLES

Diversity and Equality
American society is based on the cooperation of different groups. Each group is equal under the law with other groups.

Civilian Control of the Military
Control of the army is in the hands of ordinary public officials, reducing any threat of a military takeover.

The opening words of the U.S. Constitution are, "We, the People of the United States..." This phrase means that the true authors of the Constitution are the American people. No other words in the Constitution are more meaningful or more important. In these few words are found the very heart of our system of government: our government exists to help the American people achieve their goals.

Although some features of our national government have changed over time, one thing has remained the same. Americans have created a system of government that tries to balance the need for governmental power with the protection of individual liberties.

SUMMARIZING YOUR UNDERSTANDING

IDENTIFYING AND DESCRIBING
THE THREE BRANCHES OF GOVERNMENT

Directions: The following organizer shows the three branches of government at different levels, with their powers. For example, Congress—our national legislature—has the power to pass laws that deal with the entire nation. Complete the rest of the chart:

Branch	National Government	State Government	Local Government
Legislative (makes the laws)	The U.S. Congress makes laws for the entire nation	?	?
Executive (?)	?	The Governor carries out the laws passed by the state legislature	?
Judicial (?)	?	?	Municipal courts interpret the laws of a city

SERVICES PROVIDED BY
STATE AND LOCAL GOVERNMENT

Directions: Create a chart showing how the services of state and local government in Michigan help citizens meet their needs.

STATE GOVERNMENT	LOCAL GOVERNMENT
?	?

CITIZENSHIP

A monument honoring veterans of past wars.

Students saluting the American flag.

A political rally in front of the State Capitol Building.

In a democracy, ordinary citizens hold important political powers. They have basic rights, elect government officials and sometimes vote directly on issues. As a young citizen, you also have important rights. Your political power will increase when you begin to vote. For democracy to work, Americans must be aware of their rights and responsibilities. In this unit, you will learn what it means to be a well-informed citizen. You will explore the ways in which citizens express their views and make informed decisions about public issues.

JASIEK BECOMES
AN AMERICAN CITIZEN

 asiek Wojczuk (Ya shik Voy chuck) was dressed in his best clothes. He gave one last look in the car mirror to straighten his tie. Then he and his family crossed the street and entered the Federal Building in Detroit. Jasiek was about to be officially sworn in as a new citizen of the United States.

Jasiek had gone through a great deal of trouble to become a citizen. Eight years before, he had left his native Poland. At that time, Poland was in a crisis. A neighboring country had set up a dictatorship in Poland. People could not criticize their leaders. They were discouraged from going to church. The Polish economy was not going well. Store shelves were nearly always empty.

In 1981, Jasiek received a letter from a distant cousin inviting him to visit the United States. Jasiek traveled to New York City. Once there, he saw the Statue of Liberty, the Empire State Building and many other sights he had read about while growing up in Poland. Then he took the train to Detroit to visit his cousin.

During Jasiek's visit, something unusual was happening in his own country. Polish workers had organized themselves into a labor union. Government officials had no control over this union and were very nervous. Finally, the government cracked down, arresting those who spoke out against its policies.

Jasiek Wojczuk

The American government responded by allowing all Polish visitors to remain in the United States until the crisis in Poland came to an end. Jasiek decided to stay in America. Soon, he was taking English lessons and found a job helping to tear down old houses. He moved to a small apartment close to his cousin.

Jasiek spent little money on himself. Most of his earnings were sent to his wife and children in Poland. He missed his wife and children greatly. He decided to keep working while he thought of a plan to bring them to Michigan.

Jasiek started taking night classes at a local college. His English improved. He began to study computers. After two years, he quit his job tearing down houses. Jasiek found work making technical designs with computers.

By 1986, Jasiek had saved enough money to bring his family to America. There were still some troubles getting a government permit to enter the country. Jasiek's American cousin had to help them out. Finally, Jasiek's wife and children arrived. It was one of the happiest days of his life. Once Jasiek had re-united with his family, he decided to become an American citizen. He studied American history and learned about the U.S. government. He passed the citizenship test with flying colors.

And now the great moment had arrived. The family entered the courtroom where the ceremony would take place. Jasiek's eyes focused on the judge leading the ceremony. He was told to raise his right hand. He began to recite the Pledge of Allegiance to his newly adopted country—the United States. He smiled proudly as he gazed at the faces of his wife and children. As Jasiek said the Pledge of Allegiance, he thought about what becoming an American citizen would mean.

What rights and responsibilities would he have as an American citizen? Jasiek did not want to be just another citizen of the United States. He wanted to be a "good" citizen in his newly adopted country. He started to think of the many ways he might do this. In this unit you will find the answers to some of the questions that Jasiek asked himself as he said the Pledge of Allegiance.

HOW WOULD YOU DEFINE A "GOOD" CITIZEN?

7A You will begin this activity by examining citizenship. Then you will conduct a survey of two people in your community to find out what each one thinks makes a "good" citizen. Look for the following important words and phrases:

▶ Citizenship　　　　　▶ Naturalized Citizen　　　　　▶ Survey

A ▶ symbol appears in the margin where the **word** or **phrase** is first explained.

WHAT IS A CITIZEN?

▶ In some ways, **citizenship** (sit' i zən ship) is like a membership card. A citizen is a member of a particular nation. The idea of citizenship goes back to ancient Greece and Rome. In modern times, every nation has developed its own rules to define citizenship.

In the United States, you are an American citizen if you were born here or if your parents are American citizens. People who were not born here and whose parents are not American citizens can also become citizens. To become a citizen, a person must live in the United States for a number of years and pass a citizenship test. These people are

▶ called **naturalized citizens**.

WHAT MAKES SOMEONE A GOOD CITIZEN?

Now that you understand what a citizen is, what makes someone a "good" citizen? First, let's get your views on the issue.

> **THINK ABOUT IT**
>
> In your opinion, what makes someone a good citizen?
> Compare your answer with those of your classmates.

Do the citizens of your community agree with your answer? Let's find out how others in your community might answer this same question. You will need to interview **two** people to find out how they define a "good" citizen. At least one of these should be an adult. Let's begin by learning how to conduct a survey.

TAKING A SURVEY

The purpose of a survey (sər' vā) is to find out what people think about some topic or issue. In this survey, you will find out how people in your community define a "good" citizen. Remember, there are no right or wrong answers in a survey.

GETTING STARTED

To carry out your survey, follow these steps:

❖ Ask your parent to suggest **two** people who might participate in the project. One person might be your parent, guardian or neighbor.

❖ Begin your survey by reading the following statement to each volunteer:

> As part of a school project, I am surveying two members of our community to find their answers to the question:
> ### *How would you define a good citizen?*

❖ Take careful notes of each volunteer's answer to your question.

❖ After you have finished your discussion, thank your volunteer for his or her help in the survey.

COLLECTING DATA AND COMPARING ANSWERS

Make a copy of the following tally sheet to keep a record of the answers provided by your volunteers:

How would you define a good citizen?
❖ First Volunteer's Answer:
❖ Second Volunteer's Answer:

After your tally sheet is completed, share your answers with your classmates. The class should then choose the answers they think best define what a "good" citizen is.

Closing

HOW DO EXPERTS DEFINE A GOOD CITIZEN?

How does your class definition of a good citizen compare with definitions given by experts? The following are qualities that some experts think a good citizen should have.

A good citizen is someone who is ...

❖ **Respectful.** Good citizens treat others with respect, even when they disagree with their opinions.

❖ **Responsible.** Good citizens are responsible for their actions. They use self-control and follow the rules. They keep their promises, take responsibility and are willing to pay the penalty when they do something wrong.

❖ **Civic-Minded.** Good citizens donate their time and money to help improve the community.

❖ **Open-Minded.** Good citizens listen to the opinions of others and sometimes change their minds. They accept others with different traditions, customs and ways of living. Good citizens will **compromise** (kom' prə mīz) in order to solve problems. In a compromise, both sides settle their differences by giving up something.

THINK ABOUT IT

1. Now that you have read the views of the experts, would you change your definition of a good citizen? If so, how would you now define a good citizen?
2. Provide a specific example showing how students in your class demonstrate their good citizenship.

EXPANDING YOUR UNDERSTANDING

Creating Vocabulary Cards

Citizenship
What is "citizenship"?
What are some of the qualities of a good citizen?

Survey
What is a "survey"?
What is the main purpose of a survey?

Creating a "Good Citizen" Scrapbook

Have you ever read a newspaper story about a person who rushed into a burning building to save someone else? That person was performing an act of bravery. In addition, he or she was acting as a good citizen. Your daily newspaper often features stories about people who are outstanding citizens. Some of these citizens may perform acts of bravery. Others may donate money or volunteer time to a good cause.

Let's look for examples of good citizenship and write about them. Try to include some examples of citizens your own age. To complete this assignment, select a partner. You and your partner will create a scrapbook of "good citizenship" stories found in the daily newspaper, heard on radio or reported on television. Over the next week:

❖ find stories dealing with acts of "good citizenship."

❖ write a brief summary of each story in your scrapbook.

❖ explain why you and your partner think the person described in the story demonstrated an act of good citizenship.

Combine your stories with those of other classmates into a "Good Citizens Scrapbook" for display in your school.

Obeying the Law

One principle that guides responsible citizens is a concern for obeying the law. If citizens refuse to obey the law, society will quickly fall apart. For example, students must obey school rules. Respecting school rules creates a friendly and orderly atmosphere. It allows students to feel safe and to be able to learn.

❖ Team up with another member of your class.

❖ Think of at least **two** situations in which your behavior was guided by a concern for the rules of your school or the laws of your community.

❖ Explain how your behavior promoted a more friendly, safe and orderly environment.

HOW DO PEOPLE PARTICIPATE IN A DEMOCRACY?

7B In this activity, you will learn about representative democracy. You will explore some of the ways in which citizens participate in a democratic government. Look for the following important words and phrases:

▶ Democracy

▶ Line graph

▶ Majority Rule

▶ Trend

Imagine that your school librarian is holding a poster contest. Students are asked to create a poster for the bulletin board. The topic of the poster contest is democracy.

Introduction CITIZEN PARTICIPATION IN A DEMOCRACY

You want to submit a poster, so you ask the librarian for more details. The librarian hands you a packet with the guidelines for creating a poster. Here is what it contains:

GUIDELINES FOR THE POSTER CONTEST

▶ A ⬚democracy⬚ is a form of government in which ordinary citizens hold the greatest power. In a "representative" form of democracy, citizens elect "representatives" as their public officials. The representatives then make decisions for the people in the community.

Characteristics of Democracy

Democracies are often admired by people in other countries because of their unique characteristics:

❖ In a democracy, people are free to express their opinions, to speak freely with one another and to exchange ideas.

▶ ❖ In a democracy, community decisions are made by ⬚**majority rule**⬚. A majority is more than half the voters.

❖ In a democracy, people have the right to disagree. A democracy protects the **rights of the minority**. The minority is made up of those citizens who disagree with the majority on an issue.

❖ CONTINUED

Ways to Participate in a Democracy

In a democracy citizens should actively participate in their community. Here are some of the many ways in which citizens can participate actively in the American system of democracy.

Participation in your Community

❖ Take part in a school service project

❖ Pay taxes

❖ Serve on a jury

❖ Join a school club or organization, such as the Student Organization

❖ Run for office in a school club, community organization or school board

❖ Act directly to solve some local community problem

❖ Write letters to a local newspaper about community issues

❖ Help people in the community who are in trouble

❖ Contribute time or money to a local charity

❖ Speak at community meetings on public issues

❖ Serve as a community volunteer—firefighter or hospital volunteer

Participation in your State and National Government

❖ Discuss issues of statewide and national importance with other people

❖ Help in an election campaign

❖ Serve in the armed forces of the United States

❖ Vote in statewide and national elections

❖ Join a political party

❖ Send letters to Congressional Representatives, Senators, the President and other officials

❖ Publish articles on problems or issues of state or national importance

❖ Run for election to public office

❖ Attend public meetings or demonstrations

Poster Guidelines

Students should create a poster about our American system of democracy. The poster should:

❖ illustrate some of the actions that people do when they participate in a democracy.

❖ contain at least three illustrations. The illustrations can be pictures from newspapers and magazines, or may be students' own drawings.

Creative posters will be displayed on the library bulletin board, the local public library and businesses throughout the community.

EXHIBITING YOUR POSTER

On the day of the exhibit, students should take turns examining each other's posters. Each poster should be judged on the basis of 100 points. A panel of judges should be formed, consisting of your teacher and students elected by the class. The role of the committee is to review each poster and to award points based on the following criteria:

Name of student: _____

CRITERIA	Total Points	Points Awarded
Creativity: the uniqueness and originality of the design	30 points	
Theme: how well the poster presents the theme	50 points	
Appearance: attractiveness and artistic merit	20 points	

The poster(s) with the highest number of points will be displayed.

EXPANDING YOUR UNDERSTANDING

Creating Vocabulary Cards

Democracy
Define "democracy."
What role do representatives play in the American system of democracy?

Majority Rule
What is "majority rule?"
How are minority rights protected in a democracy?

Interpreting a Line Graph: The Voting Patterns of Americans

For a democracy to work, its citizens must **vote**. But how often do Americans come out to vote on election day? Are Americans taking their voting responsibility seriously? The following line graph provides some answers:

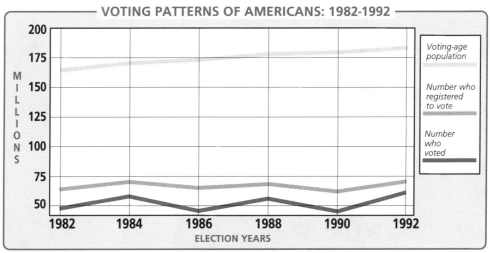

Are you having trouble understanding this line graph? If so, read the following Skill Builder.

INTERPRETING LINE GRAPHS

What is a Line Graph?

A line graph is a chart made up of a series of points connected by a line. It is used to show how something has increased, decreased or remained the same.

❖ What three items are compared in this line graph?

Keys to Understanding a Line Graph

Line graphs have a **vertical axis** or line, which runs from top to bottom. They also have a **horizontal axis**, which runs from left to right. Each axis is labeled.

❖ In this graph, what does the vertical axis show?

❖ What does the horizontal axis show?

Interpreting a Line Graph

Start by reading the **title**. It will give you an idea of the information presented in the line graph.

❖ What is the title of this line graph?

If the graph has more than one line, a **legend** is usually needed. Like the legend of a map, the legend of a line graph shows what each line represents. In this graph, the top line shows the size of the voting age population—the number of Americans who were of voting age. The middle line shows the number of Americans who were registered to vote.

❖ What does the bottom line show?

❖ CONTINUED

What was the total number of voting-age Americans in 1986? To find this answer, first go to the horizontal axis and find the line marked "1986." Next, run your finger up the "1986" line. Stop when you reach the point where the "Voting Age Population" line crosses the "1986" line. Look at the number scale to the left. Along the vertical axis, you will see the number at this point is about 175 million.

❖ What was the total number of voting-age Americans in 1988?

❖ What was the total number of registered voters in 1990?

❖ What was the total number of people who actually voted in 1988?

Looking for Trends in a Line Graph

Sometimes a line graph can be used to identify a trend. A trend is the general direction in which things are moving. A trend can be found by following the direction of the points on a line graph. For example, one trend in the graph is that the voting-age population has continued to increase from 1982 through 1992.

❖ What has been the trend for the number of people who register to vote?

❖ Do you see a trend for the number of people who actually vote?

❖ How might you explain any one of these trends?

Researching Your County Vote in the Last Presidential Election ———————

Every four years citizens in the United States vote to determine who will be their next President. In 1996, **Bill Clinton** (a Democrat) ran against **Bob Dole** (a Republican). In Michigan, a majority of voters gave their support to Bill Clinton.

Which candidate do you think most voters in your county supported? You can find the answer by looking in a current almanac. Check the index under "Elections." Under this heading find the listing, "Presidential." Turn to the page mentioned. When you locate this information for your county, complete a copy of the following chart:

NUMBER OF VOTES	1996 PRESIDENTAL ELECTION: CANDIDATES' NAMES
?	(D) Bill Clinton
	(R) Bob Dole

Ask adult neighbors, relatives and friends in your community whether or not they voted in the last election. Then ask them to explain why they did or did not vote. Make a class chart to see what factors influenced people to vote or not to vote. Then your class should create a pamphlet to encourage people to vote.

Participating in an Election Campaign

In addition to voting, many Americans participate in election campaigns. **Election campaigns** take place in the period before an election when candidates compete to be elected. During the campaign, candidates give speeches, write articles and appear on radio and television. Usually each candidate belongs to a political party. **Political parties** are groups of people with similar ideas about how government should be run. They work together to elect their candidates.

In this exercise you will interview individuals to find out the ways they have participated in an election campaign. Speak with your parents, grandparents or neighbors. Ask them if they participated in any of the following ways in the last election. Record their responses on a copy of the following chart.

Ways of Participating in an Election	Yes or No
Listened to campaign speeches by a candidate	
Spoke with others to influence their vote	
Contributed money to a political candidate	
Handed out literature for a political candidate	
Attended a political rally for a candidate	
Watched a radio or TV commercial by a candidate	
Discussed with other voters the views of candidates	
Reminded others to vote on election day	
What other ways did you participate in the election? 1._____ 2._____ 3._____	

After conducting your interview, bring your results to school. Share your results with other members of your class.

1. What was the most popular method of participating in an election campaign?

2. What methods can you and your classmates suggest for improving voter participation in election campaigns?

HOW WOULD YOU REDUCE POLLUTION IN YOUR COMMUNITY?

7C Informed decision-making is one of a citizen's most important responsibilities in a democracy. In this activity, you will look at the problem of pollution. You will learn to use a problem-solving approach to help deal with this problem. Look for the following important words and phrases:

▶ Environment   ▶ Acid Rain

▶ Pollution   ▶ Brainstorming

One problem that often occurs in a community is pollution. Just think of the large number of people in your community who drive cars, cook food, throw things into the garbage and use products made in factories. These activities seem innocent enough, but each one can cause pollution—the introduction of harmful materials into the environment. It is no wonder that protecting the environment has become a major concern for Americans in every community.

Factories sometimes pour smoke, fumes and chemicals into the air, polluting the environment.

DANGERS TO THE ENVIRONMENT

▶ Our **environment** (en vi' rən mənt) is made up of the Earth and its resources, including air, water, soil and wildlife. People used to think that because the world was so large, the actions of human beings could not damage the environment. People burned trash or dumped their garbage in rivers without thinking about it. However, the rise of industry and the growth of the world's population has greatly changed our thinking.

▶ Today, a major danger to our environment comes from pollution. **Pollution** (pə lōo' shun) is made up of the dirt, fumes, chemicals and other substances that make our environment unclean. Pollution is in the air we breathe and the water we drink. It kills plants and animals. It also causes disease among humans. Many people fear that if pollution is not controlled, it could turn our planet into a place where nothing can live.

TYPES OF POLLUTION

Pollution has a number of causes. For example, **pesticides** are chemicals used by farmers to kill insects and other pests. However, these pesticides can pose a threat to people when rain washes these chemicals into our rivers and streams. Other sources of pollution are cars that pour exhaust fumes into the air and cities that burn garbage. Some factories dump chemical **toxins** (tok' sinz) (*poisons*) into rivers, lakes and oceans. Accidents involving large ships carrying oil result in **oil spills**. Such spills often cover hundreds of miles of ocean. They have made some seashores unusable and have killed plants and animals.

Another type of pollution is **acid rain**. Factory smokestacks and automobile exhaust fumes rise into the air. These fumes form chemicals that return to the Earth in the form of poisonous acid rain or snow. Acid rain causes damage to forests, lakes, fish and even people. It is believed to have caused major damage to trees in many parts of Canada and the United States. Areas with thin soils are particularly harmed by acid rain.

Oil drilling in the Gulf of Mexico.
How does drilling for oil sometimes endanger our environment?

LOCAL POLLUTION

Pollution is not somebody else's problem. We are all affected by it. That means even the community you live in must take some steps to prevent pollution and protect the environment.

THINK ABOUT IT

What do **you** think is the greatest environmental danger to your community?

Compare your answers with those of your classmates. The class as a whole should decide which are the most serious dangers to the environment in your community.

THINK ABOUT IT

What does your **class** think are the greatest environmental dangers to the community?

Now that you have identified several dangers, what can be done about them? First, let's consider the appropriate steps to follow when trying to **solve a problem**.

Skill Builder

AN APPROACH TO PROBLEM-SOLVING

STEP 1: IDENTIFY THE PROBLEM

Begin by identifying the problem. For example, as our population has grown, a new problem has developed: where should we put the billions of tons of garbage thrown away each day? Some communities have tried towing their garbage out to sea to dump it. Other communities burn their garbage. However, both burning and dumping garbage can harm the environment.

A barge tows garbage out to sea for dumping.

> **A helpful hint**: Go through a mental checklist—*who, what, where, when*—when trying to identify or define the problem.

STEP 2: STATE THE CAUSES

Next, you will need to state **how** the problem came about. "Causes" are the different things that led to the problem. For example, many products come in packages that eventually get thrown away. This material adds to the mountains of garbage that we must get rid of every day.

STEP 3: CREATE CRITERIA

Before you look at ways to solve a problem, you must establish criteria. **Criteria** are standards for making a judgment about something. We use criteria to measure whether a solution is acceptable or not. For example, you might consider the following criteria for solving the problem of eliminating garbage:

❖ What will it cost?

❖ What effect will it have on the environment?

❖ Will it be acceptable to most members of the community?

A "good" solution will eliminate garbage, keep pollution at acceptable levels and be something people are willing to do.

❖ CONTINUED

STEP 4: PROPOSE POSSIBLE SOLUTIONS

Now you will need to explore possible solutions to the problem. Begin by listing all the ways you can think of to solve the problem. You should brainstorm with your classmates, listing as many solutions as you can.

∽   BRAINSTORMING   ∽

In brainstorming , people say whatever comes into their minds about a problem. They also suggest different ways to solve the problem. The excitement of hearing other people's ideas often helps members of a brainstorming group to think of new ideas. People in business and government often use brainstorming to help solve difficult problems. In this activity, you and your classmates might use the brainstorming technique to see what possible solutions you can come up with.

For example, one possible solution to the garbage problem is recycling. Recycling creates new products from garbage in the form of bottles, paper and plastic. Another solution could be putting garbage into a landfill. A landfill is a place where garbage can be dumped.

For each proposed solution, apply the criteria you selected in Step 3. Here is a what a sample chart might look like that applies the previous criteria to the two solutions suggested here:

	Recycling	Landfill
• What are the costs?	high	low
• What will be the effect on the environment?	good	bad
• Is it acceptable to the community?	yes	maybe

STEP 5: MAKE A CHOICE

Now you are ready to make a choice. You must compare the proposed solutions. Look at the advantages and disadvantages of each. Often there is no perfect answer. You may have to decide which advantages are more important, based on your own values. To some extent, your solution will depend on ethical considerations: what you value and what you think is "good." People sometimes value different things. As a result, people may disagree about what should be done.

APPLYING A PROBLEM-SOLVING APPROACH

Now it is your turn. Use the problem-solving approach shown on pages 318 and 319 to come up with solutions to the main environmental dangers facing your community. Your teacher will divide your class into groups. Each group should do the following:

- ❖ **Identify** an important local environmental problem.

- ❖ **State** the causes of the problem.

- ❖ **Create criteria** for judging solutions.

- ❖ **Propose possible solutions** to the problem.

- ❖ **Make a choice.** Which solution does your group prefer?

PUTTING YOUR PLAN INTO ACTION

In this activity, you thought about an important public problem: current dangers to the environment. Do you think your group has come up with a good solution to the problem? If so, think about taking steps to help put your solution into action. For example, here are some actions you might take to put your ideas into effect:

- ❖ **Sign a Petition.** Get people who support your plan to sign a petition. A **petition** is a document signed by many people asking the government to take some action.

- ❖ **Inform the Media.** Write a letter to your local newspaper, television or radio station explaining your proposal.

- ❖ **Contact Your Representatives.** Write a letter to local public officials or your elected representatives in the U.S. Congress.

- ❖ **Speak to Community Leaders.** Invite one or two community leaders to your school to discuss the problem.

- ❖ **Volunteer for a Community Organization.** Volunteer to work for a community organization that will help put your ideas into action.

> *What other ways can you think of to promote your solution?*

Discuss with your classmates how they have tried to promote their solutions.

EXPANDING YOUR UNDERSTANDING

Creating Vocabulary Cards

Pollution
What is "pollution"?
What are the dangers of pollution?

Brainstorming
What is "brainstorming"?
List five steps for solving a problem.

Asking a Social Science Question

Select a classmate to act as your partner. Then both of you should try to think of a social science question about a topic. Remember that **social science** is the study of how people behave, using the methods of science. For example, you might want to study the topic of poverty. Your social science question might be: *Does poverty lead to poor health?*

What social science question might you ask about the topic *Watching Television*? Now select your own topic and think of a social science question for it.

Topic	Social Science Question

Creating a Pie Chart about Pollution

The following table deals with different types of pollution:

Type of Pollution	Percentage of Total Pollution
Industrial processes	33%
Solid wastes	19%
Burning fuels	29%
Car and truck exhaust	19%

Use the information in the table above to complete the pie chart about pollution in the United States. The first item in the table has already been put on the chart for you.

TYPES OF POLLUTION IN THE UNITED STATES, 1995
(percentage of total pollution)

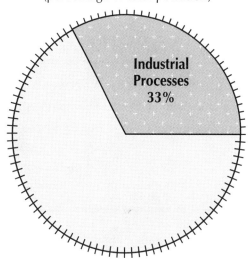

Industrial Processes 33%

SHOULD WE LIMIT THE AMOUNT OF VIOLENCE SHOWN ON TELEVISION?

7D In this activity, you will look more closely at the citizen's task of decision-making. In the pages that follow, you will be asked to examine a public issue by reading several different sources. Then you will form your own conclusions and write a letter explaining your views. Look for the following important words:

▶ Issue   ▶ Petition   ▶ Editorial

Should the President send soldiers to other countries to protect U.S. citizens there?	Should Michigan lower the age for driving a car?	Should your county raise taxes to build a homeless shelter?

These are the kinds of public issues that citizens often think about and discuss. When you are 18 years old you will be able to take a stand on these and other issues by voting. To be an informed voter, you must learn to make wise decisions on public issues. In this activity, you will have a chance to practice this important skill.

 WHAT ARE ISSUES?

Issues are not quite the same as problems. An │issue│ is something that people disagree about. Issues often concern whether or not the government should do something, such as pass a new law. There must be at least two different viewpoints for an issue to exist.

Skill Builder

STEPS TO MAKING AN INFORMED DECISION

In making **informed decisions** on public issues, you will need to:

Identify the issue	For example, you might be concerned that watching violence on television leads people to become violent in real life. Others may say that people are not affected by what they watch.

❖ CONTINUED

Get information from several sources	The more sources you look at, the more information you will find to help learn about the issue. You will also get the benefit of seeing different points of view.
Evaluate the information	Compare what each of your sources of information has to say about the issue. Be sure to separate facts from opinions.
Identify and compare different viewpoints	Find several possible ways of dealing with the issue. Then compare these different viewpoints.
Make your decision	Finally, after comparing different views, choose the one you think is best. You may also come up with a new view of your own. This could be a compromise of several views. A **compromise** is a solution in which each side gives up something, but also gets something in return.

When you need to make an informed decision, think of the illustration below. Recall that each step is part of the process of reaching a decision on an issue.

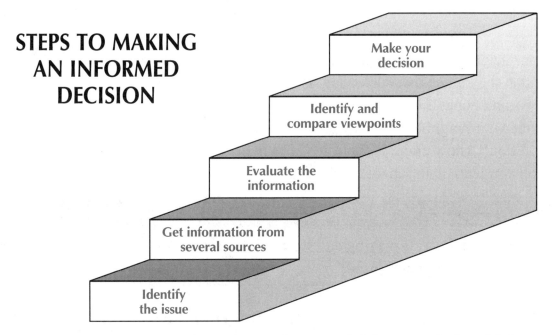

STEPS TO MAKING AN INFORMED DECISION

Now let's apply what you have learned to a real-life example in which you are asked for your opinion about a public issue. This example will help you to better understand the five steps for making an informed decision.

WOULD YOU SIGN A PETITION TO LIMIT VIOLENCE ON TELEVISION?

One evening at dinner, you are telling your parent what you learned in school about making an informed decision. Just then, the doorbell rings. It is one of your neighbors.
▶ He is holding some pamphlets and a **petition** (pə tish' un) (*a demand for action sent to someone in authority, such as a government official*).

STEP 1: IDENTIFYING THE ISSUE

Your neighbor reads the petition to both of you. It is addressed to your representative in Congress. The petition deals with television violence. It states that the violence frequently shown on television is a major reason for rising violence throughout the nation. The petition states:

> *We the undersigned believe that Congress should pass a new law limiting the amount of violence shown on television.*
>
> | Signatures | Signatures | Signatures |
> |---|---|---|
> | Robert Adams | Sally Tinsley | Kathleen Martin |
> | Gary Freno | Michael Sampson | Victor Abrams |
> | Mary Jordan | Elizabeth Thorpe | Thomas Drew II |

Your neighbor asks your parent to sign the petition. By signing the petition, people show that they agree that such a law is needed. Your parent says, "I would like a little time to think about this issue."

After your neighbor leaves, your parent turns to you. "This is an important public issue. I don't know enough about it yet to make up my mind. Why don't we use the method you learned in school today to make an informed decision?"

✔ CHECKING YOUR UNDERSTANDING ✔

The first step towards making an informed decision is to identify the issue. What issue has your neighbor raised?

STEP 2: OBTAINING INFORMATION FROM SEVERAL SOURCES

In order to make an informed decision, you must gather information about the issue from different **sources**. Using reference books is a good place to begin. They provide you with information about the issue. Also, they can tell you where to find other information, such as articles written by experts.

Encyclopedias, almanacs and the Internet are good starting points for any investigation. As you learned earlier, you must be careful to separate **facts** from **opinions**. Your parent suggests visiting the library together to find material.

✔ CHECKING YOUR UNDERSTANDING ✔

More information about the issue can be found in a variety of other sources. Name **one** other source you might look at to learn more about the issue.

STEP 3: EVALUATING THE INFORMATION

Bringing together different sources of information is only the first step in making an informed decision. Next, you have to read and compare the different sources. Let's take a look at the first of several sources you might find in the library.

Source: **THE ENCYCLOPEDIA OF SCIENCE**

Television. The first television broadcasts began in the 1930s. The introduction of television raised an important question: Should television stations be run by the government or by private companies? In some countries, the government runs all the television channels. It controls which television shows appear. In the United States, private companies run the television channels.

Americans have a tradition of free speech and a free press. As a result, the government cannot tell TV companies what to show. However, the government does not allow television stations to do anything they want. The government has the power to refuse to allow certain shows to be aired. It rarely uses this right, but it always can.

Many critics think the government should exercise this right more often, especially when it comes to limiting violence on television. They propose that the government should rate all television shows for violence. This is already done by the film industry, which rates movies. Others say America would have much better programs if the government simply took over running the television stations.

✔ CHECKING YOUR UNDERSTANDING ✔

1. What question did the introduction of television raise?
2. How was this question answered in the United States?

Now that you have learned about the background of television, let's look at a second source of information you might use—a newspaper article.

Source: THE MICHIGANDER DAILY

The Michigander Daily

First Edition   Friday

TWO TEENS DIE IN HIGHWAY "DARE"

It all began as a joke. On Thursday night, Channel 3 was showing the latest action-adventure picture. In the movie, several teenagers lie down on the center-divider line of a highway to show their friends that they are not afraid.

After watching the movie, teenagers living near Lansing began daring each other. They dared each other to lie down on the center line of the highway, just as the teenagers in the movie had done. Two teenagers took the dare. They are now dead. They were run over by a motorist who did not see them in the dark.

This is part of a growing number of violent, senseless deaths in America. Movies and television shows often influence us. Sometimes we imitate what we see, as these teenagers did. Other times, we are influenced without even knowing it.

Parents, teachers and doctors across the nation are alarmed at the increasing violence shown on television. Children watching television see thousands of acts of violence before they are even old enough to go to school. Cartoons often show violence between the characters. Some experts believe the violence on television may be partly responsible for the increasing violence in America. They are calling for Congress to pass new laws. They want to stop all violent shows on television before 10 o'clock at night.

✔ CHECKING YOUR UNDERSTANDING ✔

1. What happened to the two teenagers discussed in the newspaper article?
2. What does this newspaper story have to say about violence on television?

Next, let's look at a third source of information you might use—a newspaper editorial.

NEWSPAPER EDITORIAL

Editorials (ed i tor' e alz) are opinions presented in newspapers and magazines. They are not news articles that report facts. They usually represent the opinions of the editors. Freedom of the press is an important right enjoyed by newspapers in America. This freedom allows editors to speak out on topics that concern them. The editors try to win the public over to their viewpoint. When trying to make an informed decision, it is a good idea to read editorials in different newspapers and magazines.

Source: **EDITORIAL IN *THE ANN ARBOR TIMES***

The Ann Arbor Times

Second Edition   Tuesday

OUR VIEW OF TELEVISION VIOLENCE

A growing number of people are seeking a new law to limit the violence shown on television. Have these people carefully thought about the issue? They think that violence on television is the main cause of violence in America. They are wrong. Poverty and the large number of guns are the main causes of violence.

Have the people in favor of this new law thought about the dangers of government control? Who in the government will decide which television programs are violent and which are not? Will the government also prevent television stations from reporting violent stories on the news? Once the government controls some subjects on television, it will try to control others. Soon, the government will control everything we see. This violates our rights of free speech and a free press.

We believe it is better to let private television stations show what they want. Parents should decide what their children can watch. If parents don't want their children to watch a show because it is too violent, there is a simple remedy. The parents can change the channel or turn off the set. If we allow government to control what we can watch, where will government controls end?

✔ CHECKING YOUR UNDERSTANDING ✔

1. What stand does this editorial take on the control of private television programs by government?
2. What reasons does this editorial offer in support of its view?

Next, let's examine one last source of information—a book about raising children.

Source: "HOW TO RAISE CHILDREN: ADVICE FOR PARENTS"

Nightmares

Nightmares are dreams in which the dreamer feels helpless, afraid or sad. Children are the ones most likely to suffer from nightmares. Children may seem to enjoy television programs that show violence. However, once the children are asleep, they often suffer from terrible nightmares. These nightmares are caused by the same television programs. For this reason, many parents and educators support the use of a computer chip in televisions to prevent children from watching violent programs. The chip would get signals that would prevent the television set from showing programs considered violent.

Educational Television

Since the 1960s, there have been many attempts to create interesting television programs. Many have been created that are both educational and fun for children to watch. The most successful of these has been "Sesame Street." Tests show that three-year-olds watching Sesame Street regularly do better in learning skills than those who do not watch the program. For this reason, many parents are asking the government to sponsor more educational programs.

✔ CHECKING YOUR UNDERSTANDING ✔

1. What does the book say about nightmares?
2. What does the book say about how television can shape our behavior?

STEP 4: IDENTIFYING AND COMPARING DIFFERENT VIEWS

You have just completed reading a variety of sources. Now let's return to the original issue raised at the start of this activity:

> *Should the government limit the amount of violence shown on television?*

Think about all the different opinions you have read on this issue. Suggested answers range from having the government do nothing to banning (*forbidding*) all violence shown on television. After reading all of these different viewpoints, you may also have developed an answer of your own.

The following is a list of possible recommendations based on your reading. Make a copy of the chart. For each proposal, write down its advantages and disadvantages.

Views You Have Found— The government should:	Advantages	Disadvantages
❖ make no changes.	?	?
❖ rate television shows like movies, based on the amount of violence they show.	?	?
❖ place microchips in television sets to block violent programs.	?	?
❖ ban all violent shows before 10:00 at night.	?	?
❖ *(you provide a possible solution)* .	?	?

STEP 5: MAKING YOUR DECISION

It is time for you to make an informed decision. Compare the advantages and disadvantages of each proposal. Decide which of these are most important to you. Rank the possible actions, from the best (#1) to the worst (#5).

Possible Actions — The government should:	Number
❖ make no changes.	?
❖ rate television shows like movies based on the violence they show.	?
❖ insert microchips into television sets.	?
❖ ban violent television shows before 10:00 at night.	?
❖ (your solution).	?

WOULD YOU RECOMMEND SIGNING THE PETITION?

Closing

We first began this activity when your neighbor asked your parent to sign a petition. Now that you have made an informed decision, would you recommend that your parent sign it? ☐ Yes   ☐ No   Explain your decision.

Did you make a wise decision? If you think so, try to persuade others to your point of view. Write a letter to a newspaper, television station or your elected representative which states your view and why others should support you.

WRITING A PERSUASIVE LETTER OR ESSAY

An essay that tries to win someone over to your point of view is called a **persuasive essay**.

WHEN TO USE A PERSUASIVE ESSAY

Use a persuasive essay to get a person to change his or her mind on a particular issue. For example, let's assume you wanted others to adopt the view that it is necessary to limit the amount of violence shown on television. You would use a persuasive essay to try to win them over to your point of view.

HINTS FOR WRITING A PERSUASIVE ESSAY

You should clearly state your viewpoint. Then present logical reasons why the reader should adopt your view or suggested course of action. Avoid appeals to emotion. Instead, focus on presenting logical arguments and conclusions through the use of examples and comparisons.

WRITING A PERSUASIVE LETTER

In writing your letter, follow the "cheeseburger" format you learned about in the first chapter. Combine these steps with the format of a business letter which you learned how to write on page 294.

❖ **Introductory paragraph.** Your introductory paragraph should state the purpose of your letter. For example, your purpose might be to convince the reader that the government should limit the amount of violence shown on television.

❖ **Body of the letter.** Present as many reasons as you can in your letter. Try to convince the reader to support your viewpoint. Follow a clear and logical order. For example, each reason might be in a separate paragraph. Mention specific facts whenever you can to support your point of view. If you want to limit violence on TV, you might mention that some young people act in a "copycat" way after they see violence on television.

❖ **Closing the letter.** End with a summary of your main points. Impress the reader by concluding with a key fact or a memorable quote about the subject.

❖ CONTINUED

MAILING YOUR LETTER

If you think you have written a strong persuasive letter, mail it to your Congressperson in Washington, D.C. or to the editor of a local newspaper.

EXPANDING YOUR UNDERSTANDING

Creating Vocabulary Cards

Issue
What is an "issue"?
Identify one issue facing
Americans today.

Editorial
What is an "editorial"?
How are editorials helpful in
making an informed decision?

Looking at Important Issues Facing Americans Today

The belief that individuals may hold different views about an issue lies at the core of our democracy. Throughout history, Americans have been divided over certain issues. In the 1770s, Americans were divided over whether or not to declare independence from Great Britain. In the 1850s, Americans were divided over the practice of slavery. In the early part of the 20th century, Americans were divided over whether women should vote. This tradition of disagreement over public issues continues today. Over the next few weeks, read a national newspaper or watch a national news program on television. Make a copy of the chart below, and track a major issue facing the nation:

DATE	SOURCE OF INFORMATION	DESCRIBE THE ISSUE

What do you think is the single most important issue facing our nation today? Compare your answer with those of your classmates. Do their views agree with yours? Explain.

CORE DEMOCRATIC VALUES: PROTECTION FOR INDIVIDUALS

In this unit, you learned about some of the ways in which Americans participate in their democratic form of government. One of the reasons we are able to participate so freely in the governing process is because we have strong protections for individual rights.

Many of these protections limit the ability of the government to arrest us and put us in jail. This is very important to the success of democracy. In some countries, the government can put citizens in jail at any time without having to explain why. In those societies, many people live in constant fear of their government. They are afraid to criticize government leaders, to vote against them or to seek changes.

In such societies, government leaders have almost complete power. In these countries, the purpose of government is not to promote the good of the people. Government leaders run the government to increase their own wealth and power.

The U.S. Constitution, including the Bill of Rights prevents such abuses of government power in the United States. It provides very specific guarantees against unfair arrest, imprisonment or loss of life or property. One of the most important of these quarantees is the **right to a speedy, public trial by a jury.**

In some countries, a person accused of a crime is simply arrested and put in jail. The accused person may be briefly questioned by a judge or government official but has no trial. Often, the public is not even allowed to attend the hearing.

In the United States, a person accused of a crime is guaranteed a trial by a jury. During the trial, the government presents facts trying to show that the accused person committed the crime. The accused person has a right to present evidence to show that he or she did not commit the crime. The trial is held in public.

After hearing both sides, a jury decides whether or not the person is guilty. The jury is made up of a small of group citizens chosen at random. If the jury decides the accused person is guilty, a judge will punish the person by putting him or her in jail. The government cannot put anyone in jail without first having a jury agree that the accused person is guilty of a crime.

Some of the other important protections for individuals are the following:

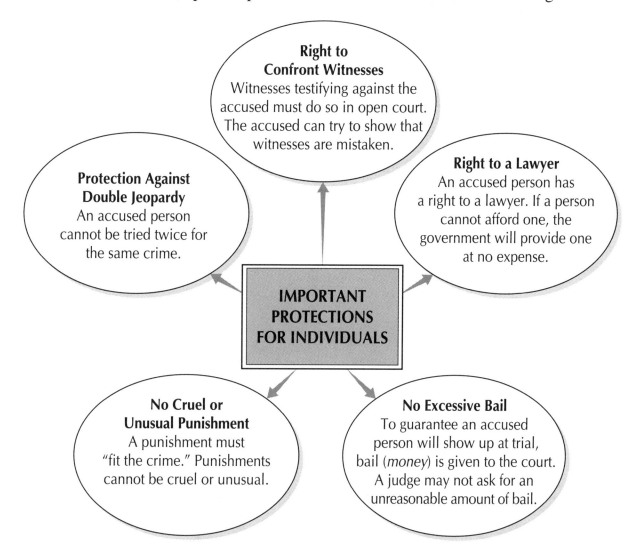

It is often very difficult to balance the needs of society with individual rights. From time to time, groups of citizens express the view that the United States has gone too far in protecting the rights of individuals accused of crimes. Under our system, it is usually very hard to prove to a jury that a person is guilty of a crime. This means that sometimes criminals may go free.

It is useful to remember that protection of the rights of the accused sends a powerful message throughout society. Individual rights are important and must be respected. Our rules make it difficult for the government to punish someone for a crime that he or she did not commit.

SUMMARIZING YOUR UNDERSTANDING

Directions: Use your knowledge to complete the following graphic organizer.

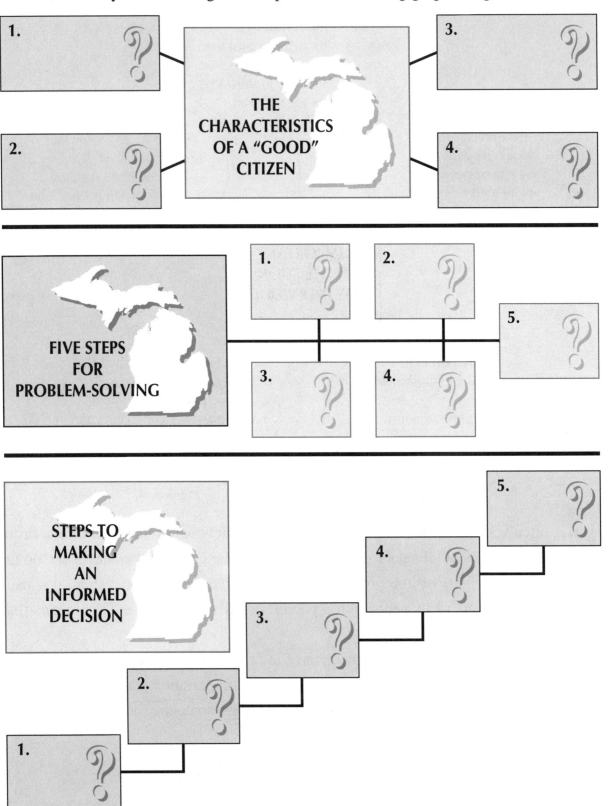

THE IMAGE I NOW HAVE
OF MICHIGAN IS ... ?

CLOSING ACTIVITY At the start of this book, you were invited to take a journey through Michigan—its land and its people. In the opening activity, you wrote what Michigan meant to you. We hope that since that time, you have learned a great deal about Michigan and your community.

WHAT DOES MICHIGAN MEAN TO YOU NOW?

Your journey is about to come to an end. You should think once again about what Michigan means to you. One way to do this is to create an "ABC" book about Michigan:

❖ Each page should have one letter of the alphabet at the top, followed by a word.

❖ The word should focus on something you have learned about Michigan's geography, history, people, economy or government. For example, on the "A" page you might write about Ann Arbor.

❖ Each page should have an illustration and a description or explanation. Illustrations can be drawings you make or pictures from a newspaper, magazine or book.

Here is a sample of how a page dealing with the letter "A" might look:

Aa
Ann Arbor

Ann Arbor is a city in the southeast corner of Michigan, located only a 45-minute ride from Detroit. Ann Arbor is home to the University of Michigan. Ann Arbor was started in 1833 when 34 German families first settled there. During the Civil War, Ann Arbor served as a stop on the Underground Railroad. Today, Ann Arbor is one of Michigan's leading cities.

Museum of Art at the University of Michigan in Ann Arbor.

To help you to organize your ABC book about Michigan, copy the following chart. As you complete your description for each letter, check it off on the chart.

LETTER	DESCRIPTION	ILLUSTRATION
A		
B		
C		
D		
E		
F		
G		
H		
I		
J		
K		
L		
M		
N		
O		
P		
Q		
R		
S		
T		
U		
V		
W		
X		
Y		
Z		

GLOSSARY

This glossary contains the meaning of many of the important words and phrases used in this book. At the end of the definition, the page number tells you where the word or phrase may be found.

	Key to Pronunciations Used in the Book						
a	bat, marry	ē	equal, bee	oi	oil, toy	ə	a in alone
ā	made, say	i	if, rig	ōō	ooze, tool		e in system
â(r)	fair, stare	ī	ice, bite	ou	out, loud		i in easily
ä	art, calm	o	ox, box	sh	shoe, push		o in gallop
ch	chief, beach	ō	over, boat	u	up, glove		u in circus
e	set, merry	ô	fought, raw	û	urge, burn		

A

abolitionists. People who opposed slavery before the Civil War. [116]

acid rain. Chemicals in the atmosphere from factory smokestacks and automobile exhaust fumes that return to the Earth in the form of rain or snow. [317]

almanac. A book of facts published each year. Almanacs cover a wide range of subjects. They often list movie stars, explorers, musicians, writers, Nobel Prize winners and athletes. [65]

American Revolution (1775–1783). The war fought between the 13 colonies and Great Britain. As a result of the war, the colonies won their independence and formed the United States of America. [130]

ancestors. Members of your family who lived a long time ago, such as great-grandparents. [181]

appointed. Officials chosen by some higher official, instead of being elected by the voters. [279]

Articles of Confederation. The agreement creating the first United States government. The government created by the Articles was unusually weak. The Articles were soon replaced by the U.S. Constitution. [105]

artifact. An object made or shaped by people, such as a tool. Ancient artifacts often provide information about lifestyles of people who lived in the past. [78]

assembly line. Method of producing goods in factories in which the product is moved from one worker to another. [134]

atlas. A special type of book that contains different kinds of maps. [63]

authority. The power of a government to act in representing the community. [275]

autobiography. A book written by a person about his or her own life. [207]

axis. The imaginary line that the Earth spins on. [17]

B

Battle Creek. Home to Kellogg's and General Foods. Battle Creek is known as the "cereal capital of the world." [128]

Bill of Rights. The first ten amendments to the U.S. Constitution, guaranteeing individual rights. [107]

board of commissioners. The governing board that is elected to represent the towns and cities in county government. The commissioners handle such matters as deciding how to spend county tax funds. [289]

budget. A plan for spending money. [292]

business. Any economic activity in which someone tries to make a profit. [231]

C

canal. A man-made ditch filled with water. The Erie Canal allowed people to travel from New York City on the east coast to the Great Lakes entirely by water. This canal helped bring settlers to Michigan from New York and New England. [110]

capital equipment. Goods that are used to make other goods or to provide services. [288]

cartographers. People who make maps. [26]

cause. The reason why something happened. [132]

chronological order. The order in which events actually happened. [161]

citizen. A person who is a member of a particular nation. [306]

Civil Rights Movement. Movement in the 1950s and 1960s aimed at ending racial segregation. [156]

civil war. Any war between citizens of the same country. The American Civil War between Northern and Southern states was fought between 1861 and 1865. [118]

classify. To arrange, organize and sort objects or information into classes or categories. Classifying is especially helpful to make sense out of many items that otherwise seem disorganized. [215]

climate. The average weather conditions of a place over a long period of time. [47]

colony. An area where people from a foreign country live. Although they live far from their original country, the mother country still governs them. [95]

compare. To identify how things are alike. [273]

compass rose. A drawing on a map in the form of a compass showing four basic directions: north, south, east and west. [28]

concept. A general idea or term that explains a group of things which, although different, have something in common. [178]

Confederate States of America. The eleven states that left the United States in 1861. The Civil War was fought to bring these states back into the Union. [118]

constituents. The people who live in an elected official's home district. [294]

constitution. A written plan for setting up a system of government. Michigan's first state constitution was written in 1836. The U.S. Constitution was written in 1787. [287]

consumers. People who buy goods and services to satisfy their needs and wants. [231]

consumption. The act of using goods and services. [231]

continents. The world's seven major land masses: Asia, Africa, North America, South America, Antarctica, Europe and Australia. [18]

contrast. To look at how two or more things are different from each other. [273]

counties. The smaller governing units every U.S. state is divided into (except for Louisiana). Michigan is divided into 83 counties. [21]

country. A place that has borders separating it from neighboring places and has its own government. People in a country usually speak the same language and have similar customs and traditions. [19]

county seat. The place where the county government is located. [290]

criteria. Conditions we create to define and classify something. [305]

D

Declaration of Independence. A document issued in 1776 that explained to the world why the American colonists had decided to seek independence from Great Britain. [262]

democracy. A form of government in which citizens govern themselves. In such a government, ordinary people hold the final power. [276]

depression. An economic downturn in which many businesses fail and millions of people are unemployed. The Great Depression occurred in the 1930s. [140]

dictatorship. A system of government in which all power is concentrated in the hands of a single person or a small group. [275]

diorama. A three-dimensional scene created by placing objects, figures and pictures in front of a painted background. [39]

due process rights. The rights that guarantee that the government cannot take away a person's life, liberty or property without a fair trial or other legal procedure. [173]

E

Eastern Hemisphere. The half of the Earth east of the Prime Meridian. [17]

economics. The study of how nations, businesses and individuals make things, buy things and use money. [228]

ecosystem. A system in which plants, animals and the physical environment work together. In an ecosystem there is a balanced relationship between land, water, the atmosphere, plants and animals. [50]

editorial. A statement written in a newspaper that gives the opinions of the newspaper's editors on important issues. [327]

effect. What happens as a result of a situation, action or event. [132]

Emancipation Proclamation. A document issued by Abraham Lincoln in 1862. It stated that enslaved people in the Confederacy would be freed on January 1, 1863. [269]

encyclopedias. Books that contain articles with information on many topics. The articles are arranged in alphabetical order. Encyclopedias usually have several volumes. [102]

entrepreneurs. People who bring the factors of production together in the hope of making a profit. [235]

environment. The Earth and the natural resources that surround us. [316]

equal protection. A guarantee in the U.S. Constitution stating that all citizens will be treated equally by any laws that the government passes. [173]

equator. An imaginary line drawn around the middle of the Earth. [32]

ethnic group. A group whose members share traditions, customs, beliefs and ancestors. Often members of an ethnic group have the same national origin, language or race. [182]

executive branch. The branch of government with the power to enforce the laws. [279]

exports. Goods and services sold from one country to people in other countries. [255]

F

factual statement. A statement that can usually be checked for accuracy by looking at other sources to be sure it is correct or incorrect. [76]

factories. Buildings in which goods are made. [242]

factors of production. All the things needed to produce goods and services. [234]

federalism. The division of government power between the national government and state governments. [276]

Fort Machilimackinac. This fort was built in the 1700s as a French trading post. The reconstructed fort now has more than a dozen restored buildings. [56]

Fort Pontchartrain. A fort built by the French in 1701. In 1760, the fort was taken over by the British. In 1796, the British turned the fort over to the United States. The city that grew up around the fort was called Detroit. [94]

free market economy. An economic system in which the government allows people to produce whatever they can and to consume whatever they can afford. [231]

French and Indian War (1754–1763). A war between England and France for control of North America. Most Native American groups sided with the French. Because of this, the war was called the French and Indian War. [95]

G

generalization. A general statement identifying a common pattern in a group of things. [186]

geography. The study of different places around the world, including a study of people, where they live and how they are linked to the world around them. [35]

geologist. A scientist who studies rocks and minerals and where they can be found. [124]

Gettysburg Address. In 1865, President Abraham Lincoln dedicated the battlefield at Gettysburg as a Union cemetery. His speech honored soldiers who had lost their lives so that the nation would remain united. [270]

glaciers. Huge sheets of ice that at one time covered Michigan. [46]

goods. Things that people make, mine or grow, usually to sell, such as foods, toys, clothes and cars. [234]

government. The organization that makes a community's rules, settles disputes and protects members of the community from hostile groups. [245]

Governor. The chief executive of a state government. [286]

Great Lakes: Five major lakes located between the United States and Canada: Lake Huron, Lake Ontario, Lake Michigan, Lake Erie and Lake Superior. [255]

Great Lakes Ecosystem. An ecosystem that includes all five of the Great Lakes and the surrounding eight states of the United States and two provinces in Canada. About 33 million people live in this ecosystem. [51]

Great Lakes Plains. An area that includes all of the Lower Peninsula and the eastern half of the Upper Peninsula. The region is characterized by generally poor soils in the Upper Peninsula and northern parts of the Lower Peninsula. [46]

Greenfield Village. A museum built by Henry Ford to house his collection of older buildings and their contents. Ford spent millions of dollars to build an outdoor museum that would show how ordinary Americans lived in the past. [59]

growing season. The period of time that plants and crops are safe from killing frost. In Michigan, the growing season of the Upper Peninsula is generally shorter than in the Lower Peninsula. In the Lower Peninsula, the growing season averages from 80 to 170 days. [48]

H

hemisphere. Geographers divide the Earth into halves; each half is known as a hemisphere because it is half of a sphere. [17]

hero. Someone who is recognized for his or her courage, talents or achievements. Heroes and heroines are the people who often make history. [309]

human capital. The labor and talents provided by people who produce goods and services. [235]

human-environment interaction. The ways in which the physical features of a place affect its people and the people affect their environment. This interaction is one of the five themes of geography. [37]

I

immigration. The movement of people into a country. An immigrant is someone who goes to another country with the intention of living there permanently. [187]

imports. Products brought into a country from other countries. [256]

income tax. A tax collected by government on the earnings of people and businesses. [291]

index. The pages of a book listing the information in the book and page numbers where that information can be found. [66]

irrelevant information. Information not related to what you are looking for. [69]

issue. A topic or question about which people have two or more opposing views. [322]

J

judicial branch. The branch of government that interprets the laws. [280]

jury. A group of unbiased citizens that sit in judgment in civil and criminal cases. [296]

K

Ku Klux Klan. An organization begun in the South that used violence to discourage African Americans from voting. [271]

L

latitude. The distance north or south of the equator, measured in degrees. Lines of latitude run horizontally around the Earth. They are also called parallels because they never cross each other. [32]

laws. Rules made by a government. A violation of a law is usually punished with a penalty. [264]

leader. A person with a vision for the future, the ability to communicate this vision to others and the ability to get others to act. [268]

legend. The part of a map that is used to unlock the meaning of the map's symbols. The legend is sometimes called the "key." [28]

legislative branch. The branch of government that makes laws. [278]

Lieutenant Governor. An elected official who assists the Governor of a state. The Lieutenant Governor carries out the duties of the Governor when he or she is out of the state. [286]

line graph. A chart made up of a series of points connected by a line. Line graphs often show how something has increased, decreased or remained the same. [313]

location. Where something can be found in relation to other things. It is one of the five themes of geography. [35]

loggers. People who make their living by cutting down trees. [126]

longitude. The distance east or west of the Prime Meridian, measured in degrees. Lines of longitude run up and down a map or globe, connecting at the North Pole and the South Pole. [33]

M

Mackinac Bridge. A bridge across the Straits of Mackinac, completed in 1957. The bridge connects the Upper and Lower Peninsulas. [45]

majority rule. A majority is more than half. In a democracy, decisions are made by a majority of the people. [300]

map. A small picture or diagram of a place, showing where things are located. [26]

March on Washington. In 1963, Martin Luther King, Jr. called for a mass rally in Washington, D.C. to focus the nation's attention on ending prejudice and discrimination. At this rally Dr. King delivered his "I Have A Dream" speech. [157]

mayor. The chief executive of a city government. [290]

mileage chart. A chart used to show the average distance between cities or places. [31]

minerals. Valuable resources found in the Earth, such as iron ore or gold. [252]

monarchy. A government in which a king or queen holds power. A monarch usually inherits his or her power. [275]

mound builders. Ancient Native American groups in North America who constructed large earthen mounds to bury their dead. [80]

Mount Arvon. The highest point in Michigan, measuring 1,979 feet above sea level. [46]

museum. Places where works of art and other interesting objects are displayed. [86]

N

national origin. The country where one's parents, grandparents or ancestors came from. [342]

nationality. The country of one's citizenship. [181]

Native Americans. The first people to live in the Americas. [76]

natural resources. Plants, animals and minerals found in nature, used to grow food, supply energy, make clothing, provide housing and serve as raw materials. [234]

naturalized citizen of the United States. A person not born in the United States and whose parents are not American citizens but who has become a citizen by living in the United States for a period of time, passing a citizenship test. and taking an oath. [306]

New Deal. A program created by President Franklin D. Roosevelt to provide work and relief to needy Americans during the Great Depression. [141]

Nineteenth Amendment. An amendment passed in 1920, giving women the right to vote. [139]

Northern Hemisphere. The half of the Earth north of the equator. [17]

Northwest Ordinance. Law passed by the American government under the Articles of Confederation to govern the Northwest Territory. It divided the Northwest Territory into smaller territories. [105]

Northwest Territory. The area northwest of the original thirteen colonies and west up to the Mississippi River. The Northwest Territory became part of the United States in 1783. Michigan was part of the Northwest Territory. [105]

O

Ojibwa. The largest Native American group in Michigan. They lived by the shores of the Great Lakes. [79]

opinion. A statement of personal beliefs, which cannot be checked for accuracy. [76]

opportunity cost. The "cost" of every economic decision, measured by the opportunity given up to do other things. [229]

oral history. Collecting and recording memories of the past through interviews of eyewitnesses. [147]

orbit. The path made by a planet, moon or satellite as it travels around a star, planet or other body in space. The Earth has an oval orbit around the Sun. [16]

Ottawa. A Native American tribe that lived in the western parts of Michigan. They were related to the Ojibwa, and followed many of their customs. [80]

P

penalty. The punishment for breaking a rule or law. [264]

per capita income. The amount of money earned by the average person in a specific area. [65]

petition. A demand for change, sent to a government official or someone in authority. [320]

physical regions. Areas with similar geographical features or climate. Physical regions can be large or small. [20]

pie chart. A circle diagram that is divided into slices of different sizes to show how the parts of something are related to the whole. [204]

political map. A map that shows where countries, states and cities are located. [63]

pollution. Dirt, fumes and other substances that make our environment unclean. [316]

Pontiac's War. A war led by Pontiac, an Ottawa chief. During this war, Native American warriors massacred the British at Fort Michilimackinac in Mackinaw City and captured every English fort in Michigan except the fort at Detroit. [95]

population density. The average number of people living in a square mile of an area. [65]

Potawatomi. A Native American group who once lived in the southwestern Lower Peninsula. [82]

precipitation. Moisture that falls to the Earth as rain, snow, hail and sleet. [47]

President of the United States. The chief executive officer of our national government. [279]

primary source. An original record of an event, such as an original letter, document or eyewitness description. [144]

Prime Meridian. An imaginary line drawn from the North Pole to the South Pole through Greenwich, England. [33]

problem of scarcity. The chief problem in economics—society has limited resources to satisfy people's unlimited wants and needs. [229]

product map. A specialized type of map that identifies where products are grown and industries are located. [248]

production. The act of making or providing goods and services. [231]

profit. The amount of money left over in a business after its expenses have been paid. [235]

provinces. Political units, similar to the states found in the United States. Canada has 10 provinces: Newfoundland, Nova Scotia, New Brunswick, Prince Edward Island, Quebec, Ontario, Manitoba, Saskatchewan, Alberta and British Columbia. [44]

Q

Quebec Act. Act passed by the British government in 1774, extending Quebec Province to the south and west. [97]

R

race. A group of people identified by some physical characteristics, such as the color of their skin. [179]

racial segregation. The separation of people by race. [271]

recycling. Creating new products from used cans, bottles, paper and plastic that would otherwise be thrown out. [319]

region. An area with places that share similar characteristics or features. People within a region usually have more contact with one another than they do with people outside the region. [36]

relevant information. Information that is useful and appropriate. It relates to what one is looking for. [69]

religion. A system of beliefs about the existence of God or of several gods. Each religion usually has a set of customs and practices and an organization, such as a church, which helps set the conduct of its members. [182]

representative democracy. A system of government in which citizens elect representatives to make government decisions. [276]

representatives. Elected officials in a democracy, who carry out the will of the people. [276]

Republican Party. A new political party which was begun in 1854 in Jackson, Michigan. The Republicans were opposed to the spread of slavery and worked to put people in public office who would be opposed to slavery. [116]

reservations. Areas set aside by the national government for Native Americans to live in. [87]

right. Something everyone in society is entitled to or allowed to do. Rights are generally protected by the U.S. Constitution. [343]

S

sales tax. A tax collected by state and local governments on purchased items. [291]

scale. A device used by mapmakers to show what distance the measurements on a map stand for in real life. [29]

secondary source. The writings and viewpoints of historians and other authors, written after an event has taken place. [144]

service industries. Industries in which workers provide useful services to others. [243]

services. Acts that people do for others. People such as electricians, plumbers and barbers provide services. [234]

social scientists. People who apply the methods and procedures used in science to the study of how people behave. They look for patterns of behavior that help explain why people act as they do. [267]

Soo Locks. The Soo Locks were opened in 1959 at Sault Ste. Marie. They raise and lower ships twenty-one feet to reach the different levels of Lake Superior and Lake Huron. [125]

Southern Hemisphere. The half of the Earth south of the equator. [17]

special district. A unit of government providing a special service that is not provided by a city or town government, such as water, garbage or snow removal. [290]

sphere. An object shaped like a ball or globe. [17]

state government. The level of government handling matters that affect people throughout the state. [283]

states. The smaller political units that many countries are divided into. The United States is divided into 50 states. Some countries are divided into provinces instead of states. [21]

strait. (*often straits*) Narrow body of water connecting two large bodies of water. [44]

suburb. A residential community located outside a city. [152]

symbol. Something that stands for or represents something else. A stop sign and the American flag are both symbols. [28]

T

table of contents. A list found in the first few pages of a book giving its main topics, divided into units or chapters, and the pages on which they can be found. [212]

table. An arrangement of words or numbers in columns used to show large amounts of information so that particular facts can be easily located and compared. [49]

tax. Money collected by the government to pay its expenses. [97]

technology. Scientific knowledge applied to a useful and practical purpose, such as building things or making goods. [243]

thesaurus. A specialized reference book used by people to help them find just the right word or phrase to express an idea accurately and effectively. [210]

timeline. A chart that shows a group of events arranged along a line in chronological order. [161]

Toledo Strip. A small strip of land that Michigan and Ohio once claimed. For a time it appeared that Michigan and Ohio might go to war over the dispute. The U.S. Congress finally settled the dispute by giving the land to Ohio. In exchange, Michigan was given the Upper Peninsula. [113]

topography. The land forms of a place, such as mountains and plains. [46]

Treaty of Paris. Treaty ending the American Revolution in 1783. Under its terms, the British government recognized the independence of the United States, and the Great Lakes were divided between Canada and the United States. [100]

U

U.S. Congress. The legislative branch of our national government, which makes laws for the entire nation. Congress is made up of two houses: the Senate and the House of Representatives. [278]

U.S. Supreme Court. The highest court in the nation. The court bases its decisions on the U.S. Constitution and federal laws. [280]

Underground Railroad. Hiding places and escape routes used by African Americans before the Civil War to escape from slavery to places where slavery was illegal. [116]

urban. Relating to a city. Detroit is an example of an urban area. [130]

V

voting. Method used by citizens of a democracy to express their views on issues or to elect public officials. [312]

W

War of 1812. War that broke out between the United States and Great Britain when British ships stopped American ships to seize deserters. The war led to fighting on the Great Lakes. The war ended in 1815. [108]

weather. An area's current temperature, wind and sunshine or precipitation. [47]

Western Hemisphere. The half of the Earth west of the Prime Meridian. [17]

World War I. A war that started in Europe in 1914. The United States entered the war in 1917. [138]

World War II. A war that started in Europe in 1939 when Hitler's armies invaded Poland. The United States entered the war in 1941 after being attacked by Japan at Pearl Harbor. [145]

PICTURE GAZETTEER

I. MAJOR LAND FORMS

Hill (hil). Hills are masses of earth and rock that are not as high as mountains. In certain areas of Michigan, hills rise 800 to 1,000 feet above sea level.

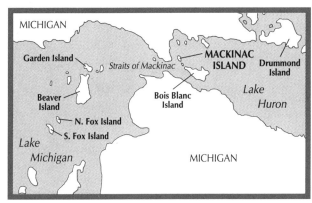

Island (ī' lənd). An island is a piece of land surrounded by water on all sides. There are about five hundred islands in the waters belonging to Michigan. Most of these islands are in the Great Lakes. Mackinac Island is an example of an island in Michigan.

Mountains (moun' tənz). Mountains are huge masses of earth and rock that rise at least 1,000 feet above the land. A group of mountains is called a **mountain range**. In Michigan, examples of mountains are the Huron and Porcupine Mountains along the southern shore of Lake Superior. Michigan's highest mountain is Mount Avron, rising 1,979 feet above sea level.

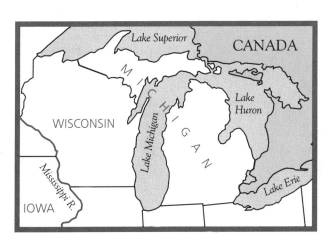

Peninsula (pə nin' sə lə). A peninsula is a piece of land surrounded by water on three sides. It is connected to a larger piece of land on its remaining side. Michigan is made up of two large peninsulas.

Plain (plān). A plain is a large area of flat or slightly hilly land. Plains are often used by people to build cities and to farm crops, because the land is flat. Part of the Upper Peninsula and most of the Lower Peninsula are part of the Great Lakes Plain.

Plateau (plat tō'). A plateau is an area of flat, level land that is raised higher than the regions around it. Sometimes plateaus are called tablelands. The northern half of the Lower Peninsula is made up of a tableland.

Shoreline (shōr' līn). A shoreline is the land that lies next to a large body of water. Michigan's shoreline is next to the Great Lakes. The shoreline of Michigan is longer than that of any other state in the nation except Alaska.

Valley (val' ē). A valley is an area of low land that runs between hills and mountains.

II. MAJOR BODIES OF WATER

Barrier Island (bar ē ər i' lənd). A barrier island is created when waves push up rock and sand to form pieces of land that rise above the surface of the ocean. A barrier island may be small, or large enough to build homes on. The Outer Banks, off the coast of North Carolina, and the island in Texas where Galveston is located are both examples of barrier islands.

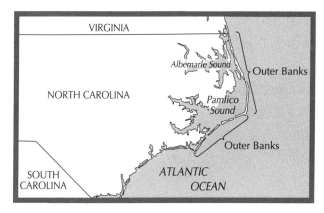

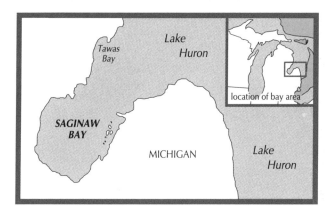

Bay (bā). A bay is a body of water, usually part of an ocean, sea or lake that forms an indentation into the land. Bays are similar to gulfs, although smaller. Michigan has several bays, such as Saginaw, Grand Traverse and Keweenaw Bay.

Gulf (gulf). A gulf is part of an ocean or sea, surrounded on three sides by land. The southern border of the United States contains an example of a gulf—the Gulf of Mexico. This gulf is connected to the Atlantic Ocean.

Harbor (här' bər). A harbor is a protected body of water usually located along a coastline. Usually a piece of land stands between a harbor and the larger body of water.

Lake (lāk). A lake is a body of water that is surrounded by land. In the United States there are five major lakes, known as the Great Lakes. Michigan borders four of the five Great Lakes. Only Lake Ontario does not touch Michigan. Michigan also has 11,000 other freshwater lakes. The largest lake entirely in Michigan is Houghton Lake.

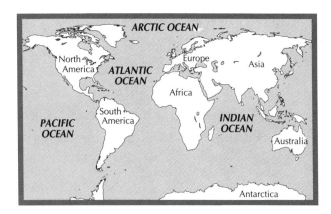

Ocean (o' shən). An ocean is an extremely large body of salt water. There are four main oceans: the Atlantic Ocean, the Pacific Ocean, the Arctic Ocean, and the Indian Ocean.

Rivers (riv' ərz). A river is a long, narrow body of flowing fresh water. Rivers flow into other rivers or into the ocean. Some of Michigan's rivers include the Muskegon, Au Sable, St. Clair and the Detroit River. Michigan's longest river is the Grand River.

Tributary (trib' yə ter ē). A tributary is a river or stream that flows into another larger body of water, such as a river.

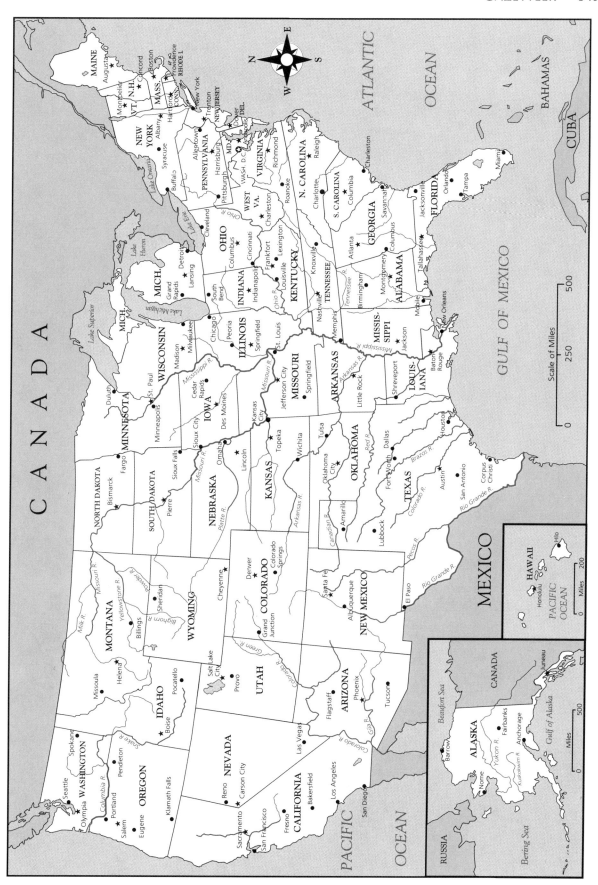

MAJOR
METROPOLITAN
AREAS

INDEX